George Sand Papers

UNIVERSITY
CENTER FOR
CULTURAL &
INTERCULTURAL
STUDIES

HOFSTRA UNIVERSITY
HEMPSTEAD, NEW YORK 11550

Hofstra University
Cultural & Intercultural Studies: 1

Other titles in this series:

No. 2. George Sand Papers. Conference Proceedings (1978). 1980
No. 3. Heinrich von Kleist Studies. 1980.
No. 4. William Cullen Bryant Studies. 1981.

ISSN 0195-802X

George Sand Papers

CONFERENCE PROCEEDINGS, 1976

Editorial Board
Natalie Datlof
Edwin L. Dunbaugh
Frank S. Lambasa
Gabrielle Savet
William S. Shiver
Alex Szogyi

Joseph G. Astman, Director
University Center for Cultural
& Intercultural Studies

AMS PRESS, INC.
NEW YORK, N.Y.

Library of Congress Cataloging in Publication Data

George Sand Conference, 1st, Hofstra University, 1976.
  George Sand papers.

  (Hofstra University cultural and intercultural
studies; 1)
  Revised selections from the proceedings.
  Includes bibliographical references.
  1. Sand, George, pseud. of Mme. Dudevant, 1804-1876
—Congresses. I. Hofstra University, Hempstead, N.Y.
Center for Cultural & Intercultural Studies. II. Title.
III. Series: Hofstra University, Hempstead, N. Y.
Hofstra University cultural and intercultural
studies; 1.
PQ2417.G4   1976   843'.7   79-21301
ISBN 0-404-61651-8

The publication of these proceedings has been made possible by
a generous grant from the Cultural Services of the French
Embassy to the United States (New York, N.Y.). Special thanks
go to M. André Gadaud, Cultural Counselor and M. Gérard
Roubichou, Cultural Attaché.

MANUFACTURED IN THE UNITED STATES
OF AMERICA

Foreword

We at Hofstra University are very proud of our tradition of serving as a center for international scholarly conferences. These conferences, coordinated by the University Center for Cultural & Intercultural Studies, manifest our firm commitment to foster the intercultural dimensions of education.

The first *George Sand Conference,* in November 1976, and the subsequent conferences on *Heinrich von Kleist* (1977) and *William Cullen Bryant* (1978), produced a rich harvest of scholarly work which will reach an even wider audience through the printed word in the *Hofstra University Cultural & Intercultural Studies.* Subsequent volumes will contain the proceedings of the following conferences: *Albert Einstein* (1979); *Renaissance Venice, Walt Whitman,* and *Nineteenth Century Women Writers* (1980); and *Fedor Dostoevski* and *Gotthold Ephraim Lessing* (1981).

Through this volume and its successors, new research will find its way to libraries. And, because the books will later be published in paper-bound editions, they will also be utilized for classroom instruction. The commitment to interdisciplinary studies, as typified by the Hofstra conferences, is wholly consistent with our university's policy of making our campus an arena for scholars in all fields of academic endeavor.

JAMES M. SHUART
President
Hofstra University
Hempstead, NY
September, 1979

George Sand. Woodbury type from a negative of 1864, by Nadar.

Preface

Several years ago I intended to include a George Sand novel in my Comparative Literature course. I noted in the margin of the syllabus to select one of the George Sand novels available in English and in paperback. I thought it was a matter of selection—but not one was available. How times have changed! Since then, at least seven biographies and 20 paperback novels have appeared—and now the present collection of essays (with a second volume to be published in 1980).

The success of our George Sand lectures and conferences has in no small measure been due to the support of the Hofstra administration: Dr. James M. Shuart, President; Dr. Harold Yuker, Provost; and Dr. Robert Vogt, Dean of the College of Arts and Sciences. At one stage or another all those participated in the program and lent their moral support throughout.

Several departments on campus were most cooperative: The Department of Comparative Literature and Languages under the chairmanship of Dr. Frank Lambasa, the French Department under Dr. Denis-Jacques Jean, and the History Department under Dr. George D. Jackson and, subsequently, Dr. John Moore.

The Editorial Board deserves a special note of thanks for services rendered far beyond the call of duty. Four members are, at present, on the Hofstra staff: Dr. Frank Lambasa of Comparative Literature and Languages, Dr. William Shiver of the French Department, Dr. Edwin Dunbaugh of History, and Ms. Natalie Datlof of the UCCIS staff. Dr. Gabrielle Savet is Professor Emerita of French at Hofstra and former chairman of the French Department. Dr. Alex Szogyi is Professor of Romance Languages and former chairman of the Department of Romance Languages at Hunter College, CUNY, and is on the staff at the Graduate Center, CUNY.

Hofstra University in general and UCCIS in particular are most grateful for the cooperation of the Cultural Services of the French Embassy in New York for both moral and financial support. Two members of the staff were especially helpful: M. André Gadaud, Permanent Representative in the U.S. of the French Universities and Cultural Counselor to the Cultural Services of the French Embassy, who spoke at one of our sessions, and M. Gérard Roubichou, Cultural Attaché to the Cultural Services of the French Embassy in New York, who at one of our banquets also honored us with a talk which is included in our publication.

We wish to express our appreciation to Ms. Rosemary Harris, distinguished actress, whose appearance in the BBC production of "Notorious Woman," brought the attention of all parts of the country to George Sand, and who honored us with her presence.

Every successful conference finds its seed in some one person's fertile mind. Nor does a conference ever succeed without someone taking hold and following through on every aspect of the program before, during, and after. That someone in this case is Natalie Datlof, Assistant to the Director of UCCIS, to whom Hofstra and George Sand scholars will be eternally grateful.

JOSEPH G. ASTMAN
Director, University Center
for Cultural & Intercultural
Studies

Editor's Preface

In 1831, a young French woman of a partially aristocratic heritage, left her husband and two children to go and live the life of a writer in Paris. The European world of 1831 had no satisfactory niche for a single woman, whatever her talent. In order to live as she knew she must, Amantine-Aurore-Lucile Dupin Dudevant was obliged to defy all accepted codes of bourgeois living. Her works, signed with the male pseudonym of George Sand, became immensely popular in her own day, and her style, the finest essence of Romanticism, influenced many of her contemporaries, not only in France but also in England, Russia, and even the United States.

Tastes invariably change with the times, and the highly personal romantically tinged novels of George Sand became far less popular than the work of her contemporaries, Balzac, Hugo, and Flaubert. For many generations, George Sand was known primarily as the highly erratic mistress of the poet Musset and the composer Chopin.

In recent years, George Sand's defiance of the existing mores of her time and her absolute insistence on living as an independent artist, has attracted the attention of both scholars and feminists. It was soon realized that she was not only a woman of fearless independence in an age of bourgeois standards, but also a great writer, too long neglected, whose works reveal a deep human understanding. She deserves her newly acquired wide audience, not only because she dared to be different but especially because of her remarkable depth of perception, her comprehension of every social stratum and human variation. The universality of works destined to be classics belongs to her.

The present collection of studies of George Sand's work emerged from a conference of scholars who convened at Hofstra University in commemoration of the 100th anniversary of her death. The interest in George Sand at Hofstra began several months earlier when Ms. Natalie Datlof, a graduate student in the History Department, then working on a biographical study of Sand, invited M. Georges Lubin, the illustrious George Sand scholar, to address a group of interested scholars and students. M. Lubin, who has accomplished more than anyone in the revival of study of Sand and her works and who has just recently completed the thirteenth volume of Sand's *Correspondance,* was at that time visiting the United States under the sponsorship of the French Cultural Services in New York.

Many of the scholars who came to Hofstra University to hear M. Lubin's talk indicated that they too had recently been working on studies of Sand, had become enthusiastic about their rediscovery of her talent, and were looking for an opportunity to discuss their studies with other scholars. With this incentive, Ms. Datlof decided to organize a George Sand conference at Hofstra University. The excitement generated by this conference was responsible for the warm friendship which soon grew among some of the devoted *sandistes* who attended. This friendship and mutual scholarly interest led to the formation of another organization, the Friends of George Sand, and its publication, *Friends of George Sand Newsletter,* printed at Hofstra University, which provides a continuing forum for those interested in studying the life, works, and influence of George Sand and to help make new scholars aware of her presence.

Since the formation of the Friends of George Sand, these scholars have continued to meet to hear papers and talks or to exchange viewpoints. Joseph Barry, Tamara Hovey, and Francine Mallet, leading biographers of George Sand, have come from Paris to meet with the group. The papers here presented are the work of the Editorial Board of the *Hofstra University Cultural & Intercultural Studies* series. The editors proudly announce that Volume 1, consisting of the proceedings of the first George Sand conference at Hofstra, will be followed by a second volume containing the proceedings of the George Sand seminar held in April, 1978. A current bibliography of writings on George Sand will be included in that volume.

ACKNOWLEDGEMENTS

The editors should like especially to thank Robert Keane, chairman of the Hofstra English Department, Valija Ozolins of the Russian Department at Hofstra, and Marie-Jeanne Pecile whose field is Women's Studies, for their assistance in editing papers within their special competencies. Many thanks also to Ms. Elaina Castro, a graduate student in the French Department, for her exemplary work in collating the index.

A special debt of gratitude is owed Dr. Joseph G. Astman, Professor of Languages and Comparative Literature and Director of the University Center for Cultural & Intercultural Studies at Hofstra University, without whose untiring efforts the George Sand conferences, and these proceedings, would not have become a reality.

Contents

George Sand Papers

The Presence of George Sand Among Us

HENRI PEYRE
Head of French Doctoral Program
The Graduate Center, City University of New York

For a number of years nothing seemed easier than to single out George Sand as the most foolish, the least sincere, and the most ludicrous paragon of what Charles Maurras belittled as "le romantisme féminin." Regrettably, the greatest successor to the Romantics, Baudelaire, was among her bitterest detractors. To her novels, he preferred *Les Liaisons dangereuses* by Laclos, and no one would find fault with such a preference today, although the two writers have nothing in common except a warm admiration for Rousseau's sentimentality. But Baudelaire, who thought he exposed and celebrated Evil and who sang litanies to Satan, could not forgive "la femme Sand" for refusing to believe in Evil. "She has excellent reasons to want to do away with Hell," Baudelaire twice remarked. He felt so repelled by her that he confided in "My Heart Laid Bare," "If I were to meet her, I could not keep myself from throwing a holy water basin at her head."

In our time, another Catholic who specializes in the extirpation of charity from his religion, Henri Guillemin, has included her in the galaxy of private foes with whom he delights in boxing—along with Joan of Arc, Benjamin Constant, Napoleon, Péguy, and a few others: a not altogether dishonorable company. He is fond, in the best Mauriac fashion, of converting agnostics and sinners on their deathbeds, or else he likes to take pity upon their long anguish at pursuing God without knowing it and not finding Him. Gladly would he save Flaubert, who occasionally pictured himself as an ascetic and, "being just" as he contended, would sink all his

1

characters and, after the Commune, all his compatriots and most of mankind, into the same slimy mud. But George Sand, on the contrary, to the very end, maintained her faith in the possibilities for self improvement lurking in human nature, and in some form of political progress and of social justice.

Few things, however, are more touching and better redeem Flaubert's cantankerous misanthropy than his letters to George Sand in the years which followed *Madame Bovary*. He entertained affection, adoration, and a friendship more moving than any love for her. He shed buckets of tears when she died. From her, he meekly accepted being admonished. While he rejoiced in never having been young and not having nourished illusions, as the safest (and, in our eyes, eminently bourgeois way not to suffer disappointments), she gently but firmly stressed her belief that living is a process of acquiring new illusions and of loving ever more generously. "No, no. . . . One cannot scorn one's species. Mankind is not an empty word. Our life is made of love, and no longer to love is to cease living." Another stern male mind, Taine, expressed a similar warm affection for George Sand and even saw her pastoral novels as not unworthy of Vergil. Renan, who in his youth had been impressed and moved by some of her novels, called her, when she died in 1876, "the Eolian harp of our age." "A string is broken in the lyre of this century," he added, alluding to one of her titles. He who had grown up among the poor and the humblest, praised her "for having lent a voice to the aspirations of those who had felt, but not known how to create." Renan remembered how, in his youth and in his native Brittany, she had been depicted as an impious woman, clad in Satanic black, trampling a crucifix under her feet. Ten years after her death, she will be saved, added the aging skeptic. In the eyes of the simple people who mourned her at Nohant, she was already a saint.

It would be preposterous, and unbearably dull indeed, to transfigure her into a saint, or into a great novelist, or even into the patron of liberated women or of the advocates of modern androgyny. Still, in this latter half of the twentieth century, which has once and for all exploded the partisan vituperations against the allegedly stupid nineteenth century and rehabilitated Romanticism, it is an act of elementary justice to grant George Sand her due. It is doubtful if France has counted a greater woman writer since 1700. Her several volumes of autobiography are among the least artificial and least insincere examples of the genre. The splendid edition of her letters, unweariedly collected and published by Georges Lubin, is not only one of the most admirable achievements of modern scholarship, it ranks with, perhaps even above, the collected letters of Mérimée, Stendhal, or Balzac. They console us for the sad disappointment experienced by the readers of the letters of Proust and, even more, of Gide. After decades of reticence, British and American audiences, who had long refused to forgive George Sand her lack of under-statement and her candid, if indiscreet, avowals, seem to have been drawn to her. At least three biographies of her, by Curtis Cate, Ruth Jordan, and Joseph Barry, have appeared within the last few years (1975 through 1977). The translation of André Maurois's *Lélia* has been widely read and admired as it deserves to be. A group of Ameri-can scholars gathered at Hofstra University in the Fall of 1976, which greatly enriched our knowledge of Sand's works, refined and deep-ened our appreciation of her. The present volume, through its range, variety, and rich content is fully worthy of the high esteem in which American scholarship in the realm of French culture is held today in Europe.

Truly great novels are few and far between. But, among the significant ones of the last two centuries written by a sizable number of women writers in the age of Mme Riccoboni, Mme de Genlis, Mme Cottin, Mme de Staël, and later by Mme de Noailles and Mme de Beauvoir, three or four by George Sand tower above the others. None but historians of literature open *Delphine* or *Corinne* today. *Lélia,* in its first version especially, even with its pathos and its Romantic weirdness, still moves us. It is in no way inferior to the more melodramatic novels of Balzac. *Lucrezia Floriani,* as Alex Szogyi has shown, is not only revealing on the puzzling personal relationship of the author with Chopin, but a technical feat as well. *Consuelo* (1843) offers one of the most attractive portrayals of women in French fiction. In a literature which has never been rich in first rate children's books, *La Mare au Diable, La Petite Fadette* (and even *François le Champi* at which Proust, or his double, shed tears, infelicitously translated as *The Country Waif* by the Univer-sity of Nebraska Press in 1977) retain much of their appeal today, not just for the young, but also for that dwindling species: *amateurs* of nature description in fiction. George Sand also proved a pioneer in attempting two other forms of fiction, a social novel and a fantastic and visionary novel on religious themes. In the latter category, stands *Spiridion* (1839), a strange and bold story, not inferior to *Seraphita* and to "Catholic" novels by Barbey d'Aurevilly, or to such twentieth-century novels around religious themes by women: *La Maison du Péché* by Marcelle Tinayre (1909) and *L'Abbaye d'Evolayne* (1933) by Paule Régnier. *Spiridion* counts no women character. It revolves around a seventeenth-century Jew who becomes first a Protestant, then a Catholic, taking on the name of a Greek bishop of the fourth century, Spiridion. He leaves a manuscript which a monk, Brother Alexis, discovers after his death. The fierce duel between the flesh and the spirit in a religious man who chooses to curb, and even to annihilate, the flesh for fear of it, is tragically depicted. The author, who had been raised in an English convent in Paris, denounces, through her protagonist, conventual life, where "the thing most dreaded is fervor and asceticism." She, who invoked God so often in her letters and could not bring herself to leave Him out of her love affairs, courageously declares at the end of the novel, "Atheists, who are justly praised for their intellectual greatness, are profoundly religious souls, who become weary or mistaken in their soaring élan towards heaven." It is no wonder that young Renan, while still a seminarist, pondered long on that novel. Sand had, in 1839, dedicated it to Pierre Leroux, "whom I revere like a new Plato, like a new Christ." He was one of the many who then believed in the imminent collapse of Christianity and groped for a new form of faith.

That faith, like that of Lamennais, with whom Sand corresponded, and that of other secular prophets, was to attract the working classes which then were becoming disaffected from traditional religion. The novelist struggled, sparing neither energy nor funds for the *Revue indépendante* (of which she took charge with the chronically impecunious Leroux). She composed novels about and for the working classes. The attempt was courageous, and probably premature. It still is in our time, and not only in bourgeois or capitalist countries, a discouraging limitation of our culture that we have not proved able to elicit a proletarian novel (or proletarian art, or music) from the so-called working classes. In French, Pierre Hamp had attempted it between the two world wars; so did Aragon in *Les Communistes,* in five volumes, in 1945-51, and André Stil, a

Communist novelist who was rewarded with the Stalin prize. George Sand had thrown herself into the advocacy of literature for the underprivileged, and by them, with naive enthusiasm. She sponsored a mason, a baker, a carpenter, a shoemaker, as storytellers or poets. She remained close to them until the Revolution of 1848 and even later. She helped them publish their works. Posterity must side with the verdict of a former liberal turned supporter of Louis-Philippe, Eugène de Lerminier, who, in December 1841 in the *Revue des Deux Mondes,* in "De la littérature des ouvriers," questioned the value of such a literature, founded on imitation. But, while he, a complacent conservative, saw in that failure the working of a natural law and a consequence of the division of functions (creative ones reserved for intellectuals and the middle classes, manual ones for workmen), Sand's generous heart fought for new conditions which, after much trial and failure, might bring about, at last, the accession of those hitherto silent classes to culture and to self-expression. Another half-century may have to elapse before that hope is at last fulfilled.

The story of George Sand's revolutionary and even "Communist" ideas has been traced, though not in the comprehensive volume which the topic deserves (for it is not just the story of one impulsive woman's utopian enthusiasms). It symbolizes the religion of the heart and the spirit of fraternity of a whole group of idealists, a number of them women, during the July Monarchy, the Second Empire, and later. A respected historian of workers' movements, Edouard Dolléans, has aptly linked the claims of the working classes and of women's rights in a volume which Armand Hoog prefaced: *Féminisme et mouvement ouvrier: George Sand* (Editions ouvrières, 1951). Before him, a sensitive admirer of Sand, Jean Larnac, treated the novelist's courageous political crusade impartially but with sympathy: *George Sand Révolutionnaire* (Hier et Aujourd'hui, 1947). Of Pierre Leroux, her inspirer and guide, from whom she later became disaffected, her biographer wisely and pointedly remarks that, until she met him, "she had only loved men. He made her love the people." As early as 1841, in a vigorous *Letter to the Rich,* the woman novelist had presented Communism as "the true Christianity, a religion of fraternity which threatens neither the purse nor the life of anybody." She was close enough to the people, peasants and artisans, to acknowledge that they were not Communist, and yet,

"France was destined to be Communist before another hundred years." The word, naturally, was not laden with the connotations which have been attached to it since Marx and Lenin. George Sand's enthusiasm, however, flagged after the first two months of the 1848 Second Republic. At least, unlike others who had also been carried away by similar illusions, she did not swing back to a reactionary and sulking mood. She visited Napoleon III whom she had known in the days when he, too, was dreaming to put an end to pauperism. But her sole purpose was to secure from him a pardon for her humble friends who were threatened with prison or deportation. She could not, like her avuncular confident, Sainte-Beuve, or like Mérimée, and not a few others, have rallied to a regime which she considered repressive of imaginative creation.

There are many ways of being a feminist, as there are many of being a political idealist and a social reformer. A number of the statements of George Sand on the rights of women might disappoint the feminists of today. That great woman, whom a legend has monotonously depicted in man's clothes and smoking a pipe, was and always remained sensitive, intuitive, impulsive, more fervent, and much less fallible in her artistic sense and in her taste than any of her male contemporaries. A bulky volume on *Romanticism and Music* (1954), by Thérèse Marix-Spire, is in fact devoted to her as the only French Romantic who truly felt and, with discrimination, judged music. One of her heroines, Consuelo, represents the finest portrayal of a musician sketched by a French Romantic. Indomitable courage and inflexible devotion to a cause often go hand in hand in a woman with a delicate sensibility. She proves readier than man to throw reasoning and cowardly prudence to the winds. "Mais aussi tu n'as rien de nos lâches prudences," Vigny declares to his symbolic Eva in "La Maison du Berger." Vigny, the lover of Marie Dorval, had no love lost for George Sand. Yet if he could have evinced a minimum of objectivity, he should have admired a woman who, already seared by the flames of a few passions and determined henceforth to challenge conventional opinion fearlessly, as early as October 1835, dared to write to her mother:

Nothing will prevent me from doing what I must and want to do. . . . I care not a fig for prejudices, when my heart orders me to prefer justice and courage. . . .

To a friend, François Rollinat, to whom she often confided, she formulated her position on the moral, social, and legal, as well as human, aspects of the question of justice for women. Women, she explained, are no longer left entirely to devout practices. Yet if they liberate themselves, however so feebly, they are condemned by public opinion. She went on:

> The opinion agrees, on one side, in finding unbearable those women who are ugly, cold, cowardly; on the other, it is the derisive and insulting blame on the part of men who no longer want devout women, who do not yet want enlightened women, and who still insist upon faithful wives. . . . Women today are neither enlightened nor devout nor chaste. . . . Society has refused to raise woman in her own eyes, to create for her a noble role and to set her up on a footing of equality which would make her capable of virile virtues. Chastity might have been a glory in free women. For enslaved women, it is a tyranny which wounds them. . . .

Few of us now open Sand's early novels, except for *Lélia*. They have suffered the fate of much literature which attempts to uphold a cause. Once the cause has been won, the demonstration appears to have been superfluous or heavy handed. Modestly, the author knew it when, at the evening of her long career, on December 8, 1872, she declared to Flaubert that in another fifty years, she would be forgotten. Unlike Stendhal, she disclaimed any ambition to be read by posterity. It requires but a minimum of historical imagination to realize how courageous such pleas for free, or at least extra-conjugal, love entitled *Indiana* or *Jacques* must have sounded in 1832-34. "The love of males has become a brothel (*un lupanar*) even under the conjugal roof." Yet, "woman cannot exprerience pleasure without love." Few women, not even Lou Andreas Salome or today's actresses, have had the good, or dubious, fortune of being loved by so many great men. She did not throw herself at their heads. If anything she endeavored to assist them, to mother them and to help them grow into their own selves. But, long before she associated with the eloquent Michel (called "de Bourges," though he hailed from Provence) and with the hypersensitive Chopin, in July 1835, she had remarked: "Of great men, I am weary. They are nasty, temperamental, despotic. God preserve me from them! The only happiness I have known in life was in friendship." Much later, to her young protégée Juliette Adam who reported it, she stated her reasons: "The superior man may be envied as a friend by the exceptional woman. But he is the same lover to all women, and often the most perfect for the vile and most stupid female. . . . If I were to live my life over again, I would be chaste!"

Inevitably when a woman has taken so many risks, has, as Lélia puts it, "sought the infinite in the creature" and has laid her successive disappointments bare, the men and the women alike who make up posterity will suspect her of a whole array of deficiencies or peculiarities. Far too much ink has been spilled over George Sand's love life by moralists, detractors from all political hues, lecturers in search of facile effects and of salacious details and amateur sexologists. Few writers have confessed more profusely than she has, in novels and especially in letters, neither Rousseau nor his twentieth century emulators, who have tried to redraft what they call "the autobiographical compact," sparing the reader nothing of their intimate lives. More objective than they, George Sand never failed to indict herself for what might be termed her failures. Her letters to Musset, after he had departed from Venice and she had become part of Pietro Pagello's incredibly mixed up life for a time, never concealed from either of those lovers that her love was to a great extent maternal. "Whether I was your mistress or your mother matters little. . . . You are right, our embrace was an incest, and we were not aware of it. . . . Poor wretched Alfred, I have loved you as a son. It is a mother's love. . . . I need to use up that surplus of energy and of sensibility which is in me. I need to feed that maternal solicitude which grew accustomed to watching a suffering and tired person." (*Correspondance,* ed. Georges Lubin, II, 561, April 15, 1834). What other women have thus nakedly confessed how much motherly genius for charity impregnated their determination to make the fullest gift of themselves?

Inevitably psychologists and biographers have found arguments to support any thesis: the most common one, which appeared to be sustantiated by the novel *Lélia*—a novel no more autobiographical, in effect, than *Les Illusions perdues* or *L'Éducation sentimentale*— was that George Sand had much of the opposite sex in her or that she was, because of some physiological or psychological defect, "frigid." In melodramatic language, Lélia, Pulchérie and others refer to one of the commonplaces of love as felt, and deplored, by the Romantics, from Rousseau to the early Flaubert in *Novembre*: the immense and disturbing role of imagination in love. The disease, of which all the Romantics were proud as of a privilege bestowed upon them by fate, similar to Moses' election by God to guide the chosen people, will later receive the name of *bovarysme*. The loving woman likes to mourn, as does Lélia, the coldness of her senses which puts her below the most abject members of her sex, at the same time as the "exaltation" of her thoughts raises her above the most passionate of men. Chateaubriand, Byron, the poet of *Jocelyn,* and Goethe himself had likewise all alluded to that abyss in themselves which no reciprocated passion ever could fill.

The difference is that while, for others, those haughty complaints found solace in their very melodious monotony, George Sand lived her sorrows and her delusions with passionate intensity. Translating her woes into literature brought her only scant comfort. No one who has read, in the third volume of Georges Lubin's edition of her *Correspondance,* her burning, imploring, and sensuous letters to a married man (Michel de Bourges) who shared her with his wife and other mistresses (1836) could still entertain the notion that George Sand's sex was in her head alone and that she was incapable of passionate surrender. No more heart-rending letters of love and jealousy were penned by any of the French Romantics. George Sand, without the recourse to debauchery, drink, or the drugs of some of her lovers, was convinced beforehand that, for her, loving meant giving ever more unstintingly of herself and being disappointed in the end; she lived over and over again the famous line of her lover in "la Nuit d'Août," "Il faut aimer sans cesse après avoir aimé." That arch-Romantic eventually became cured of her Romanticism. Flaubert, Turgenev, Renan knew her when she was serene, but never bitter or cynical. When, in 1866, it became the fashion to rail at the Romantic delusions and to substitute for them a would-be positivistic submission to reality, George Sand was the one who would not renege on the "mal du siècle" of those who had been young in the twenties. She wrote to Sainte-Beuve who had himself been too easily cured of the sorrows of his Joseph Delorme, "It may be that our so-called sickness was better than the reaction which followed it; than the greed for money, for pleasures, severed from all ideal, than those unfettered ambitions which appear to me to characterize, not too nobly, 'the health of our century.'"

George Sand: Our Existential Contemporary

JOSEPH BARRY
UNESCO
Paris, France

What do Socrates, Sartre, and Sand have in common?

For Socrates, "Only the examined life is worth living." Sartre would add the explored and exploited and inexhaustible life, insisting on the existentialist doctrine of the individual's freedom in an uncertain, contingent and apparently purposeless world, and stressing individual responsibility for fashioning the self. "The coward makes himself cowardly," he once remarked to me. "The hero makes himself heroic. What counts is total *engagement*— involvement, commitment." (Sartre is still trying to reconcile Marxism and existentialism, the dominance of social forces with the doctrine of individual freedom.)

George Sand was not born. She became George Sand, self-consciously, self-creatively, existentially. (I must confess I stole this from Simone de Beauvoir, who said in *The Second Sex,* "One is not born a woman. One becomes one"—society insists on it. The difference in our two statements however is striking, emphasizing George Sand's heroic act of achieving herself despite society's conditioning.)

The self-conscious self-examination of the person baptized Amantine-Aurore-Lucile Dupin in 1804 during the lifetime process of becoming the persona self-called George Sand, who died in 1876, is among the greatest achievements of the human spirit. Small wonder Henry James called her Goethe's sister, though one immediately adds that she was neither Goethe's, nor Byron's, nor Mozart's, nor Shakespeare's sister. She was George Sand, who cannot be defined through any man.

Nor can she be defined—discovered may be the better word—in any of her set pieces, though here one immediately recommends reading her novel *Lélia* together with a "good" biography. Rather, the discovery is to be made in the great sweeping arc of Sand's life and work, relations and influences, passions—of mind and body— and experiences. What of Flaubert, for instance, equals his reflections on himself in his letters? Similarly one must pursue George Sand in her correspondence (over 20,000 letters still in the process of publication, eventually twenty-five volumes of 1,000 pages each) and in her collected *oeuvres* (some seventy novels, two dozen plays, several score essays) in which she explores her experience as she is experiencing it, setting up a dialogue, establishing a dialectical tension, as much with herself as with her reader and correspondent. Early in her life she also established a direct communication with God, who was often herself. (Christ was a fellow Christian socialist.)

George Sand, to use Hemingway's language, did not "avoid the horns" in her writing or in her life, if one can separate the two. (Sand's writing and Sand's life never slept in separate beds.) She wrote and spoke, when women were silent or secretive, out of a carnal knowledge of contrasting experiences—of a Pagello and a Musset, a Casimir and an Aurélien, a Mérimée and a Chopin. She sought experiences and was undeterred by the failures. Those who descend into the den of lions, she once wrote to Sainte-Beuve, may well emerge "half-devoured, but are they condemned to remain mutilated the rest of their lives? . . . Long live love, despite everything!"[1] Love in the completest sense, for Sand, was a three-sided embrace of the heart or sentiment, the body or sexuality, and the mind or intelligence.

She was essentially the rarest of women, which is the unmutilated woman, unlike the Brontës, Madame de Staël, Flora Tristan, Simone de Beauvoir, despite the wounds and battle scars of her journey through—one stops to savor the full irony of the expression—"no man's land."

That journey began with the necessary, inevitable (in retrospect) first step of leaving home, husband, and children for Paris; in 1831 at the age of twenty-six—a century and a half ago—a half century before Ibsen had Nora leave her "doll's house," husband, and children.

How did it happen? How did Aurore Dudevant reach this decisive point in her journey, leaving husband, children, and home to become George Sand, herself?

Not anatomy, dear nineteenth-century Dr. Freud, but culture— the way one has been raised—is destiny. Balzac, perhaps a better observer of life, understood this and said it of George Sand. But what a struggle for a woman, whatever her upbringing, in a society warping women in a direction away from themselves. "Only with tremendous difficulty can a woman be what society has trained her *not* to be." The remark is Margot Peters's, author of a biography of Charlotte Brontë called *Unquiet Soul.*

How much of George Sand's tremendous achievement—such as becoming "the most successful of the mid-nineteenth-century French novelists" (Germaine Brée)[2]—was due to this simple fact: she had no brother? She had no brother who occupied the center of the family stage and held her parents' attentions, ambitions, and hopes. As was the case of so many remarkable women, such as her immediate predecessor, Madame de Staël, George Sand had no brother, other than an illegitimate half-brother, Hippolyte, who was brought into the big house only after she had experienced the first indispensable years of undivided love and attention and the highest, encouraged expectations. (May I suggest that someone looking for a doctoral subject might pursue this theme among other women who made it?)

George Sand when she was a little girl named Aurore Dupin was called Maurice by her grandmother, who confused her with her dead father, and was dressed as a boy by her tutor to the great confusion of a young lady in a nearby castle. Now there's a recipe for future androgynous mind and behavior! She played the hero's role in the games of her childhood, and it was George Sand in 1832, with *Indiana,* her first novel, who created the character of the woman as Hero, and not, as Carolyn Heilbrun states, "in 1880, when almost at the same moment Ibsen and James invented her."[3] Her ground-breaking study, *Toward a Recognition of Androgyny,* Ms. Heilbrun admirably admits, was based almost exclusively on English and American literature.

George Sand's first fictional creation as a child was the famous

"Corambé," who was "as pure and charitable as Christ, as radiant and beautiful as Gabriel," and as personal as a pagan god, indeed, more personal and familiar. "I completed him by dressing him as a woman," George Sand says in *Histoire de ma vie,* "for what I had loved and understood most was a woman—my mother. . . . Thus he had no sex and assumed all forms." She loved him "as a friend and a sister."[4]

Three decades later, while Chopin convalesced in Marseilles, when they returned from Majorca, George Sand with characteristic speed wrote *Gabriel,* and one wonders what debt Virginia Woolf's *Orlando* owes to it.

"My angels," Chopin wrote his friend Count Grzymala, "are finishing a new novel, *Gabriel.* Today she is going to spend all day writing it."[5] The book, George added in a postcript, such was the intensity of the self-analysis, was being delivered by "forceps."

Who were these multiple "angels" of Chopin? Gabriel-Gabrielle, we might now reply, or George-Aurore—for Chopin insisted on calling Sand Aurore. The hero of the new novel is in fact a woman raised and dressed as a man until the age of twenty-five, when, by her choice, she dressed three months a year as a woman to please her lover, the "dissolute" Astolphe, who reminds one in many ways of Musset.

The complications are as delightfully ambiguous as those of the boy actor in Shakespeare's company who pretended he was Rosalind disguising herself as a page boy. George's novel is in the form of armchair drama, heightening the similarity. Gabriel-Gabrielle would be "brother, friend, companion, and lover" of Astolphe, but he proves jealous and unworthy of her, turning to a prostitute-mistress in his pique. Our hero-heroine dies as a man, but with the word "*liberté*" on her lips.

"I have always," she had said earlier, "felt more than a woman."[6] Make that the "conventionally-defined woman," and the remark takes on its fuller meaning. Her soul, says Gabriel-Gabrielle, has no sex. Rather, it contains both sexes. Is this not depictive of the situation with Chopin, who has found a mother and a man—his guardian "angels"—in George-Aurore?

George Sand was fatherless, virtually motherless as a teenager, and raised by an invalid grandmother. In other words, she was her own young woman. "If destiny," she wrote, "had had me go directly from the domination of my grandmother to domination on the part of a husband"—as usually happened—"I should never have been myself. . . . But fate decided that from the age of seventeen there would be an interlude between the two forces, that I would belong to myself for almost a whole year, to become, for better or worse, essentially what I would be the rest of my life."[7]

She rode in male dress across the Berry countryside, feeling "alive and reborn, dominating the landscape from the saddle,"[8] fixing her eyes on the horizon and not, as one on foot or with taught lady-like modesty, on the ground. On horseback, at least, a woman is the equal of a man, and Aurore found her companions among the young men of La Châtre. Together they would clatter through the village, and there are still very old women at La Châtre who recall their grandmothers telling them, when they were very young, that the windows were shuttered against Aurore's scandalous passage through the streets with her young men.

Aurore, the young George Sand, became a conventional young woman when she married Casimir Dudevant. She loved him, I believe, for one or two years—he was no more of a brute than most country gentlemen of his period—until she was consumed by ennui, the deadly boredom of feeling wasted, which made her psychosomatically ill. "I pressed you in my arms," she wrote Casimir, "I was loved by you, yet something I could not express was missing in my happiness."[9]

In Aurélien de Sêze, her platonic lover of the Pyrenees, Aurore thought she found what she had been missing—a man who shared her intellectuality, her passions of the mind. He would be Casimir's complement—she even proposed it to husband Casimir—making for the missing wholeness. But then she made the shattering discovery: half a life plus half a life equals half a life. It could have been devastating, suicidal—in short, the fate of many intelligent women, not to speak of supremely gifted women.

Thus, Aurore left her husband for Jules Sandeau and Paris, that is, for herself. She was Nora and she inspired many Noras, if not Ibsen's very own. Though Ibsen, incidentally, always claimed he had never read George Sand, his wife Suzannah had read and reread her—especially *Consuelo,* which she read almost annually—and Nora of *A Doll's House* is a very Sandian heroine, or rather hero, if she is not George Sand herself.

So Aurore set out for Paris, as so many young Frenchmen who dreamed of becoming writers had done before her. Indeed—and I owe this to Vivian Gornick of the *Village Voice*—"the central image of a young man from the provinces going out into the world on a symbolic journey of self-discovery is the dominating image of our literature, and it is," Vivian Gornick adds, "of necessity, a male image." [10]

Why "of necessity?" Because too few women have ever made that journey from the provinces for it to have become the symbolic image even for women. In fact, young George Sand's journey of self-discovery meant emerging from two provinces—one more than for men—and that second province is "womanhood." [11] This insight is Carolyn Heilbrun's in an article for the *Saturday Review* significantly called, "The Masculine Wilderness of the American Novel."

Remember the ending of *A Portrait of the Artist as a Young Man*? "Welcome, O life! I go to encounter for the millionth time the reality of experience"—it is not the millionth time for any woman even of our time—"and to forge in the smithy of my soul the uncreated conscience of my race." [12] How exciting to substitute sex for race, as if the young Joyce embarking on life were Aurore Dudevant on the threshold of becoming George Sand, both, by the way, in Paris.

Aurore was one of the Berrichon club in Paris, its only woman, and she wanted to be one of them, not a man among men, but a writer among writers, which meant dressing as a man. The new-style male redingote, full-length and square, lent itself handsomely to her guise. She had one cut to her small, slim measure, made of strong, gray cloth—ideal for the winter weather—and ordered trousers and waistcoat to match. She tucked her long hair in the tall, felt hat students were wearing and looked for all the world like a first-year Sorbonne student. Boots, tipped at the heels with iron to cope with the slippery sidewalks, and a large, gray cravat completed Aurore's attire; and so costumed, so disguised, she tirelessly roamed Paris. No trailing skirts, no thin-soled, pointed shoes, no thin-souled, pointing fingers to hobble her. She was free, an "invisible woman,"—her phrase—as anonymous as any man in the privacy that is the gift of Paris. "To be alone in the street," she wrote, to decide for herself where to dine or where to go, to frequent the people she wished and not to have others forced upon her. To go and come at any hour, alone if she preferred, or to join her comrades in the pit rather than be confined, as were women in women's clothing, to the boxes and balconies at the theater! But above all, Aurore could go her own way unnoticed, unremarked, uninhibited, "feet solid on the slippery ice, shoulders covered with snow, hands in pockets, stomach a bit empty at times, but the head all the more filled with songs and melodies, the new colors and forms, inspirations and fantasies . . . neither *dame,* nor *monsieur,* neither woman nor man . . . walking through the desert of men." [13]

"G. Sand" appeared on the title page of George Sand's first novel, *Indiana,* when it appeared in May 1832. Presumably, the publisher welcomed the likely confusion with "J. Sand," as Aurore and Jules Sandeau signed their first and only novel, *Rose et Blanche.* Could it possibly have been Aurore's own choice? Was not the name "G. Sand" ideal for one who sought to walk through life as "neither *dame,* nor *monsieur,*" but rather as a writer among writers, a person among people? Is there a more perfect expression of the androgynous mind?

If so, it was unconscious. George Sand, alas perhaps, did not stay with it. In fact, she said, "I had resolved to remain anonymous." [14] Here one recalls the remark of Virginia Woolf: "Currer Bell, George Eliot, George Sand, all the victims of inner strife as their writings prove"—George Sand's less, I believe, after *Lélia*—"sought ineffectively to veil themselves by using the name of a man. Thus they did homage to the convention, which if not implanted by the other sex was liberally encouraged by them, that publicity in women is detestable." [15] The chief glory of a woman, she quotes Pericles, "himself a much-talked-of man," is not to be talked of.

What young man of the period, one might ask, would not have been proud to see his name on the title page of his first novel, rather than mask it, as Aurore sought?

Having said this, however, have we said everything, or indeed, much of anything? If the initial *G* had to be spelled out, Aurore obviously thought George better than Georgina. As in her wearing men's clothes—generally only in public—calling herself George enabled Aurore to pass that much more easily in a man's world.

However, George Sand went way beyond her time and ours in heroically—there is no better word—asserting, exploring, and making whole the male/female fractions of her life. Hers, I am more and

more convinced, was the creative, androgynous mind of the con-
sciously androgynous person, not only accepting, but integrating the
masculine and feminine characteristics which occur, in varying
fractions, in all human beings.

This did not mean that Sand lived a bisexual life with lovers
distributed among men and women. Androgyny is not, or perhaps
we should say not necessarily, bisexuality. It is simply recognition,
acceptance, and accomodation of our male/female impulses.

So far as can be determined, George Sand had but one woman
lover—actress Marie Dorval. And even she has been taken from her
by her biographers, who believe that a woman loving a woman, or a
man a man, is not only unbecoming but really . . . *dirty*. The androgynous character was expressed in other ways: George Sand was
knowingly the master-mistress, father-mother of Chopin as well as
other younger men, for she has told us so in the novels born from
the experience. *François le Champi,* a great success on French
television recently, was called in its time "the perfect incest." [16] The
story of a foundling raised by a woman who eventually married her
charge and lived happily ever after incidentally inspired Thackeray's
own *Henry Esmond.*

The remarkable thing, however, is that George Sand was not
unconscious of the incestuous factor in her emotional life, no more
than the androgynous aspect. To the contrary, she acted out her
nature with the full consciousness of today's realization that there
are many lives within a life. She was surrogate father for her
mother, or mother for her father, when one or the other was absent
during her childhood.

It is simply fantastic that she should have spelled out the mother-
child relationship with Chopin, who was six years younger, so
unmistakably in the novel Henry James called "splendid," *Lucrezia
Floriani.* Chopin's friends found it cruel, but Sand was no less clear
and cold-eyed in the portrayal of herself. Her Lucrezia Floriani is
George Sand, a thirty-year-old actress with four children of three
different fathers, who falls in love with a six-years-younger Prince
Karol, a transparent Chopin of soft, adolescent beauty whose finely
modeled face showed "neither age nor sex" and who was as
hauntingly beautiful as a "sad and wonderful woman."

The incestuous and the androgynous are never left in doubt. Nor
are the sexual ambivalence and ambiguity of Chopin. Prince Karol,

says Sand, had probably loved only his mother before loving
Lucrezia, and sought in his mistress, as had Musset, the prostitute
and virgin in the same person. As for Lucrezia, "Karol had become
something like her son." They even discussed it. Had Sand and
Chopin as well?

"'You are my mother, then?' Karol asked.

"'Yes, I am your mother,' she said, without reflecting that he
might think it profane. . . . which," Sand adds, "at such moments it
indeed was." [17]

This kind of cosmic serenity came to George Sand in her forties,
after the years with Chopin. It was a serenity wrestled out of a
realized life, the finest evidence is in the correspondence with
Flaubert. But the combat and the realization are the existential
essence of her meaning for us today, telling us so much about her
century and our own, about the condition of men and women,
especially creative women in their relations with creative or commonplace men, with other women, with themselves.

The black spring of 1833, when George Sand was not yet thirty, is
particularly moving and instructive. It resulted in the third of three
novels, all published within fourteen months. *Lélia* is one of the
most remarkable existentialist works ever written, the record of
a life recording itself as it was being lived. Out of the mismar-
riage with Casimir, the failure with Jules Sandeau, the fiasco
with Mérimée, the love affair with Marie Dorval, disillusionment and despair—while they were being experienced—came the
writing. The circumstances of some of the most harrowing
pages have been described by Henry James, who heard the
story, he said, from someone who had heard it "direct" from Mérimée:

> Prosper Mérimée was said to have related—in a reprehensible
> spirit—that during a term of association with the author of
> *Lélia* he once opened his eyes, in the raw winter dawn, to see his
> companion, in a dressing gown, on her knees before the
> domestic hearth, a candlestick beside her and a red *madras*
> round her head, making bravely, with her own hands, the fire
> that was to enable her to sit down betimes to urgent pen and
> paper. The story represents him as having felt that the spectacle
> chilled his ardour and tried his taste; her appearance was
> unfortunate, her occupation an inconsequence and her industry

a reproof—the result of all of which was a lively irritation and an early rupture.

To the firm admirer of Madame Sand's prose the little sketch has a different value, for it presents her in an attitude which is the very key of the enigma, the answer to most of the questions with which her character confronts us. She rose early because she was pressed to write, and she was pressed to write because she had the greatest instinct of expression ever conferred on a woman; a faculty that put a premium on all passion, on all pain, on all experience and all exposure. . . .[18]

The dawn scene described is George Sand compulsively adding to the pages of *Lélia*. Everything she has experienced and felt are in those pages—lesbianism and promiscuity, monastic retreat and suicide, and the frigidity she would ever after be accused of, which was in fact that spring's frigidity of frustration and despair. There are pages of such intensity, self-revelation and pain that no man could have written them and no man—it cannot be said too often—should fail to read them, despite the metaphysical form Sand chose partially to mask the personal pain.

"Ennui desolates my life, ennui is killing me. . . ." Lélia concludes her story, "I withdraw within myself with a quiet, somber desperation and no one knows what I suffer. . . . No man has the breadth of intelligence to understand the abysmal misery of feeling incapable of attachment or desire."[19]

Perhaps for the first time the feminine experience, examined by a woman who exhausted it, was at the center of a novel probing the inadequacies of life, where men and women find themselves in an impasse; where the writer, a woman, has faced herself—and exposed herself—at the cost of emotional agony and personal humiliation. "Filth and prostitution," cried a critic of her novel when it appeared.[20] "Frigid," was Maurois's conclusion in his biography of George Sand which he called *Lélia,* the same conclusion more recently, and more coldly, reached by Curtis Cate.

How mistaken! One black spring was not a lifetime. There was many a summer of completed passion to follow—immediately with Musset, later with Michel de Bourges and others. So many that nymphomania was added to frigid. What else can a man say of a woman who takes men as men have taken women for millennia?

When it comes to political *engagement* for George Sand we have more difficulty, if we try to discuss politics as seriously as it deserves, that is, beyond and above sentimentality, a level to which few of her time, before and shortly after 1848, ever rose. It was a period when simple slogans, such as Property is Theft, sufficed as a political philosophy and program.

Sand was a descendant of a Saxon king of Poland on her father's side (the Bourbon monarchs were her "cousins") and on the side of her mother, who was, to put it politely, a camp follower, granddaughter of a Parisian birdseller. She was raised aristocratically, which made her nicely anti-bourgeois, but her heart was on the left. She was a republican when that meant being a democrat, i.e., antimonarchical. Since monarchy was the prevalent order, being republican was revolutionary enough. It took the Revolution of 1848 to reverse the situation—temporarily. It was only after the Paris Commune of 1871 that France became truly a republic, and by then George Sand was an old woman. She was essentially an élitist socialist: socialism was to come from above. When it threatened to come from below, from the workers themselves, as in the Paris Commune, with the danger of counterrevolutionary violence, she was unprepared and responded with a Utopian pacifism.

However, the George Sand of the 1840s who would become the Muse of the 1848 Revolution, almost officially its Minister of Propaganda, was a remarkable figure. She participated in the political movements of the time, she took her risks, surely greater than Sartre's in the Algerian War. With her novels *Horace* and *Le Compagnon du Tour de France* (which a 28-year-old Walt Whitman reviewed in the Brooklyn *Daily Eagle* as *The Journeyman-Joiner* and from whose carpenter hero he would take his carpenter's garb and pose for his "carpenter portrait" in the first edition of *Leaves of Grass*) George Sand became the spokesperson not only for women, but for all the underprivileged—for nine-tenths of humanity—not only in France, but throughout Europe and beyond. "For the aristocracy of the intellect," Oscar Wilde would write appreciatively (was it in the *Soul of Man under Socialism*?), "she had always the deepest veneration, but the democracy of suffering touched her more."

George Sand tried to explain her growing political commitment to her friend Duvernet. "Many," she said, "speak of 'charity' and 'brotherhood,' but the bourgeoisie mouth the sentiments hypocritically. There is no profit in it for them—and their institutions prove it." Her own yearning for a "moral revolution" was based not so much on class against class as on a "religious and philosophical feeling for equality." When the revolution she even then called communist would come—and come it would, she believed—it might come "too quickly," before the people were prepared.

Sand continued, saying that men like her radical friend and lover Michel de Bourges say, "'Let's make a revolution, we'll see what happens afterward.' We say, 'Let's make a revolution, but let's see beforehand what we'll see afterward.'" People in revolt will inspire the great, necessary change, but on the condition that they are enlightened—"about truth, justice . . . equality, freedom and brotherhood, in a few words, about their rights and duties." She did not want "vague formulas." "What," she asked, "would be the precise freedom for the individual, what authority for the state, for society?" "What would be the form of property"—that is, of the means of production? Private, with all that implies in the way of exploitation of the worker, or collective—that is, socialist?[21]

These were the new questions of the 1840s, and as Susanne Langer has pointed out, it is the question asked by a period, and not the usually mistaken answers given, which tell us most about the period.

They are still good questions, and we've witnessed enough wrong answers, but must go on posing the questions and participating in the answers, for will it or not, participate or not, we suffer the consequences. The lesson has scarcely changed in a century and a half.

Politically and emotionally, intellectually and in what we do, is it not the wholeness of ourselves which we are really seeking? And finally is it not that we see in George Sand, when we say she is our existential contemporary?

"Only connect," E. M. Forster suggested. Only connect the disparate fractions of our alienated selves, the male and the female, the political and the esthetic, "the prose and the passion. . . . Live in fragments no longer. Only connect . . ."[22]

NOTES

1. George Sand, *Correspondance,* 13 vols. ed. Georges Lubin (Paris, 1964-78), II, p. 825.

2. Germaine Brée, "The Fictions of Autobiography," *"Nineteenth-Century French Studies,* IV, No. 4 (Summer 1976).

3. Carolyn Heilbrun, *Toward a Recognition of Androgeny,* (New York: Alfred A. Knopf, 1973), p. 49.

4. George Sand, from "Histoire de ma vie," in *Oeuvres autobiographiques,* ed. George Lubin (Paris, 1970), I, 812-823, henceforth abbreviated OA. Translations are my own.

5. Frédéric Chopin, *Correspondance,* ed. B. E. Sydow (Paris, 1953), II, 325.

6. George Sand, *Gabriel* (Paris, 1840), p. 20 and passim.

7. Sand, *OA,* II, 135.

8. George Sand, *Correspondance,* ed. Georges Lubin (Paris, 1964-78), I, 212-213.

9. Sand, *Correspondance,* I, 270.

10. Vivian Gornick, *Village Voice* (New York, May 31, 1973).

11. Carolyn Heilbrun, "The Masculine Wilderness of the American Novel," *Saturday Review (New York,* January 29, 1972).

12. James Joyce, *A Portrait of the Artist as a Young Man* (London, 1912) p. 288. First published in 1916.

13. Sand, *OA,* II, 135.

14. Sand, *OA.*

15. Virginia Woolf, *A Room of One's Own,* (London, 1970), p. 52. Originally published in 1928.

16. Joseph Barry, *Infamous Woman: The Life of George Sand,* (New York: Doubleday & Co., 1977), p. 271.

17. George Sand, *Lucrezia Floriani,* (Paris, 1847).

18. Henry James, *Notes on Novelists,* (New York, 1914), pp. 164-65. Originally written in 1897.

19. George Sand, *Lélia,* (Paris, 1960), p. 204.

20. Capo de Feuillide, *Europe Littéraire,* Aug. 9-12, 1833.

21. Sand, *Correspondance,* V, pp. 537-42.

22. E. M. Forster, *Howard's End.*

George Sand Today

GÉRARD ROUBICHOU
Attaché Culturel
de l'Ambassade de France

These papers are not only a way to honor a great French writer who played an international role in her time, but also a good opportunity to emphasize the close relationship between the French and Americans in the areas of criticism and literary and historical research. Because some interest has been focused on the work and life of George Sand, it would be worth reflecting on the contributions of this writer to our contemporary world in such a manner that our American friends could see how she is still considered in France outside of the academic community.

I do not intend to delve into the subject, as so many profound, challenging, stimulating things have been or will be said on her and/or her works, that I add but little to the expertise of the specialists and scholars whose knowledge of the period and conceptions of our author are unquestionable.

By quoting George Sand's daughter, who once said, "He who unravels my mother will be a wise one," I can easily show the impossibility of accurately saying who George Sand was, and therefore, still is for us; she was a complex personality and a very versatile talent. It is necessary for us to keep all this background in mind so that our reflection will be only an attempt to define George Sand's personality and impact.

If I tried to determine what George Sand represented to us, I would come up with very few elements: she was a writer and also a very particular type of woman! And actually, we must recognize that even for the majority of French people, the knowledge we have of her does not go far beyond these two aspects.

As a woman writer, George Sand is especially known through

some of her novels, the so-called *"romans champêtres,"* which deal
with the peasant life in the Berry region in the center of France.
There is no French child—not even today—who has not at least
once read either *François le Champi* or *La Mare au Diable* or *La
Petite Fadette.* So George Sand is a writer for youngsters!

As for the numerous other and voluminous books she wrote, they
are mostly titles, and I knew a few people—not professors, but
honnêtes hommes, educated and not specialized people—who would
be in a position to give you, if asked unexpectedly, five titles of
George Sand's, other than the above-mentioned ones, and would
refer at the drop of a hat to *Le Meunier d'Angibault, Consuelo, Lélia,
Indiana, La Comtesse de Rudolstadt,* or even *Le Compagnon du
Tour de France.*

The limitation of George Sand's talent to what she became in the
latter part of her life is rather interesting. We tend to forget that she
was one of the most celebrated writers of her time, perhaps more so
than Balzac himself, and that the real reason for this is not to be
found in the *"romans champêtres."* I shall try to explain further why
she has been eventually restricted to that minor aspect of her work.

By the turn of the century and even after, George Sand was still
considered an exemplary writer. She was even the "typical novelist,"
one who wrote the perfect type of novel. It could be remembered
that one of our most modern writers, Marcel Proust, used to read
her novels as a child, and wrote in his book, *Remembrances of
Things Past,* a few pages on George Sand, his grandmother's
favorite author, in which he praises her talent as an outstanding
writer of . . . *romans champêtres.* And this remark proves once
again the very limited approach we have to her work.

The second aspect of George Sand I referred to is that of a
woman without reserve. Smoking pipes, wearing pants, having
lovers (and generally famous ones too!), outspoken. In other words,
for the majority of us, George Sand is the "notorious woman," just
as Joan of Arc is the pure virgin of our history and Madame Bovary
the adulterous spouse of our literature. Those archetypes are rather
difficult to forget and in George Sand's case even more difficult to
correct because of all the current attention being given to the
feminist movement. Of liberated women, George Sand would be the
first: the poor sister trying desperately to fight for womens' rights in
the darkest moment of the nineteenth century.

I am not totally convinced, however, that she was such an ardent feminist, although her viewpoints were not common in some respects. We can also remember that Simone de Beauvoir, in *The Second Sex,* casually mentions George Sand only twice—not a chapter, not even a long paragraph devoted to her.

Since we have neither a very modern nor very controversial aspect of George Sand's personality and life here, I would like to look at that side of our author.

I am not convinced that George Sand was a feminist in the modern sense of the word. She felt very strongly about marriage and divorce (see *Lélia, Consuelo*), and did not share the general viewpoints of her time, especially those of the women of her time. She also had rather unusual (according to the standards of the period) conduct with men. And yet, although she was a living scandal, so to speak, I believe that the reason does not lie so much in the fact that she actually wanted to be someone to whom and by whom scandal struck, and that she actually wanted to transfer the rules of the game to the other side by giving women the rights they should have; but simply because she had an outstandingly strong personality: she actually decided that she could afford to be herself in a world mostly dominated by and made for men! Her conduct and reactions were mostly those of a woman (particularly when it came to love relationships!); but the way she behaved in her bourgeois society was exactly the same way a man would have— who, by the way, was the only one given the opportunity to act as he liked.

Is it not interesting to notice that just as all the mistresses of great authors (Balzac, Stendhal, Lamartine, etc.) are always mentioned as positive points of the creative life of their lovers as well as fundamental in their biographies, George Sand's lovers are constantly the darkest side of her life. They are carefully, and even in some instances casually, left unmentioned in the books of literature given to students. At the same time, only pipe smoking was a scandal in the context.

If we consider the literature of the period—from 1825 to 1875— we notice that there were strict female archetypes—four to be exact: the mother vs. the femme fatale, the idol vs. the "courtesan."

These four types are exactly the ones you would find in Flaubert's *Éducation sentimentale* or in several novels by Balzac. But actually, these four images of woman could easily be reduced to two: the good woman vs the bad woman. It was not conceivable not to be one or the other. George Sand was neither one nor the other: she was too intelligent, too sophisticated, and from too good a family to be considered a real courtesan (although her conduct could have been easily compared to a courtesan's); on the other hand, she was too much herself, too tempramental to accept the restrictions of the insignificant role of the typical "good woman" of her period. Certainly this complex mixture of these two elements helped build her image in her time and throughout posterity.

We must also remember that she wrote more than Musset, as much as Balzac, and that she had as many activities as many men of her period, although the majority of these were never really considered normal for a woman. Actually she lived in one of the most difficult times for a woman who wanted to take any opportunity, any chance to participate in the exciting life of her time. It was also her curiosity, her enthusiasm, so representative of her century that actually played against her; she behaved like a man!

And that is probably one of the many reasons why she is so interesting for us. She is one of the greatest witnesses of the period (her life spans three-quarters of a particularly rich century), and even more than some famous French writers she gave us (possibly because of the so-called feminine instinct) an extraordinary image and account of the evolution of the sense of the time, of the opinions and ideas of the time. She lived through the Romantic period and became romantic, capturing in many ways the romantic spirit in her books; she became interested, at the appropriate time, in the lower classes, taking part in the greatest moments of 1848. She was disappointed when it became clear that the revolution would not be brought about tomorrow. No wonder she was deeply admired by the men who wrote the best accounts of that time, by Flaubert; no wonder she was (and still is) admired in Russia as well as in England, in Germany, and Poland for her humanitarian ideas. She represented the Zeitgeist, by her works as well as by her relationship with the European intelligentsia: Chopin, Byron, Turgenev, Mickiewicz.

Her versatility, however, is also what probably hurt her because she easily accepted the qualities and the defects of her time (style, ideas, etc.). She is too much of her time for us; she has "aged" in a way. Is it really possible to read *Lélia* today except for professional reasons? This is probably why George Sand has survived as a writer and especially as the author of the "*romans champêtres,*" which do not bear, as obviously her other works do, the weaknesses and characteristics of her time: sentimentality, lyricism, poetry, etc. Because she was a full witness to the time, she also represents among the women writers of French literature, an important moment of transition. Traditionally, women writers in French literature have belonged to the best aristocratic families and were committed to literature within a circle of privileged persons who could afford to read (Mme de Lafayette, Mlle de Scudéry in the seventeenth century) or those who were writing as if literature were only preoccupied with philosophical problems (Mme de Staël).

George Sand was on her grandmother's side from an aristocratic family, and of a more modest origin on her mother's; under the difficult circumstances of the time, she oriented her work toward the social conditions of the poorer classes and, by doing so, was one of the first writers to introduce new areas to literature. She is, so to speak, the last aristocratic woman writer of French literature as well as the first new kind of woman writer preoccupied with social problems.

Finally, her complex personality is what is of most interest to us today: who was she exactly? Her biographers are questioning her homosexuality, although it seems that she was to a certain extent not indifferent to the charms of Marie Dorval. Her conduct with men was sophisticated enough to be interpreted as typically feminine, but too pathological to be only that: the way she was attracted to and then disgusted with her lovers (Musset), her relations with Mérimée, all the aspects that Rosemary Harris presented so well in her remarkable performance on TV are all excellent examples of the modern facets of her personality and help explain the interest that she has drawn.

For us, George Sand is more than just another author to be mentioned in an anthology of French literature. She is a real person whose creativity and personality still stimulate interest and research.

George Sand en 1848

GEORGES LUBIN
Boulogne-sur-Seine
France

Dans l'*Histoire de ma vie,* George Sand insiste sur la solidarité des générations entre elles, pour justifier la part qu'elle y donne à l'histoire de sa famille. De même, pour comprendre la conduite d'une personne dans un laps de temps donné, il n'est pas inutile de connaître le bilan antérieur, d'établir le solde à reporter, car il y a aussi une solidarité de l'être avec lui-même. Je ferai donc devant vous un examen, rapide, de l'évolution politique de George Sand avant la Révolution de 48.

Elle est issue d'une famille fortement teintée d'irrégularités, où les bâtards sont plus nombreux que la moyenne. Dans son ascendance disparátc, un maréchal de France, bâtard de roi, une courtisane de haut vol, des financiers fort riches, et en regard un roulier, un ferrailleur, un faïencier, un marchand d'oiseaux. Son père a dans les veines une dose de sang royal, sa mère, enfant du peuple, enfant du pavé de Paris, après une jeunesse orageuse a suivi à l'armée d'Italie un protecteur chamarré. Sang rouge et sang bleu ne se mélangeront pas sans se combattre.

L'enfance d'Aurore est marquée par des luttes entre les représentants de deux mondes aussi différents, pour ne pas dire antipodiques. Le père étant mort quand elle avait quatre ans, mère et grand-mère se disputèrent le coeur de l'enfant: voilà qui marque un être pour la vie entière, et plus tard, George Sand pourra, à bon droit, faire remonter la naissance de ses idées socialistes et démocratiques à sa naissance "*à cheval* sur deux classes" et aux contestations qui firent d'elle un enjeu.

L'instruction qu'elle reçoit est aussi irrégulière que son ascendance. D'un précepteur qui n'était sans doute pas un mauvais pédagogue, mais suffisant et pédant, elle reçut le bagage élémentaire, et même un peu plus, avant de passer trois ans dans un couvent parisien réputé où sa grand-mère l'a mise pour lui donner des manières, à cette petite paysanne, et des *maîtres d'agrément.* Elle n'y apprit que peu de choses, même en fait de manières, si ce n'est l'anglais et un peu d'italien. Mais son esprit s'y développa, et, revenue à Nohant, elle sera en mesure de se cultiver toute seule par des lectures immenses et désordonnées, au hasard des rayons d'une bibliothèque bien fournie, lectures très sérieuses dans l'ensemble: classiques anciens, français et étrangers, philosophes du XVIIIᵉ siècle—enfin les ouvrages de Jean-Jacques Rousseau, *Emile, La Profession de foi du vicaire savoyard, Lettres sur la montagne, Le Contrat social.* Elle en reçut une impression profonde, enivrante: "Je devins, en politique, le disciple ardent de ce maître, et je le fus bien longtemps sans restrictions, dira-t-elle." Mais c'est ici le lieu d'évoquer une parole célèbre: "Tu ne me chercherais pas si tu ne m'avais déjà trouvé," et on en a la confirmation par elle-même, quand elle reconnaîtra que" si les livres ont fait de l'effet sur [elle], c'est que leurs tendances ne faisaient que confirmer et consacrer les [siennes]."

La mort de sa grand-mère en 1821 (la jeune fille avait dix-sept ans), son mariage bâclé avec un homme médiocre, pour échapper à la tutelle maternelle, éloignent définitivement Aurore de ce monde aristocratique, noble ou anobli récemment, auquel Mme. Dupin de Francueil aurait voulu la rattacher avant de mourir. Le mariage la rapproche politiquement du milieu libéral qui est celui des bourgeois de La Châtre, frondeurs, ennemis de la royauté restaurée, qui appellent de leurs voeux une république, république bourgeoise, république des capacités, mais enfin une république. Ils accueillent la révolution de 1830 avec faveur, et s'accommodent, au moins au début et sous bénéfice d'inventaire, de la monarchie constitutionnelle. Mais déjà l'on sent à certains indices qui apparaissent dans sa correspondance, que la jeune femme a quelque sympathie pour un véritable gouvernement démocratique.

Tendance qui ne peut que s'accentuer dans le nouveau milieu, miétudiant, mi-journalistique, qu'elle va fréquenter à partir de 1831. C'est alors, en effet, que se produisent des changements importants dans sa vie: la première rupture du lien conjugal, son installation à Paris avec son amant Jules Sandeau, sa collaboration à un journal d'opposition, *Figaro,* enfin l'apparition sur la scène littéraire de la romancière George Sand. Ses premières oeuvres, toutes de contestation, mettant en cause l'organisation de la société, dénonçant d'abord le joug imposé à la femme, avant de s'attaquer à celui qui pèse sur le prolétaire, font beaucoup de bruit et suscitent l'indignation des uns et l'enthousiasme des autres.

Successivement, elle a pris ses "maîtres à penser" chez les saint-simoniens, chez Lamennais, chez Michel de Bourges. Chacun lui apporte une pâture pour son esprit avide, anxieux de trouver des solutions aux grands problèmes, mais elle garde les yeux ouverts, et souvent résiste devant certains aspects de la doctrine qui ne la satisfont pas. Seul Pierre Leroux obtiendra (provisoirement) une adhésion presque totale avec sa théorie du progrès indéfini, éclipsant l'influence de Jean-Jacques.

Après une longue collaboration à la *Revue des Deux Mondes,* elle reprend sa liberté en 1841, parce que Buloz pretend l'empêcher d'y écrire ce qu'elle pense, et d'introduire dans ses romans des opinions politiques. Elle crée une revue concurrente pour lui faire pièce: la *Revue indépendante.* Ses oeuvres sont de plus en plus "engagées," elle glisse dans tous ses romans des professions de foi républicaines, socialistes, et même communistes. Son communisme est assez différent des doctrines qui ont eu depuis l'extension que l'on sait, et Karl Marx, je ne l'ignore pas, a pu le considérer comme très petit-bourgeois, mais il faisait déjà l'effet d'un épouvantail auprès de la bourgeoisie de l'époque. Elle se rapproche des hommes de l'extrême gauche, notamment de l'équipe de la *Réforme* où Louis Blanc joue un rôle important. Elle est en relations épistolaires fréquentes avec le conspirateur italien Mazzini, exilé à Londres. Elle fonde dans le Berry un journal local destiné à faire la guerre aux autorités qui y représentent le pouvoir.

Puissance littéraire, elle devient une puissance politique. Des révolutionnaires comme Bakounine, Arnold Ruge, Mazzini, le général Pepe, la visitent. Nombreux sont les exilés, polonais ou autres, qui hantent sa maison.

A la veille de 1848, elle n'est plus tout à fait d'accord avec Leroux, elle le trouve "possédé aujourd'hui d'une rage de pacification, d'une horreur de la guerre qui va jusqu'à l'excès et que je ne saurais partager, écrit-elle. Il oublie que l'idéal est une conquête et qu'au point où en est l'humanité, toute conquête demande notre sang." Et elle ajoute ceci, qui est dur: "Entre le génie et l'aberration il n'y a souvent que l'épaisseur d'un cheveu." C'est que Leroux "n'espère que dans l'apostolat individuel," alors que, comme Mazzini, elle estime que les temps de l'insurrection sont venus, que les régimes corrompus ne tomberont pas tout seuls sans quelque action violente.

Disons encore que, du point de vue de sa vie intime et familiale, 1847 lui a apporté de graves déceptions. Sa fille Solange, sitôt mariée, s'est conduite en ennemie et a quitté Nohant après des scènes atroces. La rupture avec Chopin s'en est suivie (les deux événements sont liés), et a achevé de remplir à ras bord la coupe d'amertume.

Elle s'est repliée sur elle-même, essayant de s'étourdir avec un long travail solitaire qui sera l'*Histoire de ma vie.* Devant la défection des vivants, elle se tourne vers les morts, et fait revivre le passé, celui de son père pour commencer. Ce livre sera à la fois mémoires, méditation sur les problèmes du siècle, résumé d'une expérience déjà longue, histoire d'une famille dans une période historique agitée.

Faut-il s'étonner que l'annonce des journées de Février produise chez elle une réaction enthousiaste qui se traduit par des mots exaltés? Dans certaines dispositions psychologiques (chagrin violent, situation inextricable), tout ce qui vient du dehors rompre l'obsession personnelle peut être accueilli comme une délivrance, fût-ce la guerre, fût-ce la révolution. A plus forte raison lorsque l'événement répond à votre attente, à votre longue attente presque découragée. Le 7 février, George Sand se défendait de croire à une chimère qu'elle n'explique pas, mais que nous devinons sans peine quand elle ajoute: "Nous sommes une génération de foireux!" Le 16, elle n'espère pas mieux, de l'agitation commençante, que le remplacement de Guizot par Thiers. Le 18, elle écrit à son fils, "Borie est sens dessus dessous à l'idée qu'on va faire une révolution dans Paris. Mais je n'y vois pas de prétexte raisonnable dans l'affaire des banquets. C'est une intrigue entre ministres qui tombent et ministres qui veulent monter."

Mais après la victoire, c'est un tout autre son de cloche. A son ami Girard: "Les chagrins personnels disparaissent quand la vie publique nous appelle et nous absorbe. " A Poncy: "On est fou, on est ivre, on est heureux de s'être endormi dans la fange et de se réveiller dans les cieux." A Pauline Viardot: " Mes chagrins person-nels, qui étaient arrivés au dernier degré d'amertume, sont comme oubliés ou suspendus."

Dès le Ier mars, George Sand est arrivée à Paris, et a pris aussitôt des contacts avec plusieurs membres du Gouvernement provisoire.

Elle s'est employée activement à faire nommer plusieurs de ses amis à des postes-clés, comme l'en accuse une caricature de l'époque, ce n'est pas pour obéir à des considérations d'amitié, pour placer ses créatures, mais parce qu'elle voit en eux des hommes sûrs, capables de s'opposer avec énergie à la réaction qui déjà lève la tête et essaie de torpiller la jeune République.

Chaque régime nouveau opère ainsi, et il faut convenir qu'il serait bien fou de laisser aux postes de commande ses adversaires. Ardente nourrice de l'enfant au berceau, George Sand, qui n'est pas la rêveuse utopiste qu'on a voulu représenter, agit dans sa sphère d'activité pour mettre autour de lui des gardiens capables d'écarter les méchantes fées. Elle fait nommer son ami Fleury commissaire de la République pour le département de l'Indre, son ami Planet préfet du Cher, son ami Pouradier Duteil procureur général à Bourges (mais là, ce fut une erreur dont elle devait se mordre les doigts peu après, car on verra bientôt le procureur général poursuivre des . . . républicains pour écrits séditieux!), et quelques autres dans des postes secondaires (son fils, par exemple, est nommé maire de Nohant bien qu'il n'ait pas l'âge légal).

Son premier séjour à Paris lui a permis de rencontrer Ledru-Rollin, qui lui délivre un laissez-passer pour accéder auprès des membres du Gouvernement. Elle voit aussi Lamennais, Mazzini accouru de Londres, Lamartine. Ce dernier, dans son *Histoire de la Révolution de 1848* où il se donne toujours le beau rôle, raconte qu'il eut avec elle un entretien de plusieurs heures, pendant lequel il la conjura de mettre son talent au service de "la cause de l'ordre et de la moralisation du peuple." Il assure qu'elle le lui avait promis "avec cet accent d'enthousiasme passionné qui révèle la sincérité des convictions," mais qu'à son retour du Berry "les anciennes prédilec-tions de son esprit pour les théories aventurées du socialisme la rattachèrent par Louis Blanc à un centre de politique opposée." C'est apparemment parce que Lamartine et George Sand envisa-geaient de manière toute différente la définition de l'ordre et la manière de moraliser le peuple. Pour moraliser, George Sand ne s'en prive pas, mais en supposant le problème résolu, c'est-à-dire en félicitant le peuple d'être aussi doux qu'il est fort, de défiler avec ordre et décence, recueillement et politesse mutuelle. Tous ses écrits de cette période paraissent, à nos yeux, contenir une dose un peu forte de flatterie: "Le peuple de Paris est le premier peuple du monde;" "Le peuple a prouvé qu'il était plus beau, plus grand, plus pur que tous les riches et les savants de ce monde," et la première *Lettre au peuple* qu'elle lance avant de partir pour le Berry manque de mesure: "Bon et grand peuple, aujourd'hui que la fatigue de ta noble victoire commence à se dissiper . . . Tu as été grand! tu es héroïque de ta nature . . . Doux comme la force! O peuple, que tu es fort, puisque tu es si bon! Tu es le meilleur des amis, . . ."

Au cours des quinze jours qu'elle va passer à Nohant, elle prépare les élections. On la consulte comme un chef de parti. Son influence a fait admettre que l'on ne présenterait pas seulement des avocats et des propriétaires, mais un ouvrier et un paysan par département. Entre parenthèses, disons que les ouvriers et les paysans votèrent en général, non pour les leurs, mais pour des *messieurs*. La Chambre comptera seulement 34 ouvriers, et 16 agriculteurs, ceux-ci étant d'ailleurs des propriétaires, et non des prolétaires paysans. L'électorat de 1848 n'était pas mûr pour l'idée de George Sand.

C'est pendant son absence, le 15 mars, que le Gouvernement provisoire prend une décision lourde de conséquences, nous verrons bientôt pourquoi. On lit dans le registre des délibérations à cette date: "Le ministre de l'Intérieur est autorisé à s'entendre avec Mme. George Sand pour fournir des articles au Bulletin de la République. Le Bulletin de la République ne paraîtra désormais que sur le bon à tirer d'un des membres du Gouvernement provisoire.

"M. Crémieux est chargé du numéro du jeudi 16.

"M. Garnier-Pagès du numéro du samedi 18.

"M. Lamartine du numéro du lundi, 20, etc. etc."

Je vous épargne la liste complète, mais j'ai tenu à aller jusqu'au nom de Lamartine, car celui-ci a altéré par la suite la vérité en écrivant, comme s'il avait été informé par hasard de la collaboration de George Sand: "Lamartine apprit qu'elle rédigeait au ministère de l'Intérieur une feuille officielle intitulée le Bulletin de la République. Cette feuille incendiée des inspirations du communisme, rappelait par les termes, les souvenirs néfastes de la première république, elle fanatisait les uns d'impatience, les autres de terreur."

Or, cette décision, que Lamartine ne pouvait avoir ignorée, était du 15 mars, et c'est seulement le 19, dans le Bulletin n° 4, que paraît le premier texte de George Sand: *Aux Riches,* simple extrait d'un article beaucoup plus développé paru dans le journal de La Châtre. Plus développé et plus incisif, car si dans l'extrait du Bulletin, on ne trouve qu'une phrase qui nous paraisse mériter le qualificatif d'incendiaire au jugement de Lamartine ("Le communisme, c'est l'avenir calomnié et incompris du peuple"), l'article des *Petites Affiches de La Châtre* eût scandalisé le poète bien davantage. On y lisait: "Hélas! non, le peuple n'est pas communiste; et cependant *la France est appelée à l'être avant un siècle*," avec cet aveu non équivoque: ". . . moi qui suis communiste."

Dès son retour à Paris, George Sand déploie une activité fiévreuse et se dépense sans compter pour la cause. En dehors des Bulletins de la République, où sa collaboration ne peut être entièrement identifiée de façon certaine, faute de signature (mais je crois qu'on peut tabler sur cinq sûrs et cinq probables), elle publie une 2ᵉ *Lettre au peuple,* une *Histoire de la France écrite sous la dictée de Blaise Bonnin,* cinq brochures intitulées *Parole de Blaise Bonnin aux bons citoyens,* tous écrits de propagande à la portée du peuple, où elle utilise des mots et des tournures populaires et rustiques. Elle vante la nouvelle forme de gouvernement, rassure les timorés, justifie les mesures impopulaires, comme l'impôt des 45 centimes qui faisait crier les paysans,[1] tente de faire sentir l'idée de solidarité aux ouvriers des villes et à ceux des campagnes, que sépare une hostilité déclarée. Elle fait paraître en avril un journal intitulé *la Cause du peuple,* qui ne vivra que trois semaines, trois numéros. Et qui ne ment pas à son titre: c'est bien la cause du peuple qu'elle y défend, la cause du faible et de l'opprimé. A côté de la feuille qui porte aujourd'hui ce même nom, le journal de George Sand en 1848 paraîtra timide, bien sûr; il ne contient pas d'appels à la violence et à l'insurrection permanente. Mais qu'on réfléchisse un peu: *La Cause du peuple* de 1971 est un organe de combat et d'opposition, celle de 1848 était destinée aux vainqueurs (vainqueurs théoriques et provisoires plus que réels, je le veux bien, mais enfin vainqueurs des journées de février. Les thèmes et le ton ne peuvent être comparables).

A toute cette production il faut ajouter des circulaires pour le ministère de l'Intérieur et celui de l'Instruction publique, un prologue de circonstance pour le Théâtre français, *le Roi attend,* qui n'est pas un chef-d'oeuvre, et toute une série d'articles pour le journal de Théophile Thoré, l'un des plus à gauche de la presse: *la Vraie République.*

Tout cela avant le 15 mai. Et pendant toute cette période, George Sand participe à de nombreuses réunions plus ou moins secrètes, soit au ministère de l'Intérieur, soit chez elle, dans son perchoir de la rue de Condé, petit logement de garçon de son fils, où elle dort peu et écrit sans relâche.

Voici le moment venu de parler du Bulletin n° 16, qui causa un scandale énorme et eut certainement des conséquences fâcheuses pour les républicains. Je vous ai dit tout à l'heure dans quelles conditions les Bulletins devaient être supervisés par les ministres tour à tour. Officiellement établi jusqu'au Bulletin du vendredi 7 avril, ce tour aurait dû reprendre dans le même ordre par tacite reconduction pour les suivants. En fait, il semble bien que personne ne s'en soit soucié, et que les intéressés, s'en remettant à des sous-ordres, aient fait preuve de négligence. Ils avaient sans doute d'autres chats à fouetter, mais alors on comprend mal que toute cette émotion dont parle Lamartine dans son plaidoyer *a posteriori* ("Le Conseil *gémit* de cette déviation . . . qui plaçait ainsi sous la responsabilité du gouvernement des paroles et des doctrines *en contradiction ouverte* avec son esprit"), on comprend mal, dis-je, que cette émotion n'ait pas incité à une plus stricte surveillance. Quand on a peur du feu, on met un pompier de garde.

Voici le texte qui agita la France entière le 16 avril et jours suivants: ". . . les élections, si elles ne font pas triompher la vérité sociale, si elles sont l'expression des intérêts d'une caste, arrachée à la confiante loyauté du peuple, les élections, qui devraient être le salut de la République, seront sa perte, il n'en faut pas douter. Il n'y aurait alors qu'une voie de salut pour le peuple qui a fait les barricades, ce serait de manifester une seconde fois sa volonté, et d'ajourner les décisions d'une fausse représentation nationale."

"Ce remède extrême, déplorable, la France voudrait-elle forcer Paris à y recourir? A Dieu ne plaise!" G. Sand avait-elle pris cela sous son seul bonnet? C'est impossible. Quand elle écrivait à son fils, à la fin de mars, que le gouvernement et le peuple s'attendaient à de mauvais députés et qu'ils étaient d'accord pour les *ficher* par les fenêtres, ce n'est pas une opinion personnelle qu'elle exprimait, et il faut y voir le résultat de conciliabules avec les membres les plus avancés du gouvernement, qui envisageaient une sorte de coup d'Etat. Quelques mois plus tard, reconnaissant avec crânerie qu'elle était bien l'auteur de ce Bulletin, George Sand pouvait écrire: "Quand je disais, dans l'abominable 16e Bulletin, que le *peuple* a droit de sauver la *République,* j'avais si fort raison, que je remercie Dieu d'avoir eu cette inspiration si impolitique. Tout le monde l'avait aussi bien que moi, mais il n'y avait qu'une femme assez folle pour l'écrire." Peut-être en effet avait-elle raison de penser qu'il y a des moments, dans la vie d'un peuple, où il faut s'asseoir sur la légalité pour faire respecter une légitimité plus haute, et ne pas avoir peur de la formule: "Pas de liberté pour les ennemis de la liberté!" On peut en discuter, mais ce n'est pas ici mon propos. Seulement, seulement . . . était-il opportun de l'écrire? *"Inspiration si impolitique,"* disait-elle dans la lettre que je viens de citer. C'est le moins qu'on puisse dire.

Le premier résultat fut sans nul doute un recul de l'électorat flottant. Une menace aussi précise cabra beaucoup de gens, et servit de thème aussitôt à la contre-révolution, particulièrement dans les provinces qui déjà voyaient Paris avec suspicion, et regimbaient à l'idée de se faire faire la loi par la capitale. Ce n'est pas tout: après les événements du 15 mai, où l'Assemblée fut envahie et violentée par les clubs, et les journées de juin, une commission d'enquête fut constituée, dont le rapporteur n'hésita pas à mettre au nombre des causes de l'insurrection le fameux passage du 16e Bulletin que je vous ai cité. Des hommes qui témoignèrent devant la commission (Jules Favre, Carteret), ou de ceux qui auraient pu et dû prendre leurs responsabilités (Ledru-Rollin, Elias Regnault), aucun ne prit la défense de George Sand, ce qui manquait de courage et d'esprit chevaleresque. Tous s'entendirent pour prétendre qu'elle avait présenté trois projets pour ce Bulletin, parmi lesquels "on" aurait choisi, en quelque sorte *au hasard,* "celui qui a produit un si grand scandale dans le monde politique." Au hasard, vous entendez bien! Et il ne se trouva aucun commissaire pour s'enquérir de ce "on," si consciencieux et si fûté à la fois qu'il avait choisi *au hasard* un texte explosif, relu les épreuves, donné le bon à tirer, sans ressentir une seconde le poids de sa responsabilité. Pas curieux, ces commissaires! ou bien, ravis de faire porter le chapeau á cette femme qui avait le front de se dire communiste, et que la presse comparait aimablement à Théroigne de Méricourt. (*Illustration* du 3 juin)

Peu avant le fameux Bulletin, un club de femmes, désireux de recruter le plus célèbre des écrivains féminins de l'époque, l'avait fait inscrire sur une liste de candidats. Manifestation purement symbolique et platonique, mais à laquelle George Sand refusa de participer, avec une sécheresse qui déplut beaucoup à ces dames. C'est que ce défenseur de le femme n'était pas féministe au sens de "suffragette," pour employer un mot qui n'avait pas encore droit de cité. Elle n'était pas opposée à l'entrée de la femme dans la vie politique, elle la prévoyait, mais pour l'avenir et en y mettant une condition préalable: l'abolition de la dépendance de la femme, l'égalité des droits pour les deux sexes, le partage de l'autorité parentale. Moins chimérique que les rédactrices de la *Voix des femmes* elle pensait que la femme devait conquérir de haute lutte les droits civils avant de demander les droits civiques.

Peu après les élections, qui furent mauvaises comme on sait pour les républicains, et que ceux-ci n'osèrent pas corriger par la défenestration annoncée, un Anglais, Monckton Milnes, "homme d'esprit plus vif et plus fou qu'l n'appartient à un Anglais," au dire de Mérimée, réunit à dîner quelques convives marquants et assez étonnés de se trouver ensemble: Mérimée, Mignet, Alfred de Vigny, Tocqueville, Considérant, et George Sand. L'auteur de *Colomba* a conté cette rencontre dans sa *Correspondance*: il avait eu peine à reconnaître son ancienne maîtresse d'un jour, changée, évidemment, mais plutôt mieux, et ayant toujours ses magnifiques yeux noirs. Il se tint à distance, ils ne firent que s'entrelorgner. "A long spoon to eat with the devil: pour manger avec le diable il faut une longue cuiller." Mais Tocqueville, assis à ses côtés, eut droit à une intéressante conversation qu'il rapporte dans ses *Souvenirs*:

> Mme. Sand me peignit très en détail et avec une vivacité singulière l'état des ouvriers de Paris, leur organisation, leur nombre, leurs armes, leurs préparatifs, leurs pensées, leurs passions, leurs déterminations terribles. Je crus le tableau chargé et il ne l'était pas; ce qui suivit le montra bien. Elle me parut s'effrayer fort elle-même du triomphe populaire et témoigner une pitié un peu solennelle pour le sort qui nous attendait. "Tentez d'obtenir de vos amis, Monsieur, me dit-elle, de ne point pousser le peuple dans la rue en l'inquiétant ou en

l'irritant; de même que je voudrais pouvoir inspirer aux miens la patience; car, si le combat s'engage, croyez que vous y périrez tous." Après ces paroles consolantes, nous nous séparâmes et, depuis, je ne l'ai jamais revue.

Ce texte montre clairement que George Sand n'était pas si ignorante du monde ouvrier de son temps qu'on a voulu nous le faire croire. Pour être si bien renseignée sur l'état d'esprit de la classe ouvrière, il fallait qu'elle eût des rapports confiants avec ses chefs.

Parmi les journées marquantes de la Révolution de 1848, le 15 mai est une des plus troubles. L'Assemblée, où l'on discutait d'une aide à apporter à la Pologne martyre, fut, sous prétexte de pétitions à présenter, envahie par une foule armée et menaçante, à laquelle le Général Courtais, chargé de la protection de l'Assemblée Nationale, et dont le rôle est ici curieusement équivoque, avait laissé libre passage. On trouvera un vivant récit de la scène dans *Choses vues* de Victor Hugo. C'était la réalisation de la menace contenue dans un des articles de George Sand: "S'il était trahi . . . le peuple irrité violerait peut-être le sanctuaire de la représentation nationale." Article qui, publié le 5 mars dans un journal de province, avait pu passer inaperçu à Paris, mais les idées se propageaient vite, et le 16e Bulletin disait-il autre chose? George Sand n'entra pas dans la salle, mais nous savons par elle-même qu'elle était dans la foule. On l'a accusée d'avoir harangué le peuple de la fenêtre d'un café, depuis disparu, qui était au coin de la rue de Bourgogne et du quai d'Orsay. Elle l'a démenti, son fils l'a démenti aussi, plus tard. Le doute subsiste dans l'esprit de certains de ses biographes, mais quand on sait combien elle avait de complexes pour parler en public, n'étant pas du tout douée pour la parole, on demeure sceptique sur la véracité des journaux de l'époque, où fleurissent d'ailleurs les contre-vérités les plus réfutables. Les uns impriment par exemple que pour éviter les poursuites elle s'est rendue en Italie, d'autres qu'elle réside à Tours, alors que nous pouvons apporter la preuve qu'elle a tout simplement regagné Nohant.

Y est-elle tranquille? Non, pas trop, car les manifestations hostiles se succèdent. Les bourgeois conservateurs de La Châtre "ont fait accroire aux paysans, écrit-elle, que j'étais l'ardent disciple du Père Communisme, un gaillard très méchant qui brouille tout à Paris et qui veut qu'on mette à mort les enfants au dessous de trois ans et les vieillards au dessus de soixante . . . Hors de ma commune, on le croit, et on promet de m'enterrer dans les fossés." Mais à Paris on est également monté contre elle, et sa fille lui écrit un jour que les gardes nationaux se promettent de lui faire un mauvais parti. Heureusement toutes les menaces restèrent verbales, et il n'y eut pas de sang répandu à Nohant, seulement quelques défilés où l'on criait hargneusement, à la grille du château, "A bas le communisme! Mort à George Sand!"

C'est de là qu'elle suivit avec la tristesse qu'on devine les événements de juin qui lui arrachèrent cette phrase désabusée: "Je ne crois plus à l'existence d'une République qui commence par tuer ses prolétaires," et encore: "Si Jésus reparaissait parmi nous, il serait empoigné par la garde nationale comme factieux et anarchiste."

Elle ne renonce pas, elle ne met pas la tête sous l'aile. Elle signe courageusement des articles dans *la Vraie République,* élevant la voix en faveur des proscrits et des prisonniers: Barbès, Louis Blanc. En décembre, elle protestera contre la candidature de Louis-Napoléon à la présidence, et quand les jeux seront faits, elle fera dans *la Réforme* une analyse lucide des événements de cette année si fertile en surprises, où l'histoire de la France avait pris un tournant trop brusque et mal préparé. Elle note avec perspicacité que "l'histoire changera désormais de caractère. Ce ne sera plus seulement le récit des faits et gestes de certains hommes; ce sera principalement l'étude des aspirations, des impressions et des manifestations des masses. [. . .] Le souverain nouveau, l'être collectif a manqué de prudence et d'habileté. Il est jeune, l'enfant-roi; il a les travers de son âge . . . Pour mon compte, j'avoue que je me sens peuple . . ."

Avec une déception de plus dans le coeur, mais conservant cependant ses espoirs indomptés dans la naissance d'un monde meilleur, elle se remit au travail.

La littérature reprenait ses droits, après l'intermède politique, mais la politique ne perdait pas les siens. La préface de *la Petite Fadette* est assez explicite à cet égard. Répondant à Hetzel qui lui demandait une nouvelle pour un journal nouveau, elle écrivait le 29 juillet: "Je vous fais une espèce de *Champi*. Cela vous va-t-il? Il me serait impossible sous le coup des événements de faire quelque chose qui eût la couleur de mes idées, sans liberté entière. Je fais donc quelque chose que j'aurais pu faire il y a un an. Mais vous me laisserez dire un peu dans une espèce de préface pourquoi je reviens aux bergeries."

Et cette préface s'ouvre abruptement par des mots assez éloquents en eux-mêmes: "Et, tout en parlant de la République que nous *rêvons* et de celle que nous *subissons,* nous étions arrivés à l'endroit du chemin ombragé où le serpolet invite au repos." *Rêvons, subissons:* l'antithèse devait avoir un sens bien clair pour tous les lecteurs. Un peu plus loin, elle exprime, sans grandiloquence, mais avec d'autant plus de force, ses désillusions: "Je n'étais point de son avis dans ce moment-là; je ne pouvais pas si aisément prendre mon parti sur les mauvais instincts, les mauvaises passions et les mauvaises actions que les révolutions font remonter à la surface." Enfin cette longue et triste méditation dialoguée se termine par une dédicace fort claire encore que voilée: le nom du dédicataire n'apparaît point, seulement un prénom: Armand, dont on nous dit qu'il est prisonnier. Qui donc à l'époque aurait pu s'y tromper? et ne pas comprendre qu'il s'agissait d'Armand Barbès, enfermé à Vincennes depuis sa condamnation par la Haute-Cour de Bourges?

Vers la fin de l'année, tandis qu'elle travaille à tirer de son roman *François le Champi* une pièce destinée à un grand succès, elle fait une préface à un livre de Victor Borie, *Travailleurs et propriétaires,* où elle analyse le conflit en cours et insiste sur le caractère social qu'il a revêtu. Son thème est que "La propriété est de deux natures: Il y a une propriété personnelle et imprescriptible. Il y a une propriété modifiable et commune." Certaines des pages qu'elle consacre ensuite à l'examen de la doctrine communiste, sont assez prophétiques, d'autres ont été démenties par ce qui a suivi. Mais c'est ce qui arrive, n'est-ce pas, à tous les prophètes? Ce qu'il en faut retenir en tout cas, c'est qu'elle fait montre là encore, d'un courage qu'il ne faudrait pas nier comme l'ont fait quelques exégètes qui dédaignent de se remettre dans les conditions où les paroles ont été prononcées et les écrits publiés. C'était aller à contre-courant d'une opinion puissante en cette fin d'année 1848 que d'oser écrire:

> . . . comme dans le moment où nous vivons on parle encore, dans les provinces, de pendre et de brûler les communistes, moi, personnellement, je ne répudierai point ce titre dangereux. Je ne le ferais que le jour où le communisme triompherait en politique, et m'adresserait les mêmes menaces que les conservateurs m'adressent aujourd'hui. Jean-Jacques Rousseau disait: "Je suis philosophe avec les superstitieux,

religieux avec les athées." Il est des temps d'anarchie où cette parole de Jean-Jacques est nécessairement la devise de tout esprit sincère et courageux."

Est-il nécessaire d'en dire davantage, et ne convient-il pas de terminer sur une parole de George Sand elle-même? Je crois cependant qu'il ne sera pas déplacé de citer un mot de Victor Hugo, assez bien en situation: "En ces quatre mois, la France en était à ne pas distinguer le faux du vrai, entre cette femme qui s'appelait Lamartine, et cet homme qui s'appelait George Sand."

NOTES

1. Elle est loin d'approuver elle-même. Dans *La Cause du peuple,* sous la signature de Victor Borie, on lira que "cet impôt est une arme qu'une erreur du ministre des finances a mise entre le mains des ennemis de la République."

Paris—The Romantic Hub of Europe

FRANK S. LAMBASA
Dept. of Comparative Literature and Languages
Hofstra University

Paris has often been called the artistic hub of the world. The list of artists and would-be artists who came to Paris in these years from all parts of the globe would be truly enormous. There is a definite aura about Paris, a potent magnetism, a special *genius loci,* a kind of irresistible magic which attracts restless minds, making it an international artistic and bohemian center. At least, this is what Paris has become within the last 150 years.

Even medieval Paris was the reputed capital of eloquence, *le biendire* and to the Huguenot king Henry IV, Paris was "worth a mass." That is to say, the Protestant Henry was willing to convert to Catholicism to secure the support of the people of Paris. Seventeenth century Paris was the elegant center of "good taste" and "good manners" (*le bon goût*). Eighteenth century Paris was first the germinal center of the Enlightenment and Reason and later the source of revolutionary sentiment. It was, however, only in the 1830s that Paris became the accepted supranational center of literature, the crucible of arts and artistic movements, and that bohemian heaven which still attracts creative minds from all over the world.

As Curtis Cate correctly remarks in his biography of George Sand,[1] no European city prior to 1830 could claim to be the exclusive capital of the continent's arts. England, after all, could boast of having launched in the first two decades of the nineteenth century more poets of international fame—Byron, Keats, Shelley, Coleridge, and Wordsworth—but none were London-based poets. Rather they were men of the countryside and men of the world at large. While Italians had earlier dominated the world of music, by the early nineteenth century the Germans and Austrians, Mozart, Haydn, Beethoven, and Schubert, had made Vienna the musical capital of Europe.

By the 1830s, however, Paris was beginning to supplant Vienna as the musical capital of Europe. Although Rossini[2] first went to Vienna to be acclaimed, it was in Paris that the great composer settled after 1824 to become Europe's arbiter of opera. His compatriot Luigi Cherubini was already there, and Rossini's example was soon followed by the most celebrated names in music of the period. The German-born Meyerbeer, the Hungarian Franz Liszt, the master of bel canto Bellini, the Polish-born Chopin, and even the German nationalist Richard Wagner[3] all gravitated now toward Paris. And while Chopin's first ambition after finishing his lycée studies in Warsaw, was to go to Vienna (where he experienced not only his first triumphs as a pianist, but also found a publisher for one of his earliest works),[4] in Paris he ultimately made his home and enjoyed his greatest success.

To an even greater extent than for musicians, Paris became the European center for painters and sculptors. Nurtured by native talents, the Romantic revolution rebelled against the classical restraint, and rallied under the banners of painters Géricault and Delacroix. The emotive coloring of these two artists led the way to that chromatic brilliance exhibited in the second half of the nineteenth century by the Impressionists.

While the acceptance of literary Romanticism in France was rather late in comparison with England and Germany, by 1830 the Romantics held absolute power in Paris. A rare collection of youthful genius assembled there. Above all was the poet, playwright, and novelist Victor Hugo, whose play *Hernani,* at its premiere on February 25, 1830, in the Comédie Française, set the stage for the entire French Romantic revolution and whose *Notre-Dame de Paris* (1831) became the epitome of a Romantic novel. The flamboyant Alexandre Dumas, the "uncrowned king of Paris," whose melodramas linked the popular theater of the boulevards to the stately classical presentations of "Le Théâtre Français," united in his exuberant and irresistible nature both "Le Dandisme" and "La Bohême romantique," two characteristic phenomena of the period.[5] Equalling Dumas in productivity, but surpassing him in quality, was the towering figure of Balzac. Also in this group were Théophile Gautier, the bohemian author of *Mademoiselle de Maupin*; the eccentric Gérard de Nerval, translator of *Faust*; the literary critic Sainte-Beuve, whose judgement was both universally admired and feared; man-about-town and novelist, Prosper Mérimée; and, finally, but by no means least, the resolutely independent writer, George Sand, who had just made her literary début in *Le Figaro*.

The number of new plays, novels, books of poetry, painting exhibits, and musical offerings during this springtime in Paris was astounding.[6] Literary salons and clubs thrived. It was the time of Stendhal's *Le Rouge et le noir* and *La Chartreuse de Parme*, of Honoré Daumier's drawings in *La Caricature*, the exhibits in the salon of the Barbizon school, of Meyerbeer's *Les Huguenots*, of Berlioz' *Symphonie fantastique, Benvenuto Cellini, Romeo et Juliette*, Bellini's *Norma*, and *I Puritani*, Chopin's mazurkas, études, concerti, and the celebrated performances of the almost uncanny violin virtuoso, Paganini.

The artistic world of Paris was young and articulate, in Alfred de Musset's words: "Une génération ardente, pâle, nerveuse,"[7] drunk with poetry and love, a generation that created an atmosphere charged with great expectations which were, of course, not always fulfilled.

When Aurore Dupin, Baronne Dudevant, *dite* George Sand, reached Paris in January 1831, in the company of a young, budding writer Jules Sandeau, Paris seemed to her the most romantic city in the world. It was to be the place of freedom from her oppressive married life, and the place of her existential spring.[8] In true bohemian style, the two young people established themselves in a garret on the Quai des Grand-Augustins, from which they could gaze at the magnificent Notre-Dame and the sixteenth century Pont Neuf. The house, now thoroughly dilapidated, still stands.[9]

Literary life started for George Sand, however, when she moved to her "mansarde bleue" at 19 Quai Malaquais. There she experienced her first literary triumph as well as her personal heartaches during the four eventful years 1832-1836. There she wrote *Indiana*, the first work to bear the name "George Sand." In this novel Sand extended that ardent novelistic feminism of Mme de Staël in which the woman proclaims her innate right to live her own life. Feverish and tempestuous *Lélia* followed in 1833, creating a veritable storm in French literary circles.

It is also in her "blue garret" that she penned several of her famous *Lettres d'un voyageur,* the novel *Jacques,* many novellas like *Leone Leoni,* and some of the most gripping pages of her *Journal intime* of 1834. There she held court, and the number of celebrities coming to pay her homage was truly extraordinary. Besides Jules Sandeau, with whom she "collaborated" [10] on her first novel, *Rose et Blanche,* and with whom her affair was just coming to an end (in 1833), there was Prosper Mérimée, whose brief adventure with George circulated in several contradictory variations; the celebrated actress, Marie Dorval; and the very embodiment of "le dandisme poètique," Alfred de Musset.[11] From Venice came Pietro Pagello, who was Alfred's doctor during their unfortunate stay there; Michel de Bourges, the lawyer who helped her in the painful separation trial from her husband; and the Swiss Romantic poet, Charles Didier, who completed this intimate circle of lovers.[12] Among the many other intellectual and artistic as well as social luminaries in attendance were the philosopher Lamennais, the politician Arago, the literary critics Gustave Planche and Sainte-Beuve, the composers Berlioz and Liszt,[13] and so many others.

Finally into this charmed circle of poets, religious and social reformers, and musical geniuses that orbited around this most celebrated, and in some eyes the most "notorious" woman of her age, were added two famous foreign poets who contributed an additional cosmopolitan, international flavor. Both were exiles from their native countries. Both at the same time were representatives of the highest achievements of the Romantic movement in their respective homelands: the German Heinrich Heine and the Polish Adam Mickiewicz.[14]

Paris, to Heine, the *enfant terrible* among German literary prodigies, when he arrived there in May, 1831, was a city made for young poets. He was thirty-three at the time and already a celebrity for several years because of his poetry, his intrepid political writings, and an incandescent wit. Almost from the very beginning of his stay in Paris he became a friend of Théophile Gautier, and he was often in the company of Balzac, who called him "Le grand, le puissant Heine."[15] As an ingenious coiner of *bons mots,* Heine was immediately welcomed in several Parisian salons. His characterization of Musset as a "young man with a promising past," circulated everywhere.[16] For Heine, Paris was not "the capital of France but of the whole civilized world, the mecca of the intellectual élite. . . . A new art, a new life is being created here, and the creators of this new world lead tumultuously joyful lives." He saw the Romantic movement in Paris as an almost miraculous assemblage of stars, a "constellation of the first magnitude, illuminating the whole of France with the fierce light of its ideas and ideals."[17]

Heine recorded all that was happening around him. Strolling through the streets and boulevards where the great political and cultural battles of the world had been fought, Heine's enchantment seemed boundless. He succumbed easily to this seething center of Europe and got caught up in the whirl of Parisian society, literary salons, and exhibits. In his dispatches from Paris, Heine described with all the nuances of a seasoned reporter the art exhibit of 1831 and its focal attraction, Delacroix's tribute to the July Revolution, *Liberty Leading the People*.[18] But Paris, the city of light, also had its dark moments of terror. Heine's deeply moving portrayal of the cholera epidemic which descended upon Paris in the midst of its carnival season of 1832 is a vivid account of a city gripped by a malevolent force when "a masked hangman with an invisible guillotine drove about Paris."[19] While attending the funeral of a friend, finding himself suddenly surrounded by innumerable funeral processions converging at the Père Lachaise cemetery, Heine escaped to its highest hill from which he could see the city "so schön vor sich liegen."[20] "The sun was setting—its last rays seemed to bid me a melancholy farewell; twilight mists enveloped the ailing Paris like white shrouds, and I wept bitterly over the unhappy city, the city of freedom, of inspiration, and of martyrdom; the city which has already suffered so much for the temporal deliverance of humanity."[21]

While Heine was especially fascinated by the demi-monde of Paris and was in constant pursuit of the cursory amours of the boulevards, falling now for this "lorette" or that "grisette," (finally tying himself for life with one),[22] he was equally attracted to his patroness, the Princess Belgiojoso, and to George Sand, with whom he fell in love at their first meeting.[23] While he eventually recovered from his infatuation, he remained George's devoted friend until the end of his life.[24]

Next to the Princess Belgiojoso, George Sand appeared to Heine as the true ideal of a woman. The qualities of her mind, which according to his contemporaries had a vigor of "masculinity," also included all the gentleness of a tender, maternal friend. He often came to her home unannounced, finding her "sitting in an alcove in her salon, dressed as a monk or in man's clothing, her slender fingers busy rolling endless cigarettes."[25] Heine addressed her always as "ma chère cousine." He branded women who talked against her as "malicious cats who caressed her with one paw and scratched her with the other," while her male detractors are like "dogs baying at the moon," while she "gently smiles down at the dogs who bark at her."[26]

In her *Entretiens journaliers,* the continuation of her intimate diary, George Sand devotes several pages to Heine and characterizes him with a few deft strokes:

> Heine can say diabolically clever things . . . his witticisms hurt because his arrows always hit the mark. He is considered inherently wicked, but nothing is farther from the truth. His heart is as good as his tongue is mischievous. In love he is tender, romantic, and soft even to weakness . . . nevertheless he is a cynic, and a mocker. . . . He is like his poetry, a mixture of exalted sentimentality and clownish mockery. He is a humorist, like Stern. . . . As a rule I do not care for sarcastic people, yet I have always loved these two men.[27]

Paris in the 1830s was the home not only for the German Romantic poets fleeing conservative oppression at home, but also for those from Poland. In fact, the force of historical circumstances made Paris rather than Warsaw the center for Polish Romantic poets and composers. The Russians, who controlled Poland at that time, prohibited any expression of Polish nationalism. After the failure of a nationalist insurrection against the Russian oppressors in 1830-31, Polish political leaders as well as artists made Paris the home for Polish nationalists in exile.

During her romantic involvement with Frederic Chopin, perhaps the most popular of the Polish nationalist exiles, Sand came into contact with Chopin's compatriots who found in her a sympathetic listener to their nostalgic tales and recollections of their occupied homeland. George's favorite was the greatest poet of Polish Romanticism, Adam Mickiewicz, who occupies the same place in Polish literary history that Pushkin does in the Russian or Goethe in the German.[28] As the national poet of a country for which the French felt a great deal of sympathy, Mickiewicz became the first lecturer for Slavic literature at the Collège de France. He lived in Paris after the collapse of the Polish insurrection in 1831, spending twenty-three years in exile among a large number of Poles that included not only the defeated military leaders, and members of the Polish Diet and of the national government, but also almost all major artists. It was in Paris that Chopin composed most of his immortal music, and that Mickiewicz wrote one of the finest narrative poems in all European literature of the nineteenth century, *Pan Tadeusz*.[29] Also in Paris was the second of the great Polish Romantic poets, Juliusz Slowacki, Mickiewicz's younger rival and no lesser genius.[30] George was greatly impressed by Mickiewicz, calling him a "génie égal à celui de Byron"[31] and she tried, unsuccessfully, to find a producer for Mickiewicz's mystical dramatic poem *Forefathers*. Failing in her effort to have it staged, she published an article in which the drama was extolled as a greater play than Goethe's *Faust*.[32]

It was a similar situation of political oppression at home that drove young, rebellious poets of many European nationalities to Paris, giving this city, during the 1830s, a literary pre-eminence and a Romantic, bohemian attraction which lasted into the twentieth century. When Heine arrived in Paris, he wrote to a friend: "If anyone asks you how I'm getting on here, tell him, like the fish in the water. Or rather, tell people that when one fish in the sea asks another how he is getting on, the reply is 'Like Heine in Paris.'" I would like to amend this witticism of Heine's by applying it to the European Romantics of the 1830s. If one fish in the water had asked another how it was getting along, the reply should have been: "Like the Romantics in Paris."

NOTES

1. Curtis Cate, *George Sand, A Biography,* (Boston: Houghton Mifflin Co., 1975), p. XII.

2. Rossini was dubbed by his teacher in Bologna: "Il Tedeschino"—the little German, because he so quickly absorbed the scores of Haydn and Mozart.

3. Wagner and Donizetti came to Paris in 1839 and stayed until 1842.

4. It was the variations on Mozart's "La Ci Darem" for piano and orchestra.

5. Henri Murger depicted this bohemian Paris in *La Vie de bohème* on which Puccini later based his opera.

6. According to *Confessions* (translated into English under the title *Man About Paris*) by Arsène Houssaye.

7. Alfred de Musset, *Confession d'un enfant du siècle, Oeuvres complètes* (Paris: Edition Charpentier, 1902), Tome VIII, p. 3.

8. Joseph Barry, *Infamous Woman, The Life of George Sand*, (Garden City: Doubleday and Co., Inc., 1977).

9. All information concerning the Parisian lodgings of George Sand comes from lectures of M. Georges Lubin, delivered at various gatherings (the last at the Alliance Française in New York), and reported in the *Bulletin de Liaison* of the association "Les Amis de George Sand," juin 1976.

10. It was rumored that George wrote most of the novel, and that Jules's contribution was only minimal.

11. Musset's playful drawings of George and burlesque verses like:

> George est dans sa chambrette
> Entre deux pots de fleur
> Fumant sa cigarette
> Les yeux baignés de pleurs.

were a good example of Musset's jocose moods.

12. In the case of Didier, it was mostly platonic. Chopin arrived on the scene later.

13. Liszt was at that time still in the company of Marie d'Agoult, who also had a salon of her own.

14. George Sand met both Heine and Mickiewicz in the salon of Marie d'Agoult.

15. Victor Bernard, *Henri Heine*, (Paris: B. Grasset, 1946) p. 177.

16. "Heine . . . disait ce soir en parlant d'Alfred de Musset: 'C'est un jeune homme de beaucoup de passe'" (GS, *Entretiens journaliers*, 7 janv.

1841 in: *Oeuvres autobiographiques,* texte établie, présenté et annoté par Georges Lubin, (Paris: Gallimard, 1971) II, 1010.

17. Frederic Grunfeld, "When Paris Was a City for the Young," *Horizon,* v. 18, number 3 (Summer 1976), p. 33.

18. Heinrich Heine, *Sämmtliche Werke,* "Gemäldeausstellung in Paris 1831," VI, 16-20.

19. Grunfeld, "When Paris Was a City for the Young," p. 38.

20. Heine, *Sämmtliche Werke,* "Französische Umstande," VI, 177-193.

21. 'Eben war die Sonne untergegangen, ihre letzten Strahlen schienen wehmütig Abschied zu nehmen, die Nebel der Dämmerung umhüllten wie weisse Laken das kranke Paris, und ich weinte bitterlich über die unglückliche Stadt, die Stadt der Freiheit, der Begeisterung und des Martyrtums, die Heilandstadt, die für die weltliche Erlösung der Menschheit schon so viel gelitten!" ("Französische Umstände," p. 192).

22. Much has been made of Heine's relationship to Mathilde Mirat who worked in her aunt's glove and shoe shop. She was nineteen, when Heine met her in 1834, and he thirty-seven. After living with her for seven years, he married her, and this marriage lasted until the poet's death in 1856.

23. According to Vladimir Karénine (pseud. of Varvara Komarova) one of the earliest biographers of George Sand, *George Sand, sa vie et ses oeuvres,* (Paris: Ollendorff, 1899).

24. Shortly before his death, while lying paralyzed from a long illness in his "mattress grave," Heine uttered a bit of malicious gossip about George and an artist by the name of Dessauer. George dismissed it as a bitter reaction to his terrible malady: "Henri Heine m'a prêté contre lui des sentiments inouïs. Le génie a ses rêves de malade" (*Histoire de ma vie* in: *Oeuvres autobiographiques,* II, 437).

25. Antonina Vallentin, *Poet in Exile; The Life of Heinrich Heine,* trans. by Harrison Brown, (Port Washington: Kennikat Press, 1970) p. 168.

26. Heine, *Sämmtliche Werke,* "Briefe aus Deutschland," IX, 479.

27. George Sand, *Entretiens journaliers,* 7 janvier 1841 in: *OA,* II, 1010-1011. The last sentence also refers to her Berrichon friend and neighbor Jules Néraud, whom she called "mon Malgache." (Author's translation).

28. Adam Mickiewicz (1798-1855) created poetry full of patriotic pathos, a call to Romantic heroism and idealism. In 1819 he was graduated from the University of Wilno, and in 1823 he was arrested on charges of anti-Russian activity and exiled to Russia. In 1829 he was allowed to leave for Western Europe, settling in Paris in 1831. When the Crimean War broke out, he went to Constantinople to organize the Polish troops to fight against Russia. There he contracted cholera and died in 1855.

29. *Pan Tadeusz,* published in Paris in 1834, is his masterpiece. A nostalgic tale of Polish life at the time of Napoleon's invasion of Russia.

30. Juliusz Slowacki (1809-1849) was an intense poet of Romantic patriotism. Esoteric in his reveries and symbols, he is often compared to Byron, Coleridge, and Shelley.

31. *Histoire de ma vie* in: *OA,* II, 438.

32. Cate reports that she demanded a fee of 2000 francs from Buloz, the founder of the *Revue des Deux Mondes,* p. 480.

33. To Ferdinand Hiller, October 24, 1832.

George Sand's Literary Encounters

MARIE-JEANNE PECILE

"All genuine intelligence is innovating."
George Sand (*Questions d'art et de littérature*)
Paris, 1878

It is high time to demolish once and for all the rather silly notion that George Sand wrote as easily as she drew breath. In spite of Jules Janin's and Anatole France's remarks, it seems fairer and more reasonable to recognize that her ease in writing stemmed from a native talent, certainly, but also was the result of a long apprenticeship and daily discipline. Her own modesty should not mislead us. She, herself, was the first to debunk the myth of unconscious and spontaneous artistic creation. For the sake of her art, she proved capable of the same efforts and sacrifices as Balzac or Flaubert—indeed, perhaps greater ones, because she was responsible for and supported six people. Her relentless activity and the volume of her literary output were prompted by her financial responsibilities as well as by her need to communicate.

George Sand was admired by personalities as diverse as Chateaubriand, Michelet, Renan, Hugo, Taine, Heine, Dostoevsky, Turgenev, George Eliot, Matthew Arnold, Mendizabal, Mazzini, and Walt Whitman. She was held in high respect by Sainte-Beuve, Balzac, and Flaubert who dedicated works to her and solicited her critical opinion. In her time, she was more famous than Stendhal and Flaubert and she was considered the equal of Balzac and Victor Hugo. Indeed, George Sand and Victor Hugo were the two most popular writers in nineteenth-century France. In the light of this, is it conceivable that Sand who participated so intensely in the life of her age, the nineteenth century with its revitalized concern for criticism, would have remained indifferent to the works of her contemporaries and her friends? How could this woman who wrote so regularly over a period of more than forty years, not have reflected upon her art? The texts are there: we possess her prefaces, reviews, critical articles, the most important of which are collected in several volumes: *Pensées littéraires, Mélanges, Questions d'art et de littérature, Souvenirs et impressions littéraires, Autour de la table.* One must also look at her correspondence with Sainte-Beuve, Balzac, and Flaubert. Her contribution in this area, as in others, was profoundly original and displayed a remarkable acumen.

George Sand's vocation developed on fertile ground. She came of a cultured and lettered family, and enjoyed a fine and unusual education for a woman in the nineteenth century. From an early age, she was an avid reader. Her favorites and her mentors were Vergil, Montaigne, Molière, Rousseau, and Chateaubriand. She admired Vergil's simplicity and his natural, flowing style. It has been suggested that her admiration for the *Georgics* prompted her to choose the pseudonym of George. She read and reread Montaigne, deeply impressed by his wisdom and his moderation: "Montaigne does not seem to me a skeptic but a stoic. Though he hardly ever draws conclusions, he always instructs: without preaching, he conveys a love of wisdom, of reason, of tolerance and introspection. . . . His works are like all that issue from a beautiful mind: they invite reflection."[1] She was provoked, however, to vigorous protest against Montaigne's misogyny by his celebrated chapter on friendship in which he states that woman is incapable of such a strong and durable bond as existed between him and La Boétie:

> The moral inferiority attributed to woman repelled my young pride: "But that is wrong!" I cried, "this ineptitude and frivolity which you throw in our face is the result of the poor education you have condemned us to, and you aggravate the evil in confirming its existence. Put us in the best circumstances and place the men too. Make them pure, serious and of firm will. You will see that our souls have come likewise from the hand of God."[2]

She admired the temperance and common sense of Molière and she shared his philosophy of life: follow nature and do not overvalue life and death. She was deeply impressed by Rousseau. She regarded

him as the perfect man of passion and sentiment and she was
enthralled by the charm of his emotional reasoning and ardent logic.
She traveled to Les Charmettes in an effort to understand his
complex and contradictory nature: "He was a man, a true man, not
like those famous men who, drunk with their own superiority,
consent to exhibit themselves, but a man such as God makes men and
as he sends them to us. He is a being subject to every frailty and
capable of all heroism."[3] She placed his writings in their historical
context and sought to rehabilitate Rousseau by means of the most
understanding and compassionate analysis. However, she disliked
the cynicism of the *Confessions,* and she blamed Rousseau for his
self-accusations in the service of self-excuse. She stressed the need
for a new appraisal of his work:

We have too long judged the *Confessions* of Jean-Jacques from the
point of view of a purely individual apologia. He aided and abetted
this unfortunate state of affairs by mixing his personal interests
throughout his works. Now that his friends and enemies are no more,
we judge the work from a higher vantage point. We hardly care to
what point the author of the *Confessions* was unjust or insane or
to what point his detractors were impious and unfeeling. What
engages us, enlightens us and still exercises its influence, is the
spectacle of his great soul combatting the errors of his age and the
obstacles in his way as a philosopher, and the struggle of a genius
impassioned with austerity, freedom and dignity against the frivolous, faithless and corrupt society he lived in.[4]

She contrasted Rousseau, "A man of genius and meditation,
miserable, unjust and desperate,"[5] to Voltaire, Diderot and the
followers of d'Holbach: "Men of the day, active and successful
critics who propounded the philosophy of the eighteenth century,
dismantling society without a thought of the morrow. . . . Powerful
men, strong men, indispensable men, worshipped by the public,
borne in triumph, who crushed and despised the misanthropist
Rousseau, instead of defending him or avenging the verdicts of
religious intolerance, against which they should have, following their
own principles, made common cause with him."[6] She thought him
the only true philosopher of the group because he was the only one
imbued with religion. She sums up his influence,

After centuries of oblivion and ingratitude, he was the first to lead man back to the notion of truth and to the cultivation of simplicity. Literature which is the expression of the intellectual life of the masses, had grown pompous and affected. Jean-Jacques made it sincere and sublime.[7]

George Sand praised Chateaubriand as "the man of sentiment and enthusiasm."[8] His idealism moved her and his style entranced her. She admired *Le Génie du christianisme* and was deeply influenced by *René*. Because he had admired *Indiana* and *Valentine,* she sought his patronage at the time of the publication of the highly controversial *Lélia*. Nonetheless, they only met two years later in May, 1835. Chateaubriand devoted a chapter of his *Mémoires d'outre-tombe* and several pages in *La Vie de Rancé* to her.

In her first piece of literary criticism, George Sand compared René and Obermann. This article entitled "Autopsie d'Obermann" is noteworthy for its acuity and depth. In it, she defines *le mal du siècle* better than anyone. Still, these two temperaments were too different to reach any real understanding. George Sand frowned upon the *culte du moi,* and she kept at a safe distance from the great egotists of her day.

The same can be said about Vigny. If *Aldo le rimeur* prefigures Vigny's *Chatterton* and deals with the same themes, its conclusion is totally different: far from committing suicide, Aldo finds a new love for life as he discovers science. Although Sand did not finish her play, her message of courageous industry and perseverance, despite society's indifference and persecutions, is the exact opposite of that of Vigny. She was far too dynamic and optimistic to approve of haughty skepticism and solitary stoicism. She was a writer *engagé* and she believed in the didactic power of art and in the moral responsibility of the writer.

With Sainte-Beuve, however, she shared a long and fruitful communication of ideas. She hailed him as one of her "educators and intellectual benefactors"[9] and she wrote: "My intellectual life has been made up of you, M. de Lamennais and M. Leroux."[10] Sainte-Beuve praised *Indiana* and wrote a very favorable review of *Valentine.* She read him parts of *Lélia* and requested his comments. Dismayed by the critical attacks on *Lélia,* she appealed to Sainte-

Beuve who, after vacillating, wrote a long evaluation of the novel, which he described as extraordinary rather than beautiful. He depicted Sand in *Portraits contemporains*: her passionate nature frightened him, but he was won over by her youth, her spontaneity, her audacity, and her productivity. He thought highly of *Metella, Jacques, Cosima,* and her rustic novels which he praised, stressing that they were a novelty. He celebrated her in *La Revue des Deux Mondes* and bore witness to his admiration by submitting her name for the biennial prize of the Académie Française. He did, however, censure her political activities and disapproved of her tendency to mix politics and art. They became estranged when George Sand founded *La Revue indépendante* with Pierre Leroux but they resumed their friendship later and they grew closer until Sainte-Beuve's death in 1869.

George Sand admired Sainte-Beuve as a writer more than as a man. She disliked his indiscretion, his moodiness, his intolerance, and "something vaguely priestly in his manner." [11] Her description of him is masterly: "Too much heart for his spirit and too much spirit for his heart. Thus I explained this lofty nature and without daring to claim today that I understood him completely, I do think that this formula is the key to what his talent offers that is original and mysterious." [12] She attended his admission ceremony at the Académie Française in February 1845. She praised his facility and his wit but voiced reservations about his prim manner and his affected style which renders him obscure at times. Similarly, she criticized the Académie as archaic, ossified, cut off from life and she warned: "Literature considered only as the *form* of thought cannot captivate intelligent men's attention." [13]

Shortly after her arrival in Paris, George Sand made the acquaintance of Balzac. He had already made a name for himself with *Le Dernier Chouan, Un Episode sous la terreur, Le Réquisitionnaire,* and *La Peau de chagrin.* He portrayed her under the name of Camille Maupin in *Béatrix, ou Les Amours forcés,* the subject of which was suggested to him by Sand herself during a visit he made to Nohant. He sent her *L'Elixir de longue vie, La Peau de chagrin* and dedicated to her *Les Mémoires de deux jeunes mariées.* At his request, she wrote the preface in the posthumous Houssiaux edition.

Balzac and Sand had marked similarities: both were tireless

workers, both were gifted with exceptional powers of observation and imagination, but their political and aesthetic opinions differed sharply as did their literary aspirations. She quoted him as saying: "You seek man as he ought to be. I take him as he is. Believe me, we are both right. Both paths lead to the same end."[14] Far from combatting her idealism, Balzac encouraged Sand to follow her inclination which was consistent with her temperament and her convictions. George Sand relates at length a conversation between them which illuminates their respective positions: "You write the human comedy," said she, "the title is modest. You might as well say the human tragedy." "Yes," replied Balzac, "and you, you are writing the human epic. Now that title would be too exalted, but I would like to write the human eclogue. . . . You want to paint man as he is and you can, very well. But I feel impelled to portray him as I wish he would be, as I believed he should be."[15] Clearly, the idealism of George Sand was not simply a reaction against the prevailing realism but a conviction deeply held and bound to her belief in human progress.

For all their differences, the two writers esteemed each other highly and understood each other well. Their friendship lasted nineteen years. George Sand has left us a portrait of Balzac which is both affectionate and perceptive:

> Childish and mighty . . . Modest to the point of self-effacement, self-congratulatory to the point of bombast. Confident in himself and in others, very gregarious, very good and very crazy, with a sanctuary of inner reason where he withdrew to dominate entirely his creation . . . pragmatic and romantic, both in excess, credulous and skeptical, full of contrast and mysteries. . . .[16]

She praised his stamina and his productivity, his power and the comprehensiveness of his vision: "Nothing more complete has ever sprung from the brain of a writer. . . . He has said everything, seen everything, understood everything and divined all."[17] But her deep and sincere regard did not blind her to his faults: "He has grave defects: A tortured and contrived style, expressions in dubious taste. He lacks a sense of proportion in the plotting of his works. . . ."[18] She concludes her analysis by stressing the novelty, the unity and the amplitude of his *oeuvre*:

For Balzac, the novel was the framework and the pretext for an almost all embracing inquiry into ideas, feelings, customs, habits, law, art, professional life. . . . In brief, all that makes up contemporary life. Thanks to him, no earlier epoch will be known to the future generations as fully as our own.[19]

George Sand and Musset: their passion which lasted almost two years is, to quote Sainte-Beuve: "Part of the poetry of the century."[20] It has been discussed so abundantly that there is no need to dwell on it, except to point out once more that it provided mutual enrichment. Long before Sand and Musset had met, the character of Stenio the poet prefigured Musset. George Sand called Stenio an *enfant du siècle,* an expression which Musset later used as a title for his masterpiece, *La Confession d'un enfant du siècle.* She transposed their liaison in *Jacques* and she wrote *Cora, Lavinia, Metella, Aldo le rimeur, Les Maîtres mosaïstes, Leone Leoni, Les Lettres d'un voyageur.* After they parted in 1835, she expressed her suffering in the *Journal intime* and she gave her own version of what happened in *Elle et lui.* One can find echoes of their passion in *La Confession d'un enfant du siècle,* the *Nuits, Souvenir,* and even in Perdican's couplet. It has also been ascertained that George Sand, who had written *Une Conspiration en 1537,* gave Musset the idea for his *Lorenzaccio.* We recognize in this the legendary generosity of George Sand.

George Sand wrote regularly to Victor Hugo after he had sent her a letter of condolence when her grand-daughter died tragically. She was one of the first to hail his *Contemplations* and, as early as 1856, devoted a whole essay to it which was later published in *Autour de la table.* She admired Hugo's originality, his powerfulness, his mastery, and she forgave his lack of measure and proportion because she thought him genial. She shared the same manichean convictions and she believed in the redeeming power of suffering. She was an idealist too and she believed, like him, in progress. In her analysis of the *Contemplations,* she defines the poet as a seer whose mission is to aid and console mankind. She urged Hugo to forget his persona and to go forward with confidence: "You must think of yourself only to think of all! You, the most suffering of all, you must become the consolation and the support of all. Such is the mission of the poet for the true poet is a seer and it is in you that this exceptional power reveals itself the most fully today."[21] Hugo was enthusiastic over George Sand's critical essays, and he wrote to her:

> You are endowed, Madame, with every quality and the greatness of your spirit equals only the greatness of your heart. I have just read this splendid piece you wrote on the *Contemplations,* this criticism which is poetry, those effusions of thought, life and tenderness, this philosophy, this reason, this sweetness, this powerful and brilliant explanation, those drops of gold from a pen of light. . . . To thank you is almost silly, I would rather congratulate you. You are a serene character. . . . You talk about this work as you would about anything, with such calm and true simplicity that it is almost haughty when compared with the trifling finesses of all the other wits.[22]

What Hugo admired the most in George Sand was her elevation of mind. He called her "great soul" and considered her a beacon in their century and the greatest of women, perhaps of all times. He invited her to visit him in Guernsey, but, because of her many commitments, she could not go. When *La Daniella* appeared, he wrote to say how much he admired the work. When she died he wrote her funeral eulogy.

Michelet considered George Sand "The first socialist writer who in her last two works has created a new literature, immense hope of the future,"[23] and he went to see her in 1849. Sand wrote a review of his book *L'Oiseau.* She noted several contradictions, but she expressed her admiration for Michelet's style. She fully endorsed his definition of the artist's role: "The true greatness of the artist is to go beyond his goal, to do more than he envisioned and something else, to go beyond his limits, to exceed the possible and to look even beyond."[24]

George Sand's generosity came most completely into play in her relations with Flaubert. Their first exchange of letters occurred in 1863 and only Sand's death put an end to the fertile dialogue between the two writers. Their correspondence grew richer and richer over thirteen years and bears witness to a rare friendship which became deeper with the passage of time. In these extraordinary documents, we can follow the beginnings of *L'Education sentimentale, La Tentation de Saint Antoine, Trois Contes* and the beginning of *Bouvard et Pécuchet*. George Sand was the first to recognize and point out Flaubert's talent. She offered him advice and used her own influence to help him gain recognition. She wrote an article in praise of *Salammbô*, she read *L'Education* in manuscript form and recommended it to her own editor, Michel Lévy. In reply to the tepid critical response to the novel, she wrote a long and appreciative essay in which she stresses its novelty and predicts its durability. Later, Flaubert dedicated *Un Coeur simple* to George Sand and she, in turn, dedicated *Dernier amour* to him. The two writers helped each other repeatedly by mutual encouragement, advice, and criticism. Sand stressed the usefulness of these exchanges in developing as fully as possible one's individuality by tussling with another mind. Their correspondence shows the difference of their natures and convictions: she was pragmatic, tolerant, optimistic, and an idealist. A disciple of Rousseau, she built her hopes on the intelligence and the virtue of the masses and she wrote to reach them. He was hypersensitive, pessimistic, misanthropic. An aesthete, he wrote for a selected few. The artist in him engulfed the man completely. Her judgment of him is as lucid as and even more sympathetic than her portrait of Balzac. She was conscious of their differences and knew that they enriched their lives:

> What will we achieve? You certainly will spread desolation and I consolation. . . . I want to look at man as he is. He is neither good nor evil, he is good *and* evil. . . . I think that your school pays no attention to the core and hovers at the surfaces. In your obsession with form, you neglect content. You address only the literate, but nobody is literate really. One is a *man* first of all and one wants to find the man at the core of every story.[25]

Still, Sand was careful not to be dogmatic: "No, I have no theories. My life is spent in asking questions and in hearing them answered in one way or the other, without feeling that a final conclusion or a definitive answer has ever been given."[26] Over the years and whatever critical acclaim her own works received, she remained true to herself and used to say: "Criticisms are a challenge and they are stimulating."[27] She defended the right of the artist to his freedom: "The artist is an explorer. Nothing must stand in his way. He does neither good nor ill in veering to the left or to the right. His aim justifies all." [28] She also fought repeatedly for the artist's right to individuality and mutability.

George Sand did not pursue glory or money like Balzac, nor like Flaubert did she isolate herself in an ivory tower. She gave a shining example of enlightened criticism which is to say criticism proceeding from a true grasp and deep understanding of her subject and based on common sense. She was endowed with the gift of sympathy and would have liked to see critics work more feelingly. She examined the work before her, not the author, and she judged writers on the basis of their works, which she tried to place in their historical and social context. She let herself be guided by her emotion because she was convinced that "Human reason is limited, emotion goes further, soars higher and sees in the infinite." [29] This method of impressionistic criticism was supported by a vast culture and a very sure judgment, and it did not seem dangerous to her, for she was convinced that genuine and solid qualities would survive the defects due to the time and the milieu. Her critical writings show her to be less conservative than Balzac, more open minded than Chateaubriand and more direct than Sainte-Beuve. Her opinions are quite original because she was largely self-taught and did not belong to any literary group. Her modesty prevented her from thinking of herself as a visionary like Hugo or Michelet. If she shows one weakness it is to be too generous and not critical enough. Her sole criteria were simplicity and truth and she adopted Plato's definition of beauty: "Beauty is the splendor of truth." [30]

She was convinced of the didactic power of art, and for this reason she did not like Balzac's *Contes drôlatiques* or Stendhal's coarseness. She tried to be impartial, and she revised in 1845 her criticism of Lamartine written in 1839, taking into account Lamartine's evolution in religious and political matters. To make herself understood to all, she wrote in clear and simple language. She often made comparisons with paintings, sculptures, or musical works, thus illustrating her belief that art is one. She was renowned for her generosity and gave encouragement to many artists younger or less famous than she: Taine, Gautier, Dumas *fils,* Daudet, Zola, Fromentin. She provided financial aid and moral support to proletarian poets like Magu, Poncy, Lapointe, Gilland, and she wrote *L'Essai sur les poètes populaires* and the *Dialogues familiers sur la poésie des prolétaires.* She hoped that one day all classes would have access to beauty and art and she saw popular poetry as a means to begin the education of the proletariat because she believed in human perfectibility and progress. Her tremendous curiosity embraced foreign writers as well and she wrote essays on Goethe, Byron, Mickiewicz, Fenimore Cooper, and Harriet Beecher Stowe. She illustrated by her own example her conception of criticism: "The aim of criticism should be to foster literary production and to enhance creativity."[31]

In the course of her long career, George Sand was naturally led to reflect upon her craft and to formulate her own aesthetics. She wrote her own appraisal of her works in her many prefaces and in *Impressions littéraires*. She was the first to deplore that she had been obliged to write in haste because of financial necessity, and she wished that she had had more time to read and to think. In the preface of the popular edition of her complete works, she sums up her lifetime activity with characteristic modesty:

> I have been guided by the desire to have the underprivileged read works which, for the most part, were written for them. . . . I have not revealed a new truth in my works. I did not attempt to. . . . I have examined as much as I could the ideas expressed by my contemporaries. I have cherished those which struck me as generous and true. I have not always understood the practical solutions several have suggested. . . . but I did not torment myself in my powerlessness because I felt I had enough to do to put my own talents in the service of justice and love of mankind.[32]

Independently of literary groups and coteries, she elaborated her own theory of the novel which is, in her eyes, a work of poetry as well as analysis:

> I did not have the slightest theory when I started to write and I don't think that I ever had one when I felt the urge to write. Nonetheless, I have instinctively elaborated this theory according to which the novel is a work of poetry as much as analysis. There must be true situations and true characters, real characters even, grouped around a type meant to embody the main emotion or the main idea of the novel. This type is generally love. . . . It is necessary to idealize it and one must not hesitate to give it an exceptional importance.[33]

She readily admitted that she was an idealist and she defended her right to be: "I need an ideal; let those who do not need one do without one." [34] In her eyes, aesthetics and ethics are closely linked. She combatted the cult of impersonality and impassiveness. She was, long before the expression was coined, a writer *engagé,* and she declared: "It is not possible to be a poet or an artist in any genre or to any degree without being an echo of mankind. . . ." [35] She believed in the messianic role of the writer, and in this respect, she influenced Tolstoy. She watched with interest the development of realism, but she rejected naturalism, because, as she put it, "poetry is a condition of my existence," [36] and because of her high conception of art. She was quick to discern and point out the limitations of the theory of art for art's sake: "Really, never has pedantism reached such absurdity as with this theory of art for art's sake, which does not correspond to anything, is based on nothing, and which nobody in the world, no more its exponents than its opponents, can put into practice." [37] She reiterated her conviction that genius lies not in form but in the heart, and she chided her old friend Flaubert: "Before trying to be artists, let us try to be human; we have more important things to deplore than the silence of the Muses." [38] She retained her own integrity and in several instances refused to change her manuscript to please her publishers. She broke with Buloz and *La Revue des Deux Mondes,* because she felt that she could not express her views freely, and she founded *La Revue indépendante.* As a writer she tried to renew herself and also to innovate: in *Lucrezia Floriani* she broke with Romanticism and attempted to write the anti-Romantic novel. She wrote *Mademoiselle la Quintinie* to challenge Alexandre Dumas, and in *Leone Leoni* she takes up a thesis hostile to Prévost's *Manon Lescaut.*

Except for poetry, she tried every genre: she loved the theater with a passion, she wrote many plays, and she expressed many new and interesting ideas about the dramatic arts which she considered the greatest and the most complete of all the arts. She believed that theater was an excellent means of culture and better suited than the novel to educate the people. In *Le Thêatre et l'acteur* she advocated greater realism and verisimilitude, real situations, and real characters. In keeping with this theory, she used peasant dialect on the stage. She wished for a type of drama which would be closer to life and would appeal directly to the intelligence or to the heart without making use of sophisticated effects. She would have liked to see more flexibility and greater audience participation and she already envisioned a kind of theater in the round.

George Sand's curiosity and intelligence were all encompassing. Her *oeuvre* does not depict one aspect only of reality and was never deformed by one theory of art or another. She believed in the mission of the artist above all and she refused to be confined by constricting rules. Her only guidelines were common sense and simplicity, according to her belief that "In art simplicity is the greatest challenge and the highest goal."[39] To the end, she remained a disciple of Molière, and it is interesting to note that Proust hailed Molière and George Sand as the two great masters who had the most influence on him.

NOTES

1. George Sand, *Oeuvres autobiographiques* (Paris: Gallimard, 1970), II, 46. (Hereafter cited as *OA*.)

2. Sand, *OA*, II, 126.

3. Sand, *Mélanges* (Paris: Perrotin, 1873), p. 47.

4. *OA*, I, 10-11.

5. Sand, *Mélanges*, p. 144.

6. Ibid.

7. Ibid., p. 152.

8. *OA*, I, 1038.

9. *OA*, II, 274.

10. Ibid.

11. *OA*, II, 275.

12. Ibid., II, 276.

13. Sand, *Questions d'art et de littérature* (Paris: Lévy, 1878), p. 204.

14. *OA*, II, 161-162.

15. Cited by Pierre Salomon in *George Sand* (Paris: Hatier, 1953) pp. 58-59.

16. *OA*, II, 155.

17. Sand, *Autour de la table* (Paris: M. Lévy, 1876) p. 211.

18. Ibid., 212

19. Ibid., 198.

20. Sainte-Beuve, *Portraits contemporains* (Paris: Lévy, 1869) p. 201.

21. *Autour de la table*, p. 32.

22. Cited by Léon Cellier in *Archives des lettres modernes,* No 44, juillet 1962, p. 29.

23. Unpublished letter (A4822 bis F225) Biblio. Historique de la Ville de Paris.

24. *Autour de la table*, p. 63.

25. *Correspondance entre George Sand et Flaubert,* ed. H. Amic (Paris: Lévy, 1904), p. 7.

26. Ibid., 40.

27. Ibid., 192.

28. Ibid., 14.

29. *Autour de la table*, p. 40.

30. Ibid., 80.

31. *Autour de la table*, p. 56.

32. *Questions d'art et de littérature*, p. 7.

33. *OA*, II, 161.

34. *OA*, II, 160.

35. *Questions d'art et de littérature*, p. 9.

36. *OA*, II, 169.

37. *Questions d'art et de littérature*, p. 8.

38. *Correspondance George Sand-Flaubert*, p. 429.

39. *Le Compagnon du tour de France* (Paris: Perrotin, 1841), Preface.

George Sand: Social Protest In Her Early Works

NANCY ROGERS
Department of Humanities
Howard University

Many of George Sand's critics have insisted upon her lack of originality, her inability to formulate ideas of her own, or her capacity to adopt easily the notions of others, especially those of her lovers. André Maurois, the most sensitive and thorough of her twentieth-century biographers, sees this question somewhat differently: "True, she took over the ideas of Michel de Bourges, of Lamennais, of Pierre Leroux, 'but they were ideas with which she was already familiar.'"[1] Long before 1842 when Sand first specifically stated her political and social positions, collected under the title *Questions politiques et sociales,* and even before 1835 when she met both Lamennais and Bourges, the men who helped her express her socialist leanings, Sand's writings already showed a zeal for humanitarian concerns.

The major novels of this period (often called the romantic or confessional phase of her work)—*Indiana* (1832), *Valentine* (1832), *Lélia* (1833), *Jacques* (1834), and *André* (1834)—all demonstrate a critical social awareness. For Sand this is a period in which she clearly shows the influences of Bernardin de Saint-Pierre, Nodier, Senancour, and above all, her *maître de pensée,* Rousseau. It is the failures and misdeeds of society which interest the young author in these works. Far from proposing any of the radical reforms with which she was later associated, in these early novels Sand merely condemns society as she sees it, despairing of any hope for improvement or change. The grace, tranquility, and beauty of the *Vallée noire* are merely glimpsed here, overshadowed by a venomous condemnation of contemporary life. In a letter to Sainte-Beuve in 1833, she writes of society: "I believe that it is lost, I find it odious and I will never be able to say otherwise."[2] Both in her correspondence and in her prefatory writings of this early period, Sand takes great pains to deny any kind of social or political sympathies, repeatedly stating that society is beyond help and progress impossible.

While it is true that Sand did not join the *saint-simoniens* or any other such movement until much later, her spiritual sympathy is clearly evident in her novels. The subject which Sand employs in these novels to illustrate her contempt of contemporary society was the one closest to her own experiences: the injustice of marriage. Thus, all of Sand's early works deal with the question of marriage, either explicitly or implicitly. In *Lélia,* for example, the fact that none of the characters considers entering into matrimony is revealing, since, as a leading Sandian critic says, this work "cannot not be a personal novel."[3] None is a *roman de bonheur*; in every case the lovers are thwarted by social restrictions, usually familial or marital. *Indiana, Valentine,* and *Jacques* focus upon an "ill-matched couple" and the resulting injustices; in *Indiana* the solution is for the true lovers to withdraw from society and live in a harmonious relationship unsanctioned by law, whereas in the other two novels the only escape is death. *Valentine* and *André* pose the question of marriage between persons of different social status, a favorite theme of Sand's throughout her career; both end with the death of at least one of the lovers. These somewhat melodramatic plots point out an important element of Sand's early fiction: her conviction that marriage in her time is not a viable institution.

Sand's correspondence from 1833 to 1837 exhibits a similar stance in regard to divorce. In 1833, she calls marriage a "state contrary to any kind of union and happiness;" in 1834 she finds that it can be a "despicable tyranny;" and in 1837 she writes to Lamennais that she sees no way out of the "bloody injustices" and "endless miseries" of marriage except "the freedom to break and re-establish the conjugal bond." In her letters on the subject of her own marital difficulties, she describes herself as a "slave of marriage," an image which she often applies to her fictional heroines. This is especially true of Indiana who, like her creator, hides her rebellion and her disgust of her husband behind an air of submission. When accused of adultery by her husband, Indiana defends herself with the courage, force, and intelligence of the young Aurore Dudevant:

> I know that I am your slave and you are the lord. The law of this land has made you my master. You can bind my body, tie my hands, govern my actions. You have the rights of the stronger, confirmed by society; but you have no control over my will; God alone can curb it and reduce it.
>
> (*Indiana,* Garnier, p. 225)[4]

Both Indiana and Valentine fear their husbands and recognize the power of the male; yet they are courageous enough to commit adultery, both for love and for freedom. In *Valentine,* Sand considers the marriage ceremony itself, in which feelings are tacked upon church doors and girlish modesty is exposed to the obscene thoughts and gestures of the wedding guests. This public deflowering of the bride is described as a rape, in which society approves and ratifies the submission of a trembling young woman, who "falls, branded by the kisses of a detested master!"[5] Even in *Lélia,* Sand's most poetic and metaphysical novel, this problem is considered by the defiant, liberated heroine, who asks, "Is the role of woman limited to the transports of love?"[6] and who views marriage as a kind of prostitution in which women are bought and sold. In her attention to marriage and divorce, however, Sand is not a female chauvinist, but recognizes that the male suffers as well: Colonel Delmare in *Indiana* and Raymon in *Jacques* are adequate proof of this assertion.

In her writings, other than novels, of this period, Sand shows that her hatred of injustice extends beyond marriage to the whole of society. Sand's antipathy towards any kind of master—marital, political, or otherwise—is well documented, and her consequent belief in republicanism is professed throughout her correspondence. In 1835, she wrote: ". . . the love of Equality is the only thing which has not varied in me for as long as I have lived."[7] Her disgust at the inequities which resulted from differences in social rank, especially in the division of material goods, is often reiterated. Sand quite logically, decries the institution of slavery in a letter to Gustave de Beaumont, author of *Marie, ou l'esclavage aux Etats-Unis* (1835), in which she praises his "noble work" for its exposure of "false and hypocritical Democracy."[8] (Her thoughts on slavery were later elaborated more fully in her *notice* to the French translation of *Uncle Tom's Cabin* in 1852.) Yet at this time, Sand still exhibited uncertainty as to whether the conditions of human inequalities could be ameliorated. Two letters written on October 18, 1835 (there is some question about the date), well illustrate her hesitation: the first, to Liszt, states that her "fits of republican anger . . . are useless,"[9] and that she will therefore return to her armchair and do nothing; the second, to Emmanuel Arago, proposes that "we must take up the axe" and destroy society, "all the while thinking of ways to reconstruct it."[10] Sand has certainly not yet wholeheartedly arrived at the point of concrete action, preferring a more passive means of persuading, her novels.

Here, differences in rank play a vital role; both *Valentine* and *André* depict the destruction of love by social distinctions and restrictions. *Valentine,* especially, is an *étude de moeurs,* as Sand analyzes the social classes of Berry—the peasant, the "half-bourgeois, half-country-bumpkin planter class,"[11] and the aristocracy. Although critical of all classes, she is particularly savage in her condemnation of the pretentious Raimbault family, who erect obstacles between Valentine and her lover, Bénédict, a farmer's nephew. Sand makes it clear that, as Valentine says, "Our rank, our fortune are worth nothing," but that it is the aristocracy of the mind and soul which should be valued. The same is true in *André,* in which the young *fleuriste* Geneviève is the most sympathetic, sensitive, and intelligent of creatures. Both she and Bénédict must die, however, victims of a social structure which is unable to recognize their worth. In *Indiana,* Sand speaks of what God would do if He decided to interfere in human affairs: ". . . He would pass this large hand over our unequal heads and make them level like the waters of the sea."[12] Further proof of the author's commitment to the idea of erasing social inequity is the conclusion of *Indiana,* where Sir Ralph relates how the couple spends the major portion of their income to buy back slaves (in the tradition of Paul and Virginie), wishing that they were rich enough to rid the earth of that institution.

Another social problem which drew the criticism of the young Sand was that of education in her century. She felt extremely limited in her own knowledge, as stated, for example, in a letter to Hortense Allart in 1833:

I have studied nothing, I know nothing, not even my language. I have so little exactness in my brain that I have never been able to perform the simplest mathematical calculation.[13]

Echoes of her feelings of ignorance resound in the correspondence. It is not surprising, then, to find her urging her son Maurice to take advantage of education, since "without it, one lives in a kind of slavery."[14] It is precisely this lack of education which makes Sand's heroines slaves of the social system. Indiana is "ignorant like a true Creole," becoming bored whenever a question is discussed fully. Valentine is frustrated because she has learned to sing, dance, paint, and embroider, but has been taught nothing of real use; she realizes that she can neither earn her living nor develop her mind—the tools have been denied her. Fernande, the heroine of *Jacques,* is a frivolous, spoiled, convent-educated young thing who is completely unprepared to engage in meaningful conversation. Likewise, Geneviève (in *André*) is untutored and untrained, but demonstrates a lively mind when exposed to serious study. Of these heroines only Lélia (and perhaps Sylvia, the "other woman" in *Jacques*) has attained the knowledge of Mme de Staël's Corinne. Sandian women who are not brilliant poetesses are depicted as appallingly ignorant and thus unequipped to withstand the pressures of society.

In an intelligent and stimulating article in *Daedalus* (Winter 1976),[15] Tony Tanner takes a fresh look at Rousseau's *La Nouvelle Héloïse,* treating it as a paradigm of the destruction of the paternal house and an indication that the "bourgeois family would not work."[16] Sand's early novels follow the lead of Rousseau in demonstrating the lack of cohesion and stability of the *maison paternelle.* Although this does not constitute overt social criticism and although there is no mention in the correspondence of Sand's frustration with the patriarchal system, it is still interesting that the novels so obviously present a subversion of that system. In *Indiana* and *Jacques,* for example, the father figure is an older husband who is rejected by the young wife. In Indiana's case, Sand makes it explicit that her heroine, by changing her name from Carvajal to Delmare, "has only changed masters;" thus, the husband's name is merely a transformation of that of the father, and both imprison Indiana. In *Valentine* and *André* an aristocratic family lineage is the object of derision by the young heirs; Valentine is forced to sign over all of the family possessions to her dandified, aristocratic husband, an act which she gladly commits in the hope that it will permit her to lead the life she desires, that of a *fermière,* and thus escape from "the slavery of an opulent life." André also rejects his heritage—and his petty, cruel, narrow-minded father as well—choosing poverty and ignominy to marry Geneviève. None of the heroines here provides an heir to continue the family name. In all the novels except *Valentine,* the paternal house will fall; and in this case, it is ironic that the name will be continued by the bastard son of Valentine's sister, Louise, who had herself been rejected from her father's roof.[17]

In sum, Sand's first novels are hardly revolutionary works; they rarely propose action. The struggles here are useless; all her heroic characters submit to their social fate, thus reflecting Sand's belief that nothing can be changed. The only exceptions are the attempt to reduce slavery in *Indiana* and the humanitarian mission of the ex-convict Trenmor, who at the end of *Lélia* sets out to help the world "because everywhere there are duties to fill, a force to use, a destiny to be realized."[18]

Two works form the watershed in Sand's evolution from pessimism to progress: the second, revised version of *Lélia,* begun in 1836 and *Mauprat,* begun in 1835, but not given any real attention until 1837. Both works exhibit the progressive notions of the triumvirate of Sand's mentors—Bourges, Lamennais, and Leroux—and point the way to the socialist and rustic novels of the 1840s and 1850s. In April 1836, Sand wrote to the "famille saint-simonienne" in Paris, a society which she had steadfastly refused to join, stridently bidding them to lead the struggle to rebuild society:

> . . . Faithful to old childhood affections, to old social hatreds, I can not separate the idea of *republic* from that of *regeneration,* since the salvation of the world seems to rest on *us* to destroy it, on *you* to rebuild it.[19]

There is a new urgency in Sand's tone here; gone are the pessimism, the hesitancy, and the ambiguity of the early years. Instead, we find an almost messianic call to action, one reflected in her fiction of these years.

The revised *Lélia* is perhaps the most dramatic presentation of the "new" Sand. In May, 1836, she calls the first version "my best work,"[20] yet in July of the same year she writes of it: "The poison which has made me ill is now a remedy which is curing me." [21] The resulting novel, which appeared in September, 1839, contained enough changes to eradicate the essential thrust of the 1833 version. Instead of an accusation against humanity, it now became an article of faith in progress, a Bible of the poor, a new testament to humanitarianism. The romantic, suffering Lélia became an optimistic prophet, a militant believer in progress, just as her creator had become a loyal disciple of Pierre Leroux.

However, the still metaphysical and ethereal *Lélia* of 1839 was still not the real forum for Sand's constructive ideas about the future; that function was filled by *Mauprat*. This action-filled adventure story seems a somewhat bizarre choice for the presentation of the author's newly modified beliefs, yet is replaces Sand's negativism of the earlier novels by offering constructive solutions to the problems of marriage, education, patriarchy, and social equality. Marriage in *Mauprat* is no longer a barrier to happiness, but a blissful bond, offering eternal joy. This state, however, is not entered into with ease but is rewarded at the end of years of service and proof of worthiness, much in the fashion of a medieval *chevalier*. Love and marriage are complementary here, not impossible opposites; as Bernard Mauprat says:

> She is the only woman I've loved; never has any other attracted my attention or known the squeeze of my hand. I am made that way; what I love, I love eternally, in the past, the present, and the future. [22]

Education is not exclusively the realm of men in *Mauprat*; it is Edmée Mauprat, a learned, intelligent, and lucid *institutrice*, who attempts to guide her lover, Bernard, both morally and intellectually, as did Mme de Warens for Rousseau. This *éducation sentimentale* has the goal of producing an *honnête homme* in the nineteenth-century sense of a rebirth in love and virtue. Edmée's singleminded, almost violent pursuit of this renaissance of an *enfant sauvage* reflects the nineteenth century search for the absolute embodied by such romantic heroines as Corinne, la Sanseverina, and Mme de Mortsauf; the success of her mission is a vindication of the earlier Sandian heroines whose lack of knowledge keeps them chained and helpless in a world dominated by men. The *maison paternelle* of Bernard Mauprat is destined to fall in this novel; his father's branch of the Mauprat family is wild, vicious, unrestrained, a group of thieving rascals. In becoming an *honnête homme* Mauprat rejects the values of his fathers and brothers to choose those of the other branch of his family headed by his uncle, Edmée's father. By marrying Edmée, Bernard reunites his family, thus strengthening a divided house and continuing the Mauprat name through four children who hopefully "will succeed in erasing the deplorable memory of their ancestors."[23] In this case, Sand does not undermine the entire patriarchal system; rather, she depicts the demise of its most evil incarnation. The revitalized, reborn house of Mauprat is symbolized by the family home, the formerly dreaded bastion of Roche-Mauprat, now the scene of a stable, happy domestic life, a thriving salute to the possibilities of humanity.

There is much negative social criticism in *Mauprat*: the injustices of society towards women, the lack of moral integrity among the clergy, and the hypocrisy of the judicial system all receive their share of Sandian scorn. Yet, this is the first novel in which a kind of naive revolutionary radicalism appears. Although all of the main characters espouse socialistic ideals, it is the rustic philosopher Patience, one of Sand's most successful character creations, who becomes the champion of republicanism. In this novel, which begins before the 1789 Revolution, Sand traces the gathering of the storm by focusing upon the increasingly unhappy and independent peasant. Patience, a kind of Figaro of Berry, represents the rebellious peasant and predicts that "castles will fall" and the land will be equally divided. He envisions a new order in which men will live in the same peace and harmony as the stars, admires Franklin and Rousseau, and dreams of American soldiers bringing the olive branch of peace to the French nation. During the Revolution he becomes a hero among the poor of Berry and is named the judge of his district, where his impartiality and integrity towards "both the castle and the thatched hut" bring him fame and respect. This is Sand's first instance of the peasant-hero, the naive but wily activist who leads the battle for reform. The moral of the tale is that one must never merely accept things as they are but work for change and betterment, with education as the basis for solving the problems of society. This can be achieved by the Biblical message with which the novel ends, "by loving one another very much."[24] The bitter cynicism of the early novels has been transformed into a loving, active socialism by some of the strangest characters in Sand's fiction: a reformed bandit, a rat-catcher (named Marcasse), a defrocked abbé, and a bizarre old peasant philosopher, who assumes the mantle of liberty as a prophet of the new order.

Sand's later political stance and affiliations have been well established. Such works as Marie-Louise Pailleron's *George Sand et les hommes de 48,* Lucien Buis' *Les Théories sociales de George Sand,* and Edouard Dolléans's *Féminisme et mouvement ouvrier: George Sand* chart her progressively evangelical socialism of the 1840s and 1850s. Her admitted misanthropy of the earlier period (see, for example, the letter to Hortense Allart, July 1833)[25] has been transformed into a far less critical love of humanity, her former lethargy has become a militant call to action, and her statement of 1832, "I have never put my nose in politics," [26] hardly describes the writer of *Mauprat* (leaving aside as another question Sand's continued acceptance of the benefits of being a *propriétaire* in her own right). These novels and letters prove that Sand's intellectual transition from pessimism to progress was not abrupt but gradual. By the time the name George Sand had been coined in 1832, the seeds of social protest had already been sown; nurtured by the ideas of others and by the political events leading to the Revolution of 1848, they blossomed in the later novels, to inspire the whole of France.

NOTES

1. André Maurois, *Lélia: The Life of George Sand* (New York: Harper and Brothers, 1953), p. 323.

2. George Sand, *Correspondance,* II, ed. Georges Lubin (Paris: Garnier, 1966), 431. This is my translation, as are all translations in this paper.

3. Pierre Reboul, ed., *Lélia* by George Sand (Paris: Garnier, 1960), p. xliv.

4. George Sand, *Indiana* (Paris: Garnier, 1962), p. 225.

5. George Sand, *Valentine* (Paris: Lévy, 1869), p. 183.

6. George Sand, *Lélia* (Paris: Garnier, 1960), p. 292.

7. George Sand, *Correspondance,* III, ed. Georges Lubin (Paris: Garnier, 1967), p. 116.

8. Sand, *Correspondance,* III, p. 438.

9. Sand, *Correspondance,* III, p. 66.

10. Sand, *Correspondance,* III, p. 67.

11. Sand, *Valentine,* p. 6.

12. Sand, *Indiana,* p. 243.

13. Sand, *Correspondance,* III, p. 389.

14. Sand, *Correspondance,* III, p. 109.

15. Tony Tanner, "Julie and 'La Maison Paternelle': Another Look at Rousseau's *La Nouvelle Héloïse,*" *Daedalus* (Winter 1976), 23-45.

16. Tanner, p. 23.

17. This is a fascinating subject and one which has not been touched upon in Sandian criticism.

18. Sand, *Lélia,* p. 326.

19. Sand, *Correspondance,* III, p. 326. (Sand's italics)

20. Sand, *Correspondance,* III, p. 362.

21. Sand, *Correspondance,* III, p. 474.

22. Sand, *Mauprat* (Paris: Garnier-Flammarion, 1969), p. 312.

23. Sand, *Mauprat,* p. 312.

24. Sand, *Mauprat,* p. 314.

25. Sand, *Correspondance,* III, p. 389.

26. Sand, *Correspondance,* III, p. 14.

George Sand and Feminism

DENNIS O'BRIEN
Dept. of History
West Virginia University

Several months ago, while reading *Images of Women in Fiction,* I was struck by Tillie Olsen's statement that all female writers in the nineteenth century were silent on the plight of women, with the exception of George Sand.[1] I then remembered that Simone de Beauvoir singled Sand out as one of those who fought "their own battles for freedom."[2] Of course, one of the initial problems is deciding what traits define a feminist. Rather than state immediately my own definition of feminism, which would be restrictive, I should like to leave the word loosely defined initially, consider traits in Sand that most would interpret as anti-feminist, proceed to traits that most would concede as pro-feminist, and then offer a definition of feminism according to which Sand will be judged.

There is no problem in showing that Sand held many attitudes that today would appall feminists. For example, whereas Simone de Beauvoir maintains that housework is inherently degrading,[3] George Sand enjoyed such domestic duties as canning, cooking, and sewing. On this subject she said:

I have often heard women of talent say that household work, and needlework particularly, were mind-numbing and insipid and part of the slavery to which our sex has been condemned. I have no taste for the theory of slavery, but I deny that these chores are its consequence. They have always seemed to me to have a natural, invincible attraction for us, for I have felt it in all periods of my life and they have sometimes calmed great agitations of the mind. Their influence is mind-numbing only for those who spurn them and who don't know

Ed. Note: All translations are the author's.

how to look for what can be found in everything—skillful work, well done. Doesn't the man who spades have an even rougher and more monotonous task than the woman who sews? Yet the good laborer who spades fast and well is not bored by his spading, and he will tell you with a smile that he *likes the toil and the sweat of it.*

For Sand household work was not only pleasurable, but necessary for women. She said, "Is not man's life difficult and rough, in nature as in society? . . . The wife has the fatigues of housekeeping, the husband those of the establishment—two diverse yet equally necessary and thus equally noble ways of working for the family."[5] "Domestic cares have never bored me, and I am not one of these sublime spirits who cannot descend from their clouds. I see much in the clouds, certainly, and it's all the more the reason that I feel the need to find my bearings on the earth."[6]

Another way in which Sand might appear to be an anti-feminist is that she was no advocate of sisterhood. Not only did she prefer the company of men, but also she did not enjoy the presence of women.

With very few exceptions, I do not long endure the company of women. Not that I feel them inferior to me in intelligence; I consume so few of them in the habitual commerce of my life that everyone has more of them around than I. But women, generally speaking, are nervous, anxious beings who, my reluctance notwithstanding, communicate their eternal disquiet to me apropos of everything. I begin by listening to them with regret, then I let myself be caught up in a natural interest for what they are saying, only to perceive that there was really nothing to get worked up about in their puerile agitations. . . .

I thus like men better than women, and I say so without malice, that the satisfaction of the passions is only a restricted and accidental part of that attraction which one sex feels for the other, and that aside of intellectual and moral alliance, to which each sex brings what is complementary for the other. Were it otherwise, men would flee women, and vice versa, whereas on the contrary, when the age of physical passion is over, the principal element of human civilization is in their calm and delicate relationships.[7]

Likewise, her view of marriage, as expressed in a letter written in January, 1823, four months after her marriage to Casimir Dudevant, would cause most current-day feminists to cringe.

Each time then that one or the other of the spouses should like to
conserve his ideas and never yield, he will find himself unhappy. It is
necessary, I believe, that one of the two in marrying renounce entirely
himself and abnegate not only his will but also his opinion, so learns
to see with the eyes of the other, likes what he likes, etc. What
torture, what a life of bitterness, when one marries someone that he
detests. What unhappy incertitude, what future without charm, when
one marries a stranger. But also what an unfailing source of happiness when one obeys what one loves. Each privation is a new
pleasure. One sacrifices at the same time to God and to married love,
and one makes at the same time his duty and his happiness.—The
only thing left to ask is if it is the man or the woman who *remakes
themself* thus along the model of the other, and since *the bearded side
is all powerful,* and since besides men are not capable of such an
attachment, it is necessary up to us to bend in obedience.[8]

The most damning evidence for the Sand-as-a-feminist thesis is to
be found in her views on women organizing and entering politics in
order to further their cause. In 1834 she wrote,

Let the [women] set themselves right and cling to the purest examples, let them suffer and pray while waiting for marriage without
ceasing to be a sacred bond, at least cease to be a degrading tyranny.
What will they accomplish through revolt? When the male world has
been converted, woman will be converted too without anyone having
had any need to bother about her.[9]

Spurning women's organizations, Sand believed that women would
"enlarge their souls":

Too proud of their recently acquired education, certain women have
shown signs of personal ambition. . . . The smug daydreams of
modern philosophies have encouraged them, and these women have
given sad proof of the powerlessness of their reasoning. It is much to
be feared that vain attempts of this kind and these ill-founded claims
will do much harm to what is today called the cause of women. . . . If
women were rightly guided and possessed of same ideas, they would
be better placed to complain of the rigidity of certain laws and the
barbarism of certain prejudices. But let them enlarge their souls and
elevate their minds before hoping to bend the iron shackles of
custom. In vain do they gather in clubs, in vain do they engage in
polemics, if the expression of their discontent proves that they are

incapable of properly managing their affairs and of governing their affections.[10]

Eleven years later, in 1848, Sand, now forty-four years old, was still opposed to women's voting and to entering politics in order to further their cause. In February of that year the French overthrew their citizen king, Louis Philippe, and established a provisional government which hastened to elect a Constituent Assembly. On April 6 *La Voix des Femmes* contained an editorial written by a radical feminist named Eugénie Nibouyet, who advocated Sand's election to this assembly. Quickly and rudely Sand retaliated by sending a letter of reply, not to *La Voix des Femmes,* but to *La Réforme* and to *La Vraie République.*[11]

Sir: 8 April 1848
A newspaper edited by women has proclaimed my candidacy to the National Assembly. If this joke hurt only my pride by attributing to me a ridiculous pretention, I should let it pass like all those by which each of us in this world can become the object. But my silence could make one believe that I adhere to the principles of which this newspaper would like to make itself the organ. I therefore request you to receive and to consent to make known the following declaration:
    1) I hope that no elector will waste his vote by holding to the fantasy of writing my name on his ballot.
    2) I haven't the honor of knowing a single one of these ladies who form clubs and edit newspapers.
    3) The articles that could be signed by my name or my initials in these newspapers are not mine.
    I beg these ladies' pardon who, certainly, have treated me with much kindness, to take precautions against their zeal.
    I do not mean to protest beforehand against the ideas that these ladies or all other ladies want to discuss among themselves; liberty of opinion is equal for both sexes, but I cannot permit, without my consent, one taking me for the standard-bearer of a female coterie with which I have never had the least connection either agreeable or troublesome.

Sincerely,
George Sand[12]

Furthermore on the subject of women who wish to exercise political rights she wrote in April 1848,

Some women have raised this question: in order for society to be transformed is it not necessary that women intervene politically in public affairs starting today?—I dare to respond that it is not necessary because social conditions are such that women would not be able to fulfill honorably and loyally a public mandate.

Women being under tutelage and dependent upon men because of marriage, it is absolutely impossible that they present guarantees of political independence barring breaking individually and in contempt of the laws and customs, this tutelage that the laws and customs consecrate.[13]

As for you women who pretend to begin by the exercise of your rights, permit me to tell you again that you are amusing yourselves with childishness. Your house is on fire, your home is in peril, and you want to go expose yourself to railleries and public affronts when you should be defending your home and setting up again your outraged household gods. What a bizarre caprice pushes you to parliamentary struggles, you who cannot even exercise there your personal independence? What, your husband will be seated on one bench, your lover perhaps on another, and you will pretend to represent something when you are not even the representation of yourselves? An evil law makes of you the *half* of man, customs worse than the laws very often make you the half of another man, and you believe you can offer any responsibility to other men? To what ridiculous attacks, to what possible vile scandals, would such an innovation give rise? Good sense thrusts it aside, and the pride that your sex ought to have, makes nearly a crime for you to think of braving such outrages.[14]

The role of each sex is traced, its task is assigned, and Providence gives to each the instruments and resources which benefit it. Why should society upset this admirable order, . . . by giving women the same attributes as men? Women complain of being brutally enslaved, of being badly educated, badly advised, badly directed, badly loved, badly defended. All this is unfortunately true. But what confidence would women inspire if they were to demand by way of compensation, not household peace nor the freedom of maternal affections, but the right to parade in the forum with sword and helmet, the right to condemn people to death?[15]

Finally, did she believe that women's cause should receive top priority in nineteenth-century France? No, for as she said, "The people are hungry; let our leading lights allow us to think of providing bread for the people before thinking of building temples for them. Women cry out against slavery; let them wait till man is free, for slavery cannot engender liberty." [16]

By now one could readily believe that Sand was indeed a self-centered hedonist, unconcerned about the plight of her sex. To form a judgment at this point would be unfair, however, as other evidence must be considered.

As a child, Sand was aware that there were things that boys could do that girls could not. The freedom accorded to her half-brother Hippolyte and denied to her chaffed the young Aurore Dupin. As she grew older and began to read, she was bothered by the negative view of women found in the writings of the Greek philosophers and the early Christians. [17] Furthermore, she was distrustful of the future that society had assigned to her as a woman. "That boils down, I thought, to become a beautiful single woman, quite spruced up, quite starchy, playing a piano in front of people who approve without listening and without understanding, caring for no one, loving to shine, aspiring to a rich marriage, selling her liberty and her personality for a carriage, a coat of arms, some chiffons, and some money. That is not at all satisfactory for me and it never will be." [18] Searching for a positive self-image, she discovered la Marquise du Châtelet, Voltaire's great friend, the accomplished eighteenth-century mathematician, linguist, and musician. Aurore's grandmother deflated the girl's enthusiasm by reminding her that the equality with men enjoyed by that great eighteenth-century woman was not possible in the nineteenth century. [19]

Nonetheless, Aurore never abandoned her belief that women were equal to men. On this subject she said, "I am very far from thinking that woman is inferior to man. She is his equal in the sight of God, and nothing in the designs of Providence destines her to slavery. But she is not like man, and her nature and temperament assign to her another role, no less fine, no less noble, and of which I do not think she can complain unless mentally depraved." [20]

"That women differ from men, that heart and intellect are subject to the laws of sex, I do not doubt. But ought this difference, so essential to the general harmony of life, to constitute a moral inferiority? And does it necessarily follow that the souls and minds of women are inferior to those of men, whose vanity permits them to tolerate no other natural order." [21] Sand reaffirmed her belief in women in a letter to the misogynist Lamennais, who had written an anti-feminist tract, ". . . I shall dare tell you that I am not yet convinced of the inferiority of women. . . ."[22] Sand truly believed that "A woman is an adult, and has a mind of her own. We dwell under a system both archaic and pathetic in which woman must remain mute and bow to the supposedly superior wisdom of man, who may excel only in his physical strength. With all members of my sex, I eagerly await the day when the women of France will receive their equitable due under the law."[23]

This view of the equality of the sexes was fundamental to Sand's view of marriage. Although she was unhappily married to Casimir Dudevant,[24] Sand never abandoned the belief that marriage was inherently good. However, her conception of a valid marriage was one that was between equal partners. In 1848 she wrote to the members of the Central Committee of the Provisional Revolutionary Government demanding that the state "give back to the woman the civil rights that only marriage takes away from her, which the unmarried only can keep for herself; detestable error of our legislation which in effect puts woman into the greedy grasp of the man, and which makes marriage a state of eternal minority, whereas the majority of the young girls would decide never to marry if they had the slightest notion of the civil legislation at the age at which they renounce their rights."[25] How could this transformation be made? Sand anticipated Simone de Beauvoir's belief that woman's inferior status is a function of bourgeois, capitalist society. Accordingly she worked for the transformation of French society into a socialistic, or as she put it, "communistic," society. Likewise Sand used her literature as an instrument for advancing the cause of women.

In her article "Why Feminist Critics Are Angry with George Eliot," Zelda Austen said "Feminist critics are angry with George Eliot because she did not permit Dorothea Brooke in *Middlemarch* to do what George Eliot did in real life: translate, publish articles, edit a periodical, refuse to marry until she was middle-aged, live an independent existence as a spinster, and finally live openly with a man whom she could not marry."[26] She continues, "The feminist critic argues that these authors [George Eliot, Jane Austen, and Charlotte Brontë] were themselves victims of the prevailing myths of their culture and lacked the vision to allow their heroines any happy fulfillment other than marriage."[27] This lack of positive self-images for women troubled Sand who complained that "No one has wanted to raise woman in her own eyes."[28]

No one familiar with her fiction could accuse her of presenting marriage as woman's "happy fulfillment." In *Indiana*, written in 1832, Indiana states to her husband, modeled on Sand's husband Casimir Dudevant:

> I know that I am the slave and you the master. The laws of this country make you my master. You can bind my body, tie my hands, govern my acts. You have the right of the stronger, and society confirms you in it; but you cannot command my will, monsieur; God alone can bend it and subdue it. Try to find a law, a dungeon, an instrument of torture that gives you any hold on it. You might as well try to handle the air and grasp space.
>
> You can impose silence on me, but not prevent me from thinking.
>
> I passed several hours away from your domination; I breathed the air of liberty. . . .[29]

The following year Sand wrote *Lélia*, and therein Pulchérie, the attractive sister of Lélia complains:

> How many affronts one seeks to make her [woman] pay for the weakness that she has surprised and the brutalities that she has satisfied. Under what a mountain of ignominies and injustices must she be accustomed to sleeping, to walking, to being lover, courtesan, and mother, three conditions of woman's destiny that no woman escapes, whether she sells herself in the market of prostitution or by a contract of marriage.[30]

In her play *Gabriel,* written in 1839, Sand tells the story of a Florentine duke who wishes to keep his inheritance from the descendants of one of his sons. Therefore, the duke raises his granddaughter, Gabrielle, as a male, so that she/he will be able to be his heir. Smarting over Casimir Dudevant's control over her property, Sand was thereby able to air her own grievances over the injustices women sustained in matters of inheritance.

For one last example, let us look at *Lucrezia Floriani,* which Sand wrote in 1846.

> Now I have arrived, dear reader, at the end that I had proposed, and the rest will be on my part no more than an act of compliance for those who absolutely want some sort of a denouement.
>
> You sensible reader, I bet that you are of my opinion, and that you

find denouements quite useless. If, at this point, I would follow my conviction and my fantasy, no novel would end, so as to resemble real life. What then are the love stories that end in an absolute manner with a rupture or with happiness, or with infidelity or with the marriage tie? What are the events that fix our existence into lasting states? I agree that there is nothing prettier in the world than the old formula for a conclusion "And they lived happily ever after." This was said in prehistoric literature, in the time of fables. Happy times, if one would believe it, such sweet lies.

But today we no longer believe in anything, we laugh when we read this charming refrain.[31]

Nonetheless, Sand went ahead and gave her readers a conclusion to her story. "They loved for a long time, and they lived together very unhappily. Their love was a struggle to the end, to see which would devour the other. . . ."[32] I doubt if we shall see the appearance of an article entitled "Why Feminist Critics Are Angry With George Sand."

Anticipating Virginia Woolf's *A Room of One's Own,* George Sand realized that in order to be free to live her life as she pleased she would have to work, and work she did, be it painting designs on containers or writing books. Although nineteenth-century bourgeois France expected women to be household ornaments, *à la* Balzac's Madame Hulot in *La Cousine Bette,* Sand flaunted the convention with her zest for work. "What frightens me is not being penniless— I'm used to it, it's feeling incapable of working. . . ."[33]

". . . Work, . . . it is my mainstay, my nourishment, my all."[34] After her separation from Casimir Dudevant in February, 1836, Sand returned to her country home, Nohant, and wrote:

There was then an absolute solitude, and for the first time in my life I lived at Nohant with the *house deserted.* A deserted house had been for a long time one of my dreams. Until the day when I can taste without alarm the sweetness of family life, I am soothed by the hope of possessing in some ignored spot a house, be it a ruin or a thatched cottage, where I will be able from time to time to disappear and work without being distracted by the sound of the human voice.[35]

As a working woman, Sand soon became aware that women do not receive equal pay for equal work. She had been allowing the

Revue de Paris to serialize her novels before publication in book form, as was the custom in her day. However, in December, 1832, the irate author gave this right to the *Revue des Deux Mondes,* for she discovered that the *Revue de Paris* was paying the popular novelist Eugène Sue and the minor book collector P. L. Jacob more money than the 300 francs that the *Revue* was willing to pay her, better known, but a woman, for *La Marquise.*[36]

Sand followed her propinquity for work by serving as the official minister of Propaganda for the Provisional Revolutionary Government in 1848. She sent the following letter to her son Maurice, dated 23 March in which she said, "My Bouli, here I am already occupied like a statesman. I have drawn up two governmental circulars today, one for the Ministry of the Interior. It amuses me that they are addressed to all the mayors and that you are going to receive through official channels your mother's instructions."[37] It is interesting to note that she who had condemned women for entering politics had now decided to "parade in the forum with sword and helmet." Probably Sand would have justified her position in the Provisional Government, as she was not a voting member of the ministry. The role of power behind the throne is approved historically for women. Furthermore, Sand did not believe that women should necessarily be excluded from politics in the future. "Women are not suited to the posts which the laws have hitherto denied. Which in no wise proves the inferiority of their intelligence, but only the difference of their education and character. The first of these obstacles will cease with time; the second, is I think eternal."[38] In a letter written to the Central Committee of the Provisional Revolutionary Government in mid-April 1848, she wrote, "Should women participate one day in politics? Yes one day, I believe so as do you, but is this day near? No, I do not believe so, and for the condition of women to be thus transformed, it is necessary that society be radically transformed."[39] Sand labored for this transformation of French society not only by entering the Provisional Government in 1848 in order to transform bourgeois France into a socialistic society, but also by her flaunting of bourgeois society's convention on personal behavior and appearance.

With the adoption of the Code Napoléon, French women lost many of the gains that they had made before and during the French Revolution of 1789. The code subordinated women to their husbands and discriminated against them in a variety of ways. In the realm of adultery, there was no penalty for males who entered into such a relationship, unless the concubine was brought into the home. Under those circumstances the wife was entitled to a divorce. However, a woman guilty of adultery, in or out of the home, could be not only divorced by her husband, but also condemned to solitary confinement. If a husband caught his wife *in flagrante delicto* and killed her, the law could excuse this. In a letter written to François Rollinat on October 10, 1835, Sand affirmed that "chastity would have been glorious for free women. For slaves, it is a tyranny that wounds them and whose yoke they shake off audaciously. I cannot blame them for it."[40] Sand furthered expressed this attitude in a letter to the members of the Central Committee of the Provisional Goverment in a letter written in min-April, 1848. "In effect, what is the liberty that a woman can seize . . . adultery."[41] Therefore, for Sand, who did not esteem adultery, it was one way that women could shake off the shackles of bourgeois society and assert their freedom.

The popular image of George Sand is that of a woman who smoked cigarettes and who wore male clothing. Once these acts are examined in the context of their day, it will be seen that these are but two more ways that Sand asserted her right as a woman to do as she pleased in spite of the strictures of masculine, bourgeois values.

During the 1830s cigarette smoking became the vogue in France for noble and lower class males. Bourgeois men and all women, even prostitutes and actresses abstained. Nonetheless Sand began smoking cigarettes at least fifteen years before 1848, when a few Frenchwomen began to follow her example. The act gave her a notoriety that spread beyond the borders of France. Elizabeth Barrett, who visited Sand in March, 1852, lamented "Ah, but I didn't see her smoke. I was unfortunate."[42]

Yet it was in the realm of wearing masculine attire that Sand, not unlike the liberated women of today, showed that she was more concerned about comfort, practicality, and pleasure than she was with doing that which was expected of women. Even as a child she had exhibited a lack of concern about being pretty, and in 1811 her mother decided to do something to improve the child's appearance by styling her hair *à la chinoise*.

This was easily the most frightful coiffure that one could imagine and it had certainly been invented for faces that have no forehead. They teased the hair with a comb until it stood out perpendicular, and then they twisted a rod exactly to the top of the skull, in a manner to make the head an elongated ball surmounted by a little ball of hair. Thus one looked like a brioche or a pilgrim's gourd. Add to this ugliness the torture of having the hair crumbling the wrong way; it necessitated eight hours of atrocious pain and insomnia before it would take this enforced shape, and they pressed it quite well with a ribbon in order to restrain it, so that one had the skin of the forehead stretched and the corner of the eyes raised like the faces of a Chinese fan.

I submitted blindly to this torture although I was absolutely indifferent to being ugly or pretty, to following the styles or to protesting against its aberrations.[43]

About ten years later Sand learned from François Deschartres, the manager of her grandmother's estate, that a local nobleman allowed his daughter to dress in male attire so she could accompany him on the hunt. The idea appealed to Sand, and she adopted the custom. "It is necessary to remember also that at this time the skirts had no pleats and were so tight that a woman was literally like being in a box and could not decently cross a small stream without leaving her shoes there." [44] The practice disturbed Sand's eighteenth-century grandmother, who professed to confuse Sand in male attire with Sand's deceased father. However, for Sand "my manner of being so natural came out of the exceptional position in which I found myself, that it appeared quite simple to me not to live like the majority of the other girls. They judged me very bizarre, and yet I was infinitely less so than I would have been able to be if I had had the taste for affection and eccentricity."[45] Sand did not give up wearing men's clothing when she left Nohant for Paris. There she wanted to go to the theater frequently, but found that she did not have enough money to sit in the expensive places set aside for women. Attired as a man, she had access to the pit, which was reserved for men and was much cheaper. "I should like to be a jeweller or a dealer in fancy costumes in order to invent always, and in order to give, by the miracle of taste a sort of life to these rich materials. But all that is of no agreeable use for me. A beautiful dress is bothersome, jewels scratch. . . ."[46] This determination to dress with comfort, ease, practicality, and as she pleased, shows that Sand was not far in point of view from those feminists of today who are reputed to burn certain of their undergarments.

The Italian historian and critic Benedetto Croce constantly stressed that the historian, having presented the facts of a situation as best he could, must make judgments or else produce works that are "pale and bloodless." The judgment to be made in this case is whether or not George Sand should be regarded as a feminist. There are those who would maintain that a woman who enjoyed household chores, who preferred men to women, who saw no reason for women to organize, who cautioned women to avoid the political arena, who had no use for the suffrage, who counseled women to "suffer and pray" could in no way be a feminist. If one defines feminism in such a way as to limit it to such traits as a scorn of domestic work, and a preference for sisterhood, organization, and politics, then one could maintain that in no way was George Sand a feminist. However, as with life itself, the situation is not so simple. One has to recognize that this same woman worked tirelessly to combat the view that women are inferior to men, to maintain the equality of partners in marriage, to show the world via her literature the plight of women,[47] and to work in 1848 for the transformation of France from a bourgeois to a socialist society, the *sine qua non* for the liberation of women in her view. Furthermore, she pursued a career, not just for pleasure, but also in order to maintain her independence and to support her children without having to rely on her husband. As a working woman, she protested the unequal salaries that were given to women. Also, in the face of strong social pressure for the repression of women, she maintained her sexual freedom, dressed as she pleased, and enjoyed a cigarette. Finally, it must be admitted that Sand was correct in thinking that obtaining the suffrage would not immediately and inevitably lead to the rectification of women's condition.

For women of the nineteenth century there was no dilemma as to whether or not Sand was working for the cause of women. In a letter Elizabeth Barrett Browning wrote to Robert Browning in July, 1845, Mrs. Browning affirmed her belief that "there is a natural inferiority of mind in women—of the intellect. . . ." She continued, ". . . I believe women . . . all of us in a mass . . . to have minds of quicker movement, but less power and depth . . . and that we are under your feet, because we can't stand upon our own. Not that we should either be quite under your feet, so you are not to be too proud, if you please—and there is certainly some amount of wrong—: but it never will be righted in the manner and to the extent contemplated by certain of our own prophetesses . . . nor ought to be, I hold in intimate persuasion. One woman indeed now alive and only *that* one down all the ages of the world—seems to me to justify for a moment an opposite opinion—that wonderful woman George Sand. . . ."[48] This is the George Sand that should be known to the women and men of our day, Sand who would in no way accept male superiority or domination. To select several tenets of feminism held in our day by some feminists and say that all who do not hold these views are inimical to the cause of women is ahistorical. Following such specious thinking, an historian in the twenty-first century will be able to "prove" that Gloria Steinem was not a feminist. Indeed, such thinking is already leading some to question Betty Friedan's commitment to feminism. Such a fate is not deserved by the woman who, cigarette in hand, wrote in 1848, "Yes, I have the right, as a woman, and as a woman who has felt acutely the injustice of laws and of prejudices, to get excited when I see postponed, because of awkward endeavors, the reparation that is due to us."[49]

NOTES

1. Tillie Olsen, "Silences: When Writers Don't Write," in *Images of Women in Fiction, Feminist Perspectives,* ed. by Susan Koppelman Cornillon (Bowling Green, Ohio: Bowling Green University Popular Press, 1972), p. 106.

2. Simone de Beauvoir, *The Second Sex,* ed. and trans. by H.M. Parshley (New York: Bantam, 1968), p. 103.

3. Simone de Beauvoir and Betty Friedan, "Sex, Society, and the Female Dilemma," *Saturday Review,* n.v. (June 14, 1975), 18-20.

4. Curtis Cate, *George Sand* (Boston: Houghton Mifflin Company, 1975) pp. 92-93.

5. Ibid., p. 419.

6. Sand, *Histoire de ma vie,* ed. by Noelle Roubaud (Paris: Editions Stock Delamain et Boutelleau, 1949), p. 267.

7. Cate, *George Sand,* pp. 223-24.

8. Sand, *Correspondance* (13 vols.; Paris: Editions Garnier Frères, 1964-78), I, 104.

9. Ibid., II, 741.

10. Cate, *George Sand,* p. 418.

11. Sand, *Correspondance,* VIII, 401-08.

12. Ibid., pp. 391-92.

13. Ibid., p. 401.

14. Ibid., p. 407.

15. Cate, *George Sand,* p. 419.

16. Ibid., p. 418.

17. Samuel Edwards, George Sand, *A Biography of the First Modern, Liberated Woman* (New York: David McKay Company, Inc., 1972), pp. 17-18.

18. Sand, *Histoire de ma vie,* p. 129.

19. Edwards, *George Sand,* p. 19.

20. Cate, *George Sand,* p. 419.

21. Edwards, *George Sand,* frontispiece.

22. Sand, *Correspondance,* V, 303.

23. Edwards, *George Sand,* p. 33.

24. "I was not my husband's slave; voluntarily he left me to my reading and to my tranquilizers; but I was enslaved by the given situation, from which it was not for him to free me." Sand, *Histoire de ma vie,* p. 269.

25. Sand, *Correspondance,* VIII, 402.

26. Zelda Austen, "Why Feminist Critics Are Angry with George Eliot," *College English,* XXXVII (February 1976), 549.

27. Ibid., p. 550.

28. Sand, *Correspondance,* III, 58.

29. Sand, *Indiana* (New York: Howard Fertig, 1975), pp. 206-08.

30. Sand, *Lélia* (Paris: Editions Garnier Frères, 1960), p. 153.

31. The author is indebted to Professor Alex Szogyi of Hunter College for introducing him to this work.

32. Sand, *Lucrezia Floriani—Lavinia* (Paris: Calmann Lévy Editeur, 1888), pp. 264-65.

33. Cate, *George Sand,* p. 641.

34. Edwards, *George Sand,* p. 238.

35. Sand, *Histoire de ma vie,* p. 326.

36. Sand, *Correspondance,* II, 234-36.

37. Ibid., VIII, 359.

38. Cate, *George Sand,* p. 418.

39. Sand, *Correspondance,* VIII, 401.

40. Ibid., III, 58.

41. Ibid., VIII, 405.

42. Cate, *George Sand,* p. 627.

43. Sand, *Histoire de ma vie,* p. 111.

44. Ibid., p. 243.

45. Ibid., pp. 244-45.

46. Ibid., p. 123.

47. In 1848 Sand made mention of her ". . . services rendered to the cause of my sex through numerous writings. . . ." Sand, *Correspondance,* VIII, 407.

48. Robert Browning and Elizabeth Barrett Browning, *The Letters of Robert Browning and Elizabeth Barrett Browning, 1845-1846* (2 vols.; New York: Harper & Brothers, 1899), I, 116-17.

49. Sand, *Correspondance,* VIII, 407-08.

Pierre-Joseph Proudhon and George Sand: A Confrontation

AARON NOLAND
Dept. of History
The City College, City University of New York
The Graduate Center, City University of New York

George Sand's political and social thought and writings, her relations with a broad spectrum of the radical and 'advanced' theoreticians and politicians of her day, and the active role which she played in the politics of her time, particularly during the dramatic, historic period of the Revolution of 1848 in Paris, have been the subjects of critical, scholarly study in the nineteenth century and in our own day. Hippolyte Monin, Marguerite Thibert, Marius-Ary Leblond, Marie-Thérèse Rouget, Jean Larnac, as well as Sand's magnificent biographer, Wladimir Karénine, among others, have placed all *sandistes* in their debt for the detailed and carefully-researched studies they have provided concerning these important matters.[1] On the basis of the evidence presented in these studies, it is apparent that George Sand, when the occasion presented itself, brought the full weight of her talents and energies to bear on the ongoing struggle waged in France during her lifetime to transform the existing social order for the purpose of improving the conditions of the lower orders of society and creating a new world that would embody the devoutly-wished goals of the French Revolution: *Liberté, Egalité, Fraternité*.

For her continuing, deeply-felt commitment to radical social reform—a commitment that by no means precluded revolutionary action—George Sand earned in her own day the respect and affection of almost all the outstanding, influential radical and socialist theoreticians and activists, including such notables as Louis Blanc, Etienne Cabet, Armand Barbès, Agricol Perdiguier, the Social Catholic Félicité de Lamennais, and, most particularly, Pierre Leroux. Conservatives and reactionaries, *bien pensants* of various hues, put off if not enraged by her sharp attacks on marriage and the contemporary family, private property and the spirit of caste, and literary critics, who took exception to George Sand's extensive concern with social doctrines and ideologies in so many of her novels, did indeed fault her on these scores; but among socialists and other elements on the Left, George Sand's standing as novelist and apologist for the disinherited and oppressed was of the highest order, a source of pride and inspiration.

There was one striking exception to this general approbation, however, and exception that commanded attention in George Sand's own day, for this critic was the outstanding anarcho-socialist of the time in France, a man whose commitment to the revolutionary transformation of society was widely recognized and unimpeachable, and whose following among the urban proletariat in Paris and elsewhere was extensive and long lived: Pierre-Joseph Proudhon. Indeed, in the halcyon early days of the 1848 revolution, at the very time that George Sand's prestige among the elements of the Left was at its zenith[2] with her participation in the editing of the Provisional Government's *Bulletin de la République,* Proudhon was one of the few contemporaries who could speak with equal authority.[3] Already well known as a free lance writer, newspaper editor, and publisher, Proudhon was at that time editor of the newspaper *Le Représentant du Peuple,* which had a wide circulation in Parisian working class circles.[4] Proudhon was also a delegate from Paris in the National Assembly, which he used as a forum to address the country at large.

These pursuits brought Proudhon into intimate contact with a wide variety of individuals and social strata and provided him with a comprehensive, firsthand knowledge of French politics and of the profound social and economic developments of his time. He knew personally most of the leading French socialists of his day, including Louis Blanc, Auguste Blanqui, Pierre Leroux, Victor Considérant, and Charles Delescluze. He numbered among his friends and acquaintances Victor Hugo, Gustave Courbet, Jules Michelet, and Prince Jérôme Bonaparte, as well as Michael Bakunin, Alexander

Herzen, and Karl Marx—who was an early admirer of Proudhon, but who subsequently became his bitter critic and rival.[5]

In his own day Proudhon enjoyed a great notoriety. To sections of the French bourgeoisie, Proudhon was *the* class enemy, a greater threat to their notions of "law and order" than even the professed insurrectionists, such as Auguste Blanqui and Armand Barbès. Was it not Proudhon who had repeatedly proclaimed in his books and newspaper articles that French society was "menaced by dissolution?" Had he not scandalized and outraged the *bien pensants* in affirming that "Property is theft" and that "God is evil?" If George Sand offended segments of French public opinion by her attacks on the sanctity of marriage and the status of women, Proudhon certainly aroused protest from these same quarters with his sweeping indictment of the entire social order of his day, an order ruled and exploited, as he put it, by a new "mercantile and landed aristocracy, a thousand times more rapacious than the old aristocracy of the nobility." [6]

In view of all this, it would appear that Proudhon and Sand should have been natural allies in the struggle for a new and more equitable society. And yet, paradoxically, there was absolutely no common ground between them; Proudhon found no virtue in any of George Sand's writings, neither in her fiction nor her more explicit political and social essays and tracts. On the contrary, Sand probably did not have, in her lifetime, a more intransigent, unrelenting, fervent, and vituperative enemy than Proudhon.

How is one to account for this? What did Proudhon find in the writings and conduct of George Sand that led him to take up his pen in implacable opposition to one of the leading figures of the Left? From Proudhon's notebooks it would appear that his acquaintance with Sand's work was quite thorough and dated from the early eighteen-forties.[7] At that time he read some of her pieces in newspapers and periodicals, and on the basis of what he himself called these "fragments," he conceived, as he put it, "a strong repulsion toward the author." [8] Friends, whose opinions carried weight with him, however, reassured him that his initial reaction was unfair and prejudiced. "Mme Sand, they told me," Proudhon reports, "is a writer of genius, and, more important, she is a good woman. Read her, and you'll see." [9] Proudhon has informed us that he then undertook to read a number of Sand's works, some eleven novels, including *Indiana, Lélia, Mauprat, Le Compagnon du tour de France, Spiridion,* and *Leone Leoni.* Some of these novels contain Sand's most explicit formulations of her social thought, of her "socialism," as students of Sand's work have noted,[10] and they render most apparent the pervasive influence on Sand of the social philosophy, metaphysics, and religious notions of such contemporaries as Leroux, Lammenais, and Blanc.[11] Proudhon scrutinized carefully Sand's important journalistic writings at the time of the 1848 Revolution, and he also claimed to have read Sand's multivolume *Histoire de ma vie* and to have witnessed the performance of three of her plays: *Champi, Claudie,* and *Maître Favilla.*[12]

One of Proudhon's basic criticisms of George Sand as a social thinker and reformer was that, although she spoke with considerable authority on matters of social policy and readily proffered schemes aimed at redressing social, political, and economic problems—most emphatically at the time of the 1848 Revolution[13]—she did not have a really comprehensive theory of society or of social change, a "science of society," as it was currently phrased. Rather her social philosophy, Proudhon wrote in 1858, was an artificial construction, an eclectic patchwork of ideas and slogans gathered from a variety of sources, some contemporary—the writings of Leroux, Lamennais, Blanc, the Saint-Simonians, and Jean Reynaud—and some drawn from the eighteenth century, especially from Jean-Jacques Rousseau and the legacy of "babouvisme."[14] What was needed, what the times called for, in Proudhon's view, was certainly *not* another "gospel," a new gospel according to George Sand to be added to "the gospel according to Philippe Buchez, the gospel according to Pierre Leroux . . . Lamennais, Victor Considérant . . . Mme Flora Tristan . . . Constantin Pecquer, and still so many others."[15] Certainly not: since the French Revolution when, in Proudhon's view, the critical issue had come to be generally recognized as the need to establish natural order in society, the public had been offered a plethora of social reform programs which were intended to resolve the problems posed by the transformation of traditional institutions and values that had been initiated by the great French Revolution and by the impact on Europe of the ongoing Industrial Revolution. As Proudhon put it in 1851, "Systems abound; schemes fall like rain."[16] Yet not one of these schemes or programs, in his view, was adequate to the task, for not one was anchored in a scientific understanding of the true nature of society, nor was the basic principle (if any) of the restructuring of society organic in nature, immanent in the very fabric of human society itself. All of these theorists and would-be reformers—and this included George Sand—were in some degree dogmatic, absolutist, arbitrary, sentimental and subjective, and motivated by "the spirit of exclusion, of reaction." [17]

The problem of social reform, the heart of the matter, in Proudhon's view, was not simply to formulate a constitution for the future social order on the basis of pure logic, or common sense, or personal wishes, or on the basis of generous sentiments or effluent feelings and longings such as the brotherhood of man or some vaguely-defined "religion of humanity." The essence of the matter was not to legislate into existence the true order of a just and equitable society, but to discover what are—and, indeed, have always been—the fundamental principles of that order, principles and processes that, in Proudhon's words, were *organique, régulateur,* and *souverain.* [18] And the method by which these governing principles were to be discovered, Proudhon affirmed in 1848, was that of "interrogating the people," [19] that is, by carefully studying the history of past civilization and observing how mankind, from time immemorial, evolved from its "entrails," in answer to its needs, spontaneously, without conscious design for the most part, social institutions—laws, religions, governments, domestic arrangements, economic structures, etc.—which embodied and made manifest the immanent principles of the natural order of society.

Because George Sand was not, in Proudhon's estimation, a serious student of history or political economy or any of the related disciplines, and because she lacked, in Proudhon's words, "a taste for metaphysics," [20] she constructed her social philosophy, her brand of socialism, on eminently acceptable humanitarian sentiments and on ostensibly self-evident truths and maxims. In short, as far as Proudhon was concerned, Sand's writings were in large measure simply "verbiage," as affirmed in a letter dating from 1847, and Sand herself a *romancière philanthrope,* characterized by a striking *incapacité philosophique.* [21] In his unpublished notebook dating from 1848, Proudhon was less restrained, describing her as a *parolière* and declaring: "Cette femme écrit comme elle pisse." [22]

Proudhon's critique of George Sand as a social theoretician and avant-garde reformer can be brought into sharper focus by an examination of his reaction to her often reiterated and, in her own time, rather sensational (in some circles, quite notorious) views on marriage and the status of women. What Sand demanded was the equality of the sexes in law and marriage. The Code Napoléon, as it concerned marriage and the family, the code which today remains the foundation of the French legal system, institutionalized in Sand's day the legal inferiority of a wife vis-à-vis the husband, and in its treatment of adultery in particular, assigned to the wife the status of a morally inferior being.[23] "That women differ from men," Sand affirmed, "that heart and intellect are subject to the laws of sex, I do not doubt. But ought this difference, so essential to the general harmony of things, to constitute a moral inferiority?"[24] Marriage, in her view, could be a viable and just and morally acceptable relationship only if women enjoyed the same civil rights and were entitled to the same consideration as men. Mutual respect and more, far more, the recognition of love as the fundamental element in the relationship between man and wife—"To marry without love," Sand had written, "is to serve a life-sentence in the galleys."[25]—could alone justify the institution of marriage; and in their absence, divorce as a means for redressing an unjust state of affairs must be available on equal terms to both husband and wife.[26]

In Proudhon's concept of how all of society should be reconstructed, both the role he assigns to the institution of marriage and the status he reserves for women are in direct opposition to the views of George Sand.[27] If Proudhon managed to offend and enrage so many of the *bien pensants* of his day with his opposition to private property and religion, he certainly occasioned dismay among his colleagues on the Left, particularly among the mass of radical social theoreticians and activists, with his insistence on the inferiority of women—all women—and his affirmation that the latter had to choose between being a "courtesan or a housewife." At a time when almost all socialists, the Saint-Simonians, Fourierists, as well as Louis Blanc and Pierre Leroux, among others, were supporters of feminist movements and promoted the cause of the enfranchisement of women, Proudhon struck a sharply opposing stance, coining and propagandizing the slogan: "Plutôt la réclusion que l'émancipation!"[28]

For the purpose of this paper, it is not necessary to determine whether Proudhon's remarks are simply the expressions of traditional male chauvinism, a peasant superstition, an atavistic embodiment of Roman paterfamilias sentiments, a perversity, or something more or less reputable. Proudhon's anti-feminism—if that be the appropriate designation—has little bearing on his fundamental criticism of George Sand's views, and this criticism can be considered and evaluated on its own merits.

At the heart of this criticism were two considerations. The first was that Sand, in Proudhon's view, conceived of the relationship between husband and wife as analogous to the various kinds of contracts that make up the web of social relations in the society at large: that marriage was a contract not unlike those that individuals, of their own free will, enter into with other individuals in order to secure certain ends, to satisfy specific needs or interests. In such contracts there was equal exchange and reciprocity. Assumed in this notion of a contract was the view that the family, posited by the marriage, was comparable to the larger units that constituted the society as a whole—that the rights and obligations, the laws and regulations that obtained in the society at large were not essentially different from those that related to the family unit. Secondly, Proudhon noted that for Sand the bond between the husband and wife was, above all, the bond of love, a purely private element with which the laws of society could have no concern. How could a society legislate in matters of the heart? The marital relationship was viable, "legitimate," if the word can properly be employed in this context, only as long as love ruled all. "When Mme Sand speaks of marriage," Proudhon wrote, "it is always love that is being spoken of . . . because marriage is nothing but love."[29] Proudhon cited passages in Sand's novel *Jacques* in which the husband-to-be writes to his finacée:

> La société va vous dicter une formule de serment; vous allez jurer de m'être fidèle et de m'être soumise, c'est-à-dire de n'aimer jamais que moi et de m'obéir en tout. L'un de ces serments est une absurdité, l'autre une bassesse. Vous ne pouvez pas répondre de votre coeur, même quand je serais le plus grand et le plus parfait des hommes; vous ne devez pas promettre de m'obéir, parce que ce serait nous avilir l'un et l'autre.

The young lady, Proudhon goes on, responds: "Ah! tenez, ne parlons pas de notre mariage; parlons comme si nous étions destinés seulement à être amants." Why, then, bother to get married?

Jacques replies: "Parce que la tyrannie social ne nous permet pas de nous posséder autrement." [30]

Since she had an artistic temperament, was a creator of "erotic" novels and not a student of society and history, it was to be expected, Proudhon contended, that George Sand would have an idealized notion of love and marriage, that love would be hypostatized into an autonomous, pre-eminent and absolute value and that she should fail to comprehend the central position that marriage and the family played in the construction of a viable social order. "The female artist, or writer of novels," Proudhon declared, is easily "seduced by the ideal and by the sensual." [31] But what civilization ever based marriage and the family on an emotion as "inconstant as nature has made it" as sexual love? What code of laws in the history of civilization had ever anchored the security and stability of the connubial state, of the family, on this love? Concerning this matter, Proudhon found the Code Napoléon a representative and "admirable" case in point. He noted that Articles 212, 213, 214, and 203 of the Civil Code, one of the five parts of the Code Napoléon, provided that:

1. The spouses owe to one another mutual fidelity, aid and assistance.
2. The husband owes protection to his wife, the wife obedience to her husband.
3. The wife is required to reside with the husband and to follow him wherever he judges it appropriate to reside. The husband is obliged to receive her and to furnish her with the necessities of life, in accordance with his capacities and his station in life.
4. The spouses together have a contractual obligation, by the sole fact of marriage, to nourish, maintain, and raise their children. [32]

"The word love is not mentioned," Proudhon affirmed, "and it should not be—it is in that respect that the legislation appears to me to be admirable." [33]

In Proudhon's sociology, in his theory of society, [34] the family was the nuclear cell, the core unit, of the social order, embodying not simply the private interests and concerns of the connubial partners and their offspring, but those of the society as a whole and, indeed, of all generations to come. A marriage might well be the issue of love, but the union brought into existence by the act of marriage was a "moral entity," governed not by sexual love, but by "the essential attribute of humanity," the "organizing principle" at the center of human life and society, and "the force which assures the progress of man and society"—Justice. Space is lacking to develop in any detail Proudhon's conception of the role of justice in the history of civilization and in the creation of an equitable, truly human social order; suffice it to say that in his view justice—"the respect, spontaneously experienced and reciprocally guaranteed, for human dignity, in all individuals and in whatever circumstances it [human dignity] may find itself compromised, and at whatever the risk may be that we expose ourselves in its defense" [35]—was the superior, sovereign force, the dominant factor in marriage and the family. A true marriage, in Proudhon's view, of necessity involved "the subordination of love to justice," marriage being, in Proudhon's words, the *vainqueur de l'amour,* the guarantee . . . against the failings of love;" and he cited with approval the proverb: "Le marriage est le tombeau de l'amour." [36] It was in subordinating sexual love to the superior force of justice and the larger, more permanent interests of the social order that the transient, inconstant character of human love is transformed and, in Proudhon's words, rendered "stable, equal, durable, and indissoluble . . . and superior to itself." [37] Sexual love is transformed into devotion, and "to the ephemeral reign of love succeeds, for the rest of life, the more serious reign of conscience." The family then comes into its own as the "embryonic organ of justice," with the spouses "constituting but one body, one soul, one will, and one intelligence, devoted to one another unto death. . . ." [38] The family, spouses and children, now serve effectively, in Proudhon's view, as a moral agency, "the effective core and foundation," as one Proudhon scholar put it, "of moral life."

> Here youngsters receive their basic moral education, and from both instruction by their parents and the family experience itself they can acquire the basis of a moral perspective and inclination out of which justice in the larger society will evolve. [39]

Although husband and wife form, through marriage, a single moral entity, "an androgynous unit," there was, as Proudhon saw it, no equality between them in the sense in which men who enter into contracts, into mutual agreements, in the market place and in the public area at large are said to be equal before the law, enjoying the same prerogatives and status. The egalitarianism, which Proudhon believed in all sincerity should reign in the society as a whole, had no place—could have no place—within the connubial union as he conceived of it. The marriage contract, to him, was not like other kinds of pacts or contracts, and the family, contrary to what such conservatives as Louis Bonald and Frédéric Le Play contended, was not a prototype, a model or paradigm for other institutional units that constituted a society.[40] Proudhon is far from clear in this matter of the particular character of the marriage contract, and there appears to be a mystical element, not to speak of a strong dose of prejudice, in his conception of it. What is clear, however, is that in his mind the moral dimension of the family did not include the notion of the equality of husband and wife. The ultimate authority within the family in Proudhon's view, as in the Code Napoléon, rested squarely with the husband.

As Proudhon saw the matter, the man and the woman brought different, disparate faculties and characteristics to a marriage, elements that were complimentary and "equivalent" in some sense, but in no way of equal status, weight or interchangeability. "The qualities of a man and a woman," Proudhon affirmed, "are incommutable values; to appraise, to estimate the qualities of one by the other, is to reduce them equally to nothing."[41] To Proudhon, marriage was

> the union of two heterogeneous elements, *power* and *grace,* with the first represented by man, the producer, inventor, scholar, warrior, administrator, and magistrate; the second, represented by woman, of whom the only thing that can be said is that she is, by nature and by destination, the achieved, living idealization of all that the man possesses in himself, in a higher degree of power and ability, in the three spheres of work, knowledge and rights.[42]

Proudhon acknowledged that there was an apparent paradox involved here: what could justify the fact that in the family, "cet organisme formé pour la Justice," as Proudhon himself defined it, in which one would thus suppose that everything would be balanced and in which equality would reign, man legitimately exercised the supreme authority, while the woman was assigned a definitely subordinate status? Writing in 1860, Proudhon endeavored to explain away the paradox by affirming that in every case where "supremacy" was claimed for the husband and "subordination" for the wife, it was a question "exclusively of the exercise of virile attributes."

> Because of the predominance of their respective faculties, the man is the Producer and Warrior; the woman the mistress of day-to-day affairs and the idealizer. As a consequence of this, the attributes of the former are those identified with work, hunting, fishing, agriculture, industry, commerce, science, politics, war, peace, and justice—in a word, all that concerns the world at large. The attributes of the woman are love, children, the home, religion, when there is a religion to be considered—all that relates to the ideal and to ordinary existence, in a word, the home. I do not deny that the woman exercises an influence on all the activities of the man; but it is only an influence, not an initiative. . . . the fixed character of these different attributes consequently entail different responsibilities, which in turn imply different degrees of initiative.[43]

It was in the context of these conceptions of love, marriage, and the family that Proudhon took strong exception to George Sand's writings in support of women's rights and the revision of the Civil Code. While asserting in print that of all the "so-called emancipators" of women, George Sand was "the most worthy of esteem,"[44]— Proudhon nevertheless insisted that her influence on public opinion in France was undeniably deleterious. "Is it not true," Proudhon queried George Sand in print in 1860, "that in *Valentine, Indiana, Lélia*—and above all, in *Jacques*—you attacked marriage as being an immoral and barbaric institution? Is it not true that you have consistently held free love to be superior to legalized love?"[45] In short, the "idealized eroticism" which, in Proudhon's view, permeated Sand's fiction—"The collected novels of Mme Sand are a *garland* offered to love"—served only to promote the debasement of domestic morality.[46]

This last charge by Proudhon can well serve as a bridge to a consideration of his final, broader indictment of George Sand and her writings. As has been indicated previously, Proudhon, perhaps the most "moralistic" of the major radical thinkers of his time, was very much concerned with the spiritual health of the France of his day, almost haunted by the vision that the basic institutions of his country were "menaced by dissolution." Writing in 1862, he took a quite pessimistic stance, expressing a lack of confidence in France and her ability to survive. "I no longer believe in France; I no longer expect anything from her. . . . Decadence in France has made frightful progress during the past ten years. . . . Corruption, stupidity, venality and laziness alone have doubled—that's your progress."[47] An "entire generation *est gangrenée.*"[48] France was "*une nation prostituée,* the foyer of all the corruptions that blighted the old order of society, and just as France had once held aloft the flag of liberty and right, she now carries the banner of universal dissolution."[49]

Proudhon contended that the basic causes of the decadence of France could be traced back to the mid-eighteenth century; and while a full consideration of this matter lies beyond the scope of this paper, one of the crucial factors in the decline of French civilization as Proudhon conceived of it merits examination, for it bears directly on his critique of George Sand. This factor, as Proudhon isolated it, was the increasing "effeminization" of almost every aspect of French life—that is, the increasing pre-eminence, in Proudhon's view, of sentiments and feelings, of the subjective and romantic, of the aesthetic principle, over the "masculine element," the will and power to act, objectivity and reason, juridical and moral principles, and discipline and self-denial. In a viable, progressive social order, Proudhon maintained, the masculine element, which represented "l'intégralité de l'esprit," dominated, providing the society with its *élan,* its forward thrust, and assuring for that order its increasing mastery over its environment.[50] Proudhon insisted that history disclosed that a nation, after having manifested "a virile energy," could become effeminized and, as a consequence, "fall into decay." This is what had happened to "the Persians after Cyrus, to the Greeks after the Peloponnesian War, and to the Romans themselves, following their immense conquests and their civil wars."[51]

One of the means by which this effeminization of French life was advanced was literature. This "efférmination littéraire," Proudhon affirmed, "began with Rousseau." The writings of Jean-Jacques Rousseau manifested, in Proudhon's estimation, a certain fuzziness of ideas, the dominance of "passion or affectivity over reason." Rousseau's *Nouvelle Héloïse* (1761) prepared the way for the "dissolution" of marriage—"from the publication of this novel dates in our country the enervating of souls by love, an enervation that must be followed closely by a frigid and sombre impudicity."[52] Rousseau's influence on the public opinion in his day was "immense," and it had continued to be felt strongly in Proudhon's own day. As Proudhon explained it, this was due in large measure to the fact that Rousseau had

> put the fire to the gunpowder that French letters had been amassing for two centuries. It is indeed something to have kindled in human souls such a conflagration: the force and virility of Rousseau consists of this; in all other respects he is like a woman.[53]

Proudhon, in 1858, discussed the "successors" to Rousseau, noting the contributions made to the effeminization of French institutions and the undermining of traditional French moral values by such notables as Germaine de Staël, Pierre-Jean de Bèranger, Alphonse de Lamartine, and, lastly, George Sand.[54]

This, then, was the ultimate, the most weighty indictment that Proudhon brought against his great contemporary: Sand might well plead the cause of the equality of the sexes, the sacred character of love whether sanctioned by the laws of society or not; she might well argue for the liberation, the emancipation of women. This was what was manifest, according to Proudhon, in Sand's writings. The latent function of her writings, however, was, in Proudhon's view, something quite different. Beneath her rhetoric, concealed by her *bavardage,* her *excitation érotique,* her social poetry and utopianism, Proudhon discerned a concerted assault on the moral and ethical values of traditional French society, a powerful resentment of the masculine element, a demand for the "systematic depression of the male sex"—"a black androphobia," as he called it.[55] Writing in 1860, Proudhon affirmed that Sand was indeed "in revolt against society," but, he noted, not like anarcho-socialists such as himself, rebels who had a vision of a future society that would be based on a morality that would demand stringent self-discipline and Spartan self-denial.[56] The upshot of Sand's efforts, the inevitable, all-encompassing, deleterious consequences that would follow upon the triumph of her theories and teachings, would be not simply the disappearance of the existing family structure, but an unparalleled disruption of the entire social order, the final realization of "social effemination," and the inauguration of a regime which Proudhon called "la pornocratie," the reign of the courtesan, of the prostitute. "Alors, c'est fini de la societé," were Proudhon's final words in the matter.[57]

What was George Sand's response to Proudhon's sweeping attacks on her writings? As far as the written record is concerned, apparently Sand did not respond. Proudhon himself, in 1860, reported that he had heard that Sand had intended to bring an action for libel against him, but had not done so upon learning that the Imperial Prosecutor was initiating an action against Proudhon for his *De la Justice dans la révolution et dans l'église,* on the grounds that it was offensive to civic and religious morality.[58] Sand did have some things to say about Proudhon in a letter which she wrote to Giuseppi Mazzini in 1852, years before Proudhon had published his major criticisms. Proudhon, she informed Mazzini, really had no doctrine. His writings were "a tissue of dazzling contradictions, of brilliant paradoxes which will never constitute a school of thought. Proudhon may have his admirers, but he will never have adepts." She acknowledged that he was an "incontestable polemicist . . . very militant, impassioned, incisive and eloquent . . . an informed economist, ingenious, but powerless due to the uniqueness of his conceptions. . . ." Her final judgment of the man was unequivocal in the extreme: "Proudhon is the greatest enemy of socialism."[59]

ACKNOWLEDGMENT

The author is indebted to Judy Cory for her invaluable assistance in the preparation of this paper.

NOTES

1. H. Monin, "George Sand et la république de février 1848," *La Révolution française,* XXXVII (1899), 428-448, 543-561; XXXVIII (1900), 53-64, 167-185; M. Thibert, *Le Féminisme dans le socialisme français, de 1830 à 1850* (Paris, 1926); M.-A. Leblond, "Notes sur George Sand socialiste," *La Revue socialiste,* XL (1904), 28-49, 174-190; M.T. Rouget, *George Sand 'socialiste'* (Lyons, 1931); J. Larnac, *George Sand révolutionnaire* (Paris, 1948); V. Karénine (pseud.

Varvara Komarova), *George Sand: sa vie et ses oeuvres,* 4 vols. (Paris, 1899-1926).

2. Larnac, *George Sand révolutionnaire,* p. 145.

3. See Edouard Dolléans and J.-L. Puech, *Proudhon et la révolution de 1848* (Paris, 1948), and Mary B. Allen, "P.J. Proudhon in the Revolution of 1848," *The Journal of Modern History,* XXIV (March 1952), 1-14.

4. In the words of his most recent biographer, Proudhon was "brilliant" as a political journalist, the role in which "he made his mark in the history of the Revolution." Robert L. Hoffman, *Revolutionary Justice: The Social and Political Theory of P.-J. Proudhon* (Urbana, 1972), p. 130. See also pp. 119-144, *passim.*

5. See in this connection, J. H. Jackson, *Marx, Proudhon, and European Socialism* (New York, 1962), and Pierre Haubtmann, *Marx et Proudhon* (Paris, 1947).

6. Quoted in Aaron Noland, "History and Humanity: The Proudhonian Vision," *The Uses of History,* edited by H.V. White (Detroit, 1968), p. 61.

7. *Carnets de P.-J. Proudhon* (Paris, 1960), I, 51.

8. Proudhon, *De la Justice dans la révolution et dans l'église* (Paris, 1935), IV, 246.

9. Ibid.

10. David Owen Evans, *Le Socialisme romantique: Pierre Leroux et ses contemporains* (Paris, 1948), pp. 105-131, *passim;* Karénine, *George Sand: sa vie et ses oeuvres,* III, 217-635, *passim.*

11. Evans, *Le Socialisme romantique,* pp. 16-19, 105-107; Maxime Leroy, *Histoire des idées sociales en France,* 3 vols. (Paris, 1946-54), II, 419, III, 56-65, 144-145.

12. Proudhon, *De la Justice dans la révolution et dans l'église,* IV, 246.

13. Larnac, *George Sand révolutionnaire,* pp. 163-188; Edouard Dolléans, *Féminisme et mouvement ouvrier: George Sand* (Paris, 1951), pp. 85-98.

14. Proudhon, *De la Justice dans la révolution et dans l'église,* IV, 255-256. "George Sand n'a jamais eu, au sens propre, de doctrine. Les éclats de sa sensibilité et son talent d'écrivain ont pu faire illusion. Elle

a des idées, des sentiments, sans vues systématiques, sans grande ordonnance logique." (Leroy, *Histoire des idées sociales en France,* III, 55-56.)

15. *Correspondance de P.-J. Proudhon,* 14 vols. (Paris, 1875), II, 131, letter to A.M. Maurice, July 27, 1844.

16. Proudhon, *Idée générale de la révolution au XIXe siècle* (Paris, 1924; 1st edition, 1851), p. 157.

17. Ibid.

18. Proudhon, *De la Justice dans la révolution et dans l'église,* I, 280.

19. Proudhon, *Solution du problème social* (Paris, 1868; 1st edition, 1848), p. 18. "Le problème de la reconstitution sociale est posé, il faut le résoudre. Cette solution, nous ne l'apprendrons que du Peuple," p. 14. See also Proudhon, *De la création de l'ordre dans l'humanité, ou principes d'organisation politique* (Paris, 1927; 1st edition, 1843), pp. 381, 388.

20. Proudhon, *De la Justice dans la révolution et dans l'église,* IV, 255. See also *Correspondance de P.-J. Proudhon,* II, letter 'A Madame,' February 17, 1847, 238. Jean Larnac, in his *George Sand révolutionnaire,* published in 1948, without referring to Proudhon's views, has lent support to the latter's estimate of Sand's inadequacy as a social thinker, noting that "it does not appear that George Sand ever undertook to study history, theology, sociology or law—studies which would have permitted her to base her convictions on documentary materials or closely reasoned arguments," p. 39. See in this connection Pierre Salomon, *George Sand* (Paris, 1953), pp. 51, 64-65, 158.

21. *Correspondance de P.-J. Proudhon,* II, letter 'A Madame,' February 17, 1847, 238.

22. *Carnets de P.-J. Proudhon,* III (Paris, 1968), 33.

23. On the Code Napoléon, see Leo Gershoy, *The French Revolution and Napoleon* (New York, 1964), p. 456, and Robert B. Holtman, *The Napoleonic Revolution* (New York, 1967), pp. 88-98.

24. Quoted in André Maurois, *Lélia, the Life of George Sand* (New York, 1968), p. 389.

25. Quoted in Maurois, *Lélia,* p. 429.

26. Ibid., pp. 392-393. See also Thibert, *Le Féminisme dans le socialisme français de 1830 à 1850* (Paris, 1926), p. 274.

27. Proudhon submitted Sand's views on love, marriage, and the status of women to extensive analysis both in his multi-volume *De la Justice dans la révolution et dans l'église* published in 1858 and in his *La Pornocratie, ou Les Femmes dans les temps modernes* published posthumously in 1875. A detailed treatment of Proudhon's arguments would require a monograph; only a summary account is possible here.

28. Proudhon, *La Pornocratie* (Paris, 1875), p. 203.

29. Proudhon, *De la Justice dans la révolution et dans l'église*, IV, 251.

30. Quoted in Proudhon, *De la Justice*, p. 250.

31. Proudhon, *La Pornocratie*, p. 91.

32. Proudhon, *De la Justice dans la révolution et dans l'église*, IV, 291.

33. Ibid.

34. On Proudhon's theory of society, see my article, "Proudhon: Socialist as Social Scientist," *The American Journal of Economics and Sociology*, XXVI (July 1967), 313-328, and Georges Gurvitch, *Les Fondateurs français de la sociologie contemporaine* (Paris, 1955); Gurvitch, *Pour le Centenaire de la mort de Pierre-Joseph Proudhon* (Paris, 1964), pp. 98-100.

35. Proudhon, *De la Justice dans la révolution et dans l'église*, I, 215, 423, 324, 426, 323, 329, 324, 217. See also pp. 314-315, 328, 433; III, 345-347, 513-516.

36. Ibid., IV, 56, 209, 251, 259; III, 638.

37. Ibid., IV, 12, 24, 26, 46, 292-293, 297-298. "Le mariage, exprimant, selon moi, la charte primitive de la conscience, doit être indissoluble, parce que la conscience est immuable. Les voeux sont une symbolique du mariage, l'homme, se saisissant lui-même n'a plus que faire du symbole" (Proudhon, *La Pornocratie*, p. 140). See also *La Pornocratie*, p. 210.

38. Proudhon, *La Pornocratie*, pp. 57-58, 51-53, 210.

39. Hoffman, *Revolutionary Justice*, p. 251.

40. Proudhon, *De la Justice dans la révolution et dans l'église*, IV, 295-308, *passim*.

41. Ibid., IV, 271; *idem, La Pornocratie*, pp. 5, 8-13.

42. Proudhon, *De la Justice dans la révolution et dans l'église*, IV, 276.

43. Ibid., p. 321. "L'homme et la femme pourraient-ils, dans le commerce de leur vie, échanger, par convention mutuele, leurs attributions? Pourraient-ils, à volonté, vaquer indifféremment l'un et l'autre, tantôt aux soins domestiques, tantôt aux soins du dehors; la femme à monter à cheval et aller à la guerre, l'homme se friser et faire joli coeur? . . . Non, puisque ce serait aller à l'encontre de leur facultés respectives, confondre leurs sexes, et bannir, autant qu'il serait en eux, de leur société, la dignité, le respect et bientôt l'amour" (ibid., pp. 321-322).

44. Ibid., p. 314. Why was Sand the "most worthy of esteem?" Because ". . . elle est la seule qui ait eu la franchise de mettre sa vie et ses écrits d'accord avec ses sentiments," her words matching her actions (ibid.).

45. Ibid., p. 314.

46. Ibid., p. 47, 56, 249, 259.

47. *Correspondance de P.-J. Proudhon,* XII, letter J.-A. Langlois, April 12, 1862, 47-48.

48. Ibid., letter Gouvernet, May 23, 1862, 112.

49. Quoted in Koenraad W. Swart, *The Sense of Decadence in Nineteenth-Century France* (The Hague, 1964), p. 102. See also, *ibid.,* 103.

50. Proudhon, *La Pornocratie,* pp. 71-73, 228; Proudhon, *De la Justice dans la révolution et dans l'église,* IV, 182, 216.

51. Proudhon, *La Pornocratie,* 72.

52. Proudhon, *De la Justice dans la révolution et dans l'église,* IV, 240, 217-219. Concerning Proudhon's ambivalent attitude towards Rousseau, see my article, "Proudhon and Rousseau," *Journal of the History of Ideas,* XXVIII (1967), 33-54.

53. Proudhon, *De la Justice dans la Révolution et dans l'Eglise,* III, 636; IV, 217-219; *idem, Pornocratie,* 241. "Le bon sens public et l'experience ont prononcé définitivement sur Jean-Jacques: caractère faible, âme molle et passionnée, jugement faux, dialectique contradictoire, génie paradoxal, puissant dans ses aspirations, mais faussé et affaibli pas ce culte de l'idéal qu'un instinct secret lui faisait maudire" (*De la Justice,* IV, 217).

54. Ibid., pp. 219-256; Proudhon, *La Pornocratie,* pp. 166-167. As has often been noted, Rousseau's influence on George Sand was profound. In her writings, references to him are innumerable, far more than any other writer. Monin put the matter simply and accurately: Sand was the "fille

intellectual de Rousseau" ("George Sand et la république de février 1848," *loc. cit.,* 440). See also George Sand, "Quelques Réflexions sur Jean-Jacques Rousseau," *Revue des Deux Mondes,* XXVI (1841), 703-716; Leblond, "Notes sur George Sand socialiste," *loc. cit.,* 183-185, 28; Karénine, *George Sand,* III, 370-371.

55. Proudhon, *De la Justice dans la révolution et dans l'église,* IV, 248-249, 253.

56. Ibid., p. 315; Proudhon, *La Pornocratie,* pp. 241, 252. See also Georges Sorel, *Matériaux d'une théorie du prolétariat* (Paris, 1929), 198-200; Jeanne Duprat, *Proudhon, sociologue et moraliste* (Paris, 1929).

57. Proudhon, *La Pornocratie,* 74, 139, 184, 242. "Le mariage, organe naturel et formateur de la justice, est base de la société: il produit la liberté et la République. La pornocratie, son antagoniste, est le dernier mot de toute usurpation et tyrannie" (ibid., 174).

58. Proudhon, *De la Justice dans la révolution et dans l'église,* IV, 312. See also Hoffman, *Revolutionary Justice,* 209.

59. *Correspondance de George Sand,* III, letter May 23, 1852, 340-341. See also G. Sand, "Sur Proudhon et Jules Janin," (1848), in *Souvenirs et idées* (Paris, 1904), pp. 40-41.

George Sand and Balzac

JANIS GLASGOW
Department of French and Italian
San Diego State University

Are the similarities between George Sand's little known *Metella* (1833),[1] and Balzac's *La Femme abandonnée* (1832)[2] merely fortuitous, or was Balzac's *nouvelle* the point of departure for one of her literary creations? Balzac has often been accused of using George Sand as a fictional model,[3] and no-one has ever before discerned the corollary. The more I have investigated this possibility, the more I have become convinced that George Sand was inspired to retort to Balzac's tale with a version of her own in which she also asserted women's rights for freedom.

These two *nouvelles* of approximately the same length now seem often amusing to us; both our literary styles and our life styles differ enormously from those of the nineteenth century. The life styles described, however, are fascinating for the radically opposing views they offer of the two authors' attitudes.

When Balzac was first presented to Aurore Dudevant some time between January 12 and April 8, 1831,[4] he was already an established Parisian literary figure. From the beginning of his acquaintance with the mistress of Jules Sandeau, he had found Aurore, five years his junior, both *sympathique* and courageous. He paid frequent visits to the couple's apartment on the Quai Saint-Michel and later on the Quai Malaquais, but when they separated, probably on March 6, 1833,[5] Balzac quickly took Sandeau's side of the argument, and in letters to Madame Hanska wrote some malicious quips about the author of *Indiana* and *Valentine*.[6] Therefore, because of Balzac's preference for Sandeau, at the time she composed *Metella*, George Sand was not on the same friendly terms with her colleague as when he had published *La Femme abandonnée*.[7]

Before Balzac wrote his *nouvelle,* Aurore Dudevant had published only three short pieces and the novel *Rose et Blanche,* in collaboration with Sandeau and under the name J. Sand, followed by her own first novel, *Indiana,* and the *nouvelle, Melchior,* under the name George Sand.[8] In the thirteen months that intervened before *Metella,* however, George Sand had become famous. She had published a poem, two short stories, two *nouvelles,* a short play, plus her second and third novels, *Valentine* and *Lélia.*[9]

Although we cannot know Balzac's exact degree of familiarity with all George Sand had published at the moment she composed *Metella,* from the titles he mentioned in his correspondence we can assume that he had read almost all of her works.[10] From George Sand's own letters, we know she was equally familiar with his works as they appeared.[11] Perhaps because of their temporarily strained relations, Balzac was less indulgent toward *Jacques* and *Le Secrétaire intime,* which followed *Metella.*[12] After they met at the Opera on August 23, 1834, on her return from Italy, George Sand sent him *Lélia* and two volumes of *Le Secrétaire intime,* which contained the nouvelles *La Marquise, Lavinia* and *Metella.*[13] It is interesting to note that although Balzac spoke of all of the other works in the volume, he either chose to remain silent about *Metella,* or else the correspondence has been lost.

In order to approach the two works through this vision of George Sand's initial inspiration, let us return to the genesis of Balzac's *nouvelle,* which was largely inspired by the author's affective world: *La Femme abandonnée* contains many recognizable autobiographical elements. The links between the heroine and the four women who, during the summer of 1832, held an important place in Balzac's past and present, are of primary importance.

Balzac's first model for an abandoned woman was provided by the Comtesse d'Hautefeuille;[14] his former mistress, the Duchesse d'Abrantès gave him the details about a suicide which he used for his hero.[15] The hero's suicide was arranged to assuage Madame de Berny, twenty-two years older than Balzac, with whom he had had a liaison for nearly ten years. At the time he wrote this *nouvelle,* Balzac was actively seeking a younger love. However, by criticizing himself in the hero who commits suicide (because he cannot replace the greatest love of his life with a younger woman)—he appeared far more loyal to Mme de Berny.[16] But the woman who exercised the predominant role in this story is Mme de Castries. It was she whom Balzac was trying ardently to seduce, she whom he met in Savoie shortly after completing this *nouvelle,* she to whom he finally presented the manuscript.[17]

> Claire-Clémence-*Henriette*-Claudine de Maillé de la Tour-Landry (Dec. 8, 1796-July 7, 1861) had married the Marquis, later the Duke, of Castries in 1816. The marriage was unhappy, but in 1822, the young marquise met Victor de Metternich, the eldest son of the Austrian Chancellor. A passionate liaison ensued and she gave birth to his son in 1827. Shortly after, Mme de Castries suffered a fall from horseback which caused her, from that time on, to walk with difficulty. On November 30, 1827, her lover died of tuberculosis. Heart-broken, and no longer accepted by the Faubourg Saint-Germain society, Mme de Castries spent her time in her hôtel on the rue de Grenelle, and she visited her father in his château or her uncle in Normandy. She began to surround herself in her salon with writers and artists, her guests being, among others, Balzac, Sainte-Beuve and Alfred de Musset.[18]

A number of situations in Balzac's story parallel those in the life of Mme de Castries. The heroine, Mme de Beauséant (also named Claire) having been born into an illustrious family, is ostracized by her aristocratic society, because she betrayed her marriage vows to follow her lover. When abandoned, she has nothing other than her name, her fortune and her memories. Balzac's fiction amplifies this theme, and he portrays the heroine as forced to lead a discreet and secluded life. The rest of Balzac's story is, as Pierre-Georges Castex has so admirably stated "une manoeuvre stratégique destinée à vaincre la résistance que sa nouvelle amie opposait à ses assiduités."[19] His hero, Gaston de Nueil, who pursues the heroine to Geneva and lives an idyll of three years there, represents Balzac's dream: to join Mme de Castries at Aix-les-Bains, to leave with her for Geneva, and to become her lover.

The real-life developments that followed bear little resemblance to his fiction. Balzac worked all day, suffered a leg injury on his trip to Savoie, and Mme de Castries, wanting to remain faithful to her memory of Metternich, maintained her reserved attitude. The month at Aix was, therefore, a big disappointment for Balzac, and his separation from Mme de Castries followed in Geneva, where they spent only four or five days.[20] Before leaving Aix, Balzac had already determined not to accompany Mme de Castries, her son, her uncle, the Duke of Fitz-James, and his family to Italy.[21] Miserable, he confided to his friend Mme Carraud that he could not face returning to Paris, but would "remain unknown at some modest distance in order to avoid the teasing and the jokes of people who mock everything."[22] Balzac took refuge with Mme de Berny, and he did not return to Paris until December.[23] Mme de Castries did not return from Italy until the following June.[24]

Since *La Femme abandonnée* was not yet published in book form when *Metella* appeared in the *Revue des Deux Mondes,* George Sand could only have had access to the text in the *Revue de Paris*. She read the magazine faithfully, and was publishing her own works in it at the time. For further proof, she mentions the issue of August 12 in her letters, and she wrote from Nohant (on September 3, 1832) for copies of the magazine which had not yet reached her.[25] *La Femme abandonnée* was printed on September 9 and 16 in the *Revue de Paris* and in December they published Sand's *La Marquise.*[26] With the success of *La Marquise,* Sand signed a more advantageous contract with François Buloz of the *Revue des Deux Mondes* and she subsequently changed her loyalties.[27] We also note that, given certain plot similarities to the Balzac text in the *Revue de Paris,* it was in her favor to publish *Metella* in another periodical.

The possibilities for George Sand's sources of information about Balzac and Mme de Castries are numerous. Balzac had requested his mother to send a copy of his *Contes philosophiques* to Jules Sandeau and George Sand while he was staying at Aix-les-Bains,[28] and, on his return to Paris, he promptly paid a visit to the couple.[29] It is highly likely that he himself may have spoken to them of his *nouvelle* and of Mme de Castries. Furthermore, at the time of *Metella,* George Sand and Balzac had in common many acquaintances, not all of whom were equally well disposed to him. Among the best known were Emile Régnault, Gustave Planche, H. de La Touche, François Buloz, Sainte-Beuve, Mérimée, and last, but never least, the personal friend of Mme de Castries, Alfred de Musset.

During the months intervening between the two publications, George Sand had not only established her literary reputation, she had also lived and suffered a great deal. Following the break-up with Sandeau and the cooled relationship with Balzac, she had had a liaison with Planche, a deep friendship with Marie Dorval, an unfortunate week with Mérimée, and, on July 29, 1833, had begun her celebrated relationship with Musset.[30] Her last novel, *Lélia,* had been judged scandalous, and she had been deeply hurt by the criticism. Her arm-chair play which preceded *Metella, Aldo le rimeur,* voiced these reactions: the poet protagonist bewailed his heart placed nude before a public of vultures.[31] *Metella* now gave George Sand the chance to offer her version of an abandoned woman. At twenty-nine, she was already judged to be a woman with a heavy past.

Desirous of fleeing Paris to avoid more slander, needing money for the trip to Italy with Musset, and still sensitive to Balzac's siding with Sandeau, she launched her retort. More now than at any previous time, George Sand's ideas were not in tune with Balzac's. George Sand could show that a woman had more options than Balzac's Mme de Beauséant. Her heroine, also with a past, would have the courage to live her life, in public if she so desired; she would be free-thinking; she was capable of not withdrawing from the world at the end of an adventure.

Obviously, Balzac's heroine interested George Sand far more than did Gaston de Nueil. This was not the only time that she used another work as her source of inspiration. In *Leone Leoni* she had been moved to reverse the male and female roles of *Manon Lescaut.*[32] It remained to her to show how the theme of *La Femme abandonnée* could be elucidated by someone having other tastes than Balzac's, other convictions, another viewpoint.

In each *nouvelle,* the heroine has, by choice, broken ties with her social milieu to be with a lover who, in the long run, abandons or has already abandoned her. She then becomes the mistress of a much younger man and is left again. Both young men conceive romantic plans to make the lady's acquaintance, but Sand's hero, Olivier, has more doubts about the validity of his project and would probably never have carried it through were it not that the first lover himself arranges the introduction. As in most Romantic novels, neither the women nor their lovers have any financial cares, and they know love only outside of marriage. Both depart for Geneva where they live their idyll with the young lover. Gaston de Nueil and Claire de Beauséant spend three years in a villa, rented by the heroine, beside Lake Geneva; Olivier spends every summer with

Metella Mowbray in a chateau she has purchased beside "Lac Léman."[33]

Above all, both women worry about their age: they are uncertain of their powers to hold a younger lover. A revealing statement of Metella about her first lover, the Comte de Buondelmonte, is that she fears using the vocabulary "des femmes abandonnées."[34] In separating from Buondelmonte, Metella announces: "Je vous rends votre liberté."[35] This recalls Claire de Beauséant's sentence, written in a letter to Gaston at the end of their liaison: "Si tu as hésité entre quelque chose et moi, je te rends ta liberté."[36] Later, on an envelope containing Gaston's declaration of eternal love, written nine years earlier, Claire writes: "Monsieur, vous êtes libre."[37]

Another parallel is that, at the end of the narration, each hero uses a gun to kill game—rabbits in Sand's printed version, but in the manuscript "innocent birds,"[38] to be equated with Balzac's "*gibier*" and "*perdrix*."[39] The main difference is that her hero will not end by killing himself.

There are also a number of fascinating parallels between the lives of Metella and of Mme de Castries. Sand's hero, for example, has heard of Lady Mowbray last season at Aix.[40] George Sand had never been to Aix-les-Bains and had asked François Buloz if the spelling "Aixe" was correct.[41] Her heroine departs for Geneva as Balzac had planned to do with Mme de Castries. (George Sand's first trip to Geneva did not take place until August, 1834.[42]) The places where Metella is said to have passed are Aix, Bern, Genoa, Florence, and Naples.[43] At the beginning of Sand's *nouvelle,* Metella lives in Florence (Manuscript: Venice). Mme de Castries had spent time in all of these areas with Metternich, and, more recently, had spent the winter and spring in Italy.[44] Metella is also half English. Mme de Castries' mother and her uncle, the Duke of Fitz-James, descended from the royal English Stuart family.[45] Metella is well over thirty, *"l'âge indéfinissable d'une femme."*[46] Mme de Castries when she was with Balzac, was thirty-five. (George Sand, at that time, was only twenty-nine.)

The styles and literary devices of George Sand and Balzac differ radically. She plunges immediately into the action of her story, economizes her descriptions to accentuate the effects, and uses considerably more dialogue, which is both spontaneous and comical. Each character has his own individuality. The humor derives from the character's personal traits and weaknesses. Balzac's humor is more cynical: that of the omniscient author, who limits himself to poking fun at secondary provincial stereotypes rather than at the protagonists themselves.

While Balzac's narration is simple and direct, following a strict chronological order, Sand prefers to use dialogues in which she emphasizes the characters' confrontations, hesitations, "thought-meanderings," and gestures which underscore other traits. In attempting to show the difference between the actual thoughts and the appearance a character wishes to present, she creates an impression of psychological depth. Lightness alternates with more serious considerations, while, with Balzac, the atmosphere is almost continually serious. Sand's characters are not always rational; they follow their instincts, change their minds, recognize their own complexities. Balzac's protagonists are what they are; their behavior (with the exception perhaps of Gaston's suicide) is more or less forseeable. Rather than being three-dimensional, they tend to be flat.

The two authors' caterings to outmoded literary artifices and false situations are unwittingly humorous and can be spotted by any sensitive person immediately. What is worth exploring, however, are Balzac's and Sand's differing preoccupations and attitudes.

At the beginning of *Metella,* Sand is primarily interested in extolling the exoticism and freer way of life to be found in Italy. Balzac, on the contrary, used his talents to describe traditional mores and the life styles of provincial aristocrats, who are both attracted to and repulsed by anything too Parisian. Mme de Beauséant's superiority lies in the fact that she is Parisian. Lady Mowbray is more international.

When once he finally enters into his story, Balzac puts the weight of the action on the two protagonists. He only alludes to Mme de Beauséant's previous lover (far in her past), while Metella's two lovers are shown openly. Buondelmonte dominates the heroine in the first half of the *nouvelle,* while Olivier has replaced him in the second half.

Metella Mowbray, like her creator, has had a more vivid past than Mme de Beauséant. This was undoubtedly George Sand's intention. Metella is easily touched, open, liberal; she lives her life with intensity. Although, before he has made her acquaintance, she conquers Olivier by her legend, afterward, she holds him by her need of him and by her weakness. Olivier wants to protect her. Mme de Beauséant, victim of the inhibitions of her milieu, attracts Gaston by her legend also, but she wins him even more strongly by the obstacles she places before him. While Metella and Olivier openly agree to meet and go together to Geneva, Mme de Beauséant flees Gaston, who follows her there.

George Sand's Olivier surely owes far more to Alfred de Musset (who represented a young savior offering happiness in Italy) than he does to Gaston de Nueil. The ending of Sand's work, however, reveals that her dreams were mixed with uncertainties, and that she sensed Alfred's love would not resist the corrosive effects of time. Since she wanted to present an ideal image of her hero, unlike Gaston, Olivier remains pure and blameless. Victim of his attraction for Metella's niece (who is young and innocent), he is in no way really guilty towards Metella, for he still loves her tenderly. Gaston is condemned by Balzac. Caught in his own games, like Constant's Adolphe, he only recognizes what he has lost when it is too late.

With Gaston's suicide, the world of Balzac's characters, always contracted, is now closed. His heroine's existence will end as well, for she will be forced to live completely retired within herself.

Sand's ending in *Metella* projects a very different atmosphere, both in the 1833 version, as well as in the short paragraphs added in 1852. The loves which Metella has lived have disintegrated slowly, naturally, unyieldingly. But life will continue for her, modified but filled. She will seek and find other solutions. She will love her niece. Sand's conclusion appears more realistic than Balzac's dramatic one.

The *nouvelle* of Balzac, therefore, presents the closed moral universe of a traditionalist man, while the work of George Sand represents the open moral universe of a somewhat disillusioned young woman, who was both emancipated and liberal. Both *nouvelles* contain the authors' dreams, their desires, their fantasies; in George Sand's case hers also contains her doubts.

Balzac created a hero seeking an absolute love which he could not recognize existing as such. Gaston, discovering that he has already lived his love and that it cannot be recaptured, commits suicide, thereby destroying the mediocrity to which he will be doomed. The literary world has become a prison encompassing everything. The life and behavior of his characters are determined by the society which dominates them. The only escape from his stifling world is passionate love, total and invading, or suicide.

George Sand, in *Metella,* seems not to believe in a single love which, if unhappy, blocks all escape routes. Love exists, love dominates in life, and her female protagonist profits to the maximum from all the moments in which she can experience it. Sand, however, recognizes all the complexities of human relationships. Love, for that reason, cannot lean on codes too rigorously established. The greatest destructor of love should not be *society:* it is *time.* With this idea, Balzac would have agreed. For George Sand, nevertheless, life is open to those who answer its call; experience should teach wisdom; if passion no longer exists, small happinesses are perhaps what remain to be savored. Human beings, in assuming their liberty, also assume responsibilities and moments of anguish. It is their liberty, not society, which creates their suffering; but existence will hopefully bring other fulfilling moments. Sand is freer than Balzac.

ACKNOWLEDGMENT

This paper has been extracted from Professor Janis Glasgow's book, *Une Esthètique de comparaison: Balzac et George Sand, La Femme abandonneé et Metella.* It is published by Editions A.-G. Nizet, Paris and contains a chronology of the entire Balzac-Sand relationship.

NOTES

1. First published in the *Revue des Deux Mondes,* IV (15 octobre 1833), 121-170.

2. Published in the *Revue de Paris,* XII (9 et 16 septembre 1832), 113-138, 172-190.

3. Balzac may have used George Sand as a model in *La Fille aux yeux d'or* (See Pierre-Georges Castex, introduction to Balzac's *Histoire des Treize* (Paris: Garnier, 1956), pp. 359-361) and also in *Les Illusions*

perdues (See Maurice Regard, "Charles Didier et George Sand," *Revue des Sciences humaines,* LXLVI (oct.-déc. 1959), pp. 476-477). George Sand suggested Balzac's plot for *Béatrix,* and played roles in both *Béatrix* and in *La Muse du département* (See Maurice Regard, introduction to *Béatrix* (Paris: Garnier, 1961) pp. i-lx; Balzac's text in any edition of *La Muse du département*). In addition, Balzac dedicated his *Mémoires de deux jeunes mariées* to George Sand, copied, almost verbatim, her dedication in *La Dernière Aldini* in his *Le Curé du village* (See Sand, *Correspondance,* textes réunis, classés et annotés par Georges Lubin (Paris: Garnier, 1964-1978), IV, 7; 240, note 1; 853-854; V, 207; Balzac, *Correspondance,* textes réunis, classifiés et annotés par Roger Pierrot, IV (Paris: Garnier, 1966), 31, 245, note 1.

4. Sand, *Correspondance,* I, 998.

5. Ibid., II, 210-11.

6. Ibid., II, 212.

7. Balzac lodged Sandeau with him for a time expecting Jules to collaborate in writing plays, but he rapidly became disenchanted by Sandeau's nonchalance and laziness. A few years later, he consequently renewed his friendship with George Sand. (See Balzac, *Oeuvres complètes: Lettres à l'étrangère,* I, 1832-1840 (Paris: Les Bibliophiles de l'originale, 1967), p. 394; Balzac, *Corres.,* II (1962), pp. 445-446.)

8. Sand, *Corres.,* I, 767-769; II, 3, 5.

9. Ibid., II, 6; 159 and note 3; 210-214.

10. Balzac, *Corres.,* I, 522-523 and Sand, *Corres.,* II, 87, note 3.

11. Balzac, *Corres.,* I, 573; 720-721 and note 1; Sand, *Corres.,* I, 933-934.

12. Balzac, *Oeuvres complètes, Lettres à l'étrangère,* I: 259, 586.

13. Sand, *Corres.,* II, 472, 682-683 and note 1; Balzac, *Corres.,* II, 545-546 and notes.

14. See Balzac, *Oeuvres complètes: La Comédie humaine: Etudes de moeurs, Scènes de la vie privée,* Vol. III (Paris: Club de l'Honnête Homme, 1956), pp. 11-18 and Pierre-Georges Castex, *Nouvelles et contes de Balzac (Scènes de la vie privée)* (Paris: Centre de Documentation universitaire, 1961), pp. 61-70.

15. Anne-Marie Meininger, *"La Femme abandonnée, L'Auberge rouge* et la duchesse d'Abrantès," *L'Année balzacienne 1963* (Paris: Garnier, 1963), pp. 65-81.

16. See note 14.

17. Bernard Gagnebin, "Balzac à la Fondation Bodmer," *L'Année balzacienne 1973* (1973), pp. 4-5.

18. Shortened translation of Roger Pierrot's data found in Balzac, *Corres.*, I, 751-752.

19. Castex, *Nouvelles et contes de Balzac,* p. 64.

20. *L'Année balzacienne 1963* (1963), pp. 352-353 and notes; Balzac. *Corres.,* II, 4.

21. Balzac, *Corres.,* II, 132-133.

22. Ibid., II, 153.

23. Ibid., II, 4.

24. Marcel Bouteron, *Etudes balzaciennes* (Paris: Jouve, 1954), p. 103.

25. Sand, *Corres.,* II, 146-147 and notes; 155.

26. Ibid., II, 6.

27. Ibid., II, 7, 193, 235-237.

28. Balzac, *Corres.,* II, 104 and note 1.

29. Ibid., II, 203.

30. Sand, *Corres.,* II, 213.

31. Sand, *Mélanges* (Paris: Perrotin, 1843), pp. 11-13.

32. Sand, Prèface printed in *Souvenirs et idées* (Paris: Calmann-Lèvy, 1904), pp. 115-117.

33. Sand, *Nouvelles* (Paris: Michel Lévy, 1861), p. 289.

34. Ibid., p. 273.

35. Ibid., p. 283.

36. Balzac, *La Comédie humaine (II), Etudes de moeurs: Scènes de la vie privée, Vol. II.* Texte établi par Marcel Bouteron (Paris: Bibliothèque de la Pléiade, 1951), p. 239.

37. Ibid., p. 242.

38. Manuscript of *Metella* (first titled "Lady Mowbray") (Chantilly, Bibliothèque Spoelberch de Lovenjoul, Folio E 826).

39. Balzac, *La Comédie humaine (II),* p. 243.

40. Sand, *Nouvelles,* p. 255.

41. Sand, *Corres.,* II, 429.

42. Ibid., II, 472.

43. Sand, *Nouvelles,* pp. 260, 262.

44. Gabriel Ferry, *Balzac et ses amies* (Paris: Calmann Lévy, 1888), pp. 92-93.

45. Bouteron, *Etudes balzaciennes,* p. 94.

46. Sand, *Nouvelles,* p. 271.

George Sand and the Victorians: Matthew Arnold as Touchstone

PAUL G. BLOUNT
Department of English
Georgia State University

Periodical reviews and numerous references in personal letters of Victorians tell us that George Sand was one of the most widely read foreign writers in Victorian England, second in popularity only to Goethe. English readers, eager to escape insularity, turned to continental writers; an England that in 1835 was importing one French volume for every fifty-three of its population[1] could not ignore the French writer who produced more than one hundred volumes between 1832 and her death in 1876.

The events of George Sand's personal life, reported in detail to Victorians, her separation from her husband, and her liaisons with Jules Sandeau, Alfred de Musset, and Frédéric Chopin, actually increased the popularity of Sand's works while confirming English suspicions about the immorality of the French. Basically, however, Sand's popularity with the Victorians rested on her literary merit. Readers admired her characterizations, and a generation nurtured on Wordsworth could not help admiring her descriptions of nature. A large number of readers felt that Sand's writings contained a message for the times, a warning against despair over problems arising from social, economic and religious changes. Sand's search for the "ideal life" appealed to people like George Henry Lewes, Charlotte Brontë, and Matthew Arnold, who were repelled by the coarser, more realistic portrayal of life found in the works of Sand's French contemporaries such as Balzac or Stendhal.

Whether or not they were in agreement over her qualities, leading

Victorian writers and critics took ample note of Sand, and it is a tribute to her many-sided personality that this woman, whom the vitriolic critic J.W. Croker saw as a moral degenerate, could be an influence in religious matters upon Matthew Arnold. In fact an examination of Arnold's works shows how much he was influenced by Sand, and Arnold can be used as a "touchstone," to borrow one of Arnold's own phrases, to illuminate the reception of Sand as a writer in Victorian England.

The basis for Arnold's interest in Sand was laid at Rugby, where Thomas Arnold, his headmaster father, stressed the study of writers in other European languages. One result of Thomas Arnold's European outlook was his son's intense interest in French literature. And the chief French writer of Arnold's youth was George Sand, whose novels he read in the original.

Later, at Oxford in 1842, Arnold and his close friends enjoyed discussions on contemporary writers and politics. It was at this time that Arnold and his friend Arthur Hugh Clough reached the conclusion that they could not become sound critics if their knowledge was limited to English literature. As a result, Arnold subsequently increased his reading in German and French writers. It was to be expected that Arnold and his university associates—all still young and imbued with youthful ideas of romantic protest—would be stimulated by George Sand, whose writing had already stirred the Germans, Russians, Italians, and the French. Sand seemed to this group "the incarnation of a new spirit of revolt and renovation,"[2] and besides, there was the appeal to these young men of being bold and even wicked in reading her works.

In July, 1846, two years after taking his degree at Oxford, Arnold made a sentimental pilgrimage to Nohant and became one of many Englishmen who often importuned Sand by their visits. Writing thirty years later, Arnold recalled with nostalgia his trip to Berry. At Boussac the young Briton addressed a letter conveying to Sand "in bad French, the homage of a youthful and enthusiastic foreigner who had read her works with delight."[3] Sand received what Arnold calls his "infliction" good-naturedly and sent a message by a servant from Nohant, saying she would welcome him if he chose to call.

When he arrived at mid-day, Sand, as he no doubt had expected, was surrounded by a large group of admirers. Arnold admits that he entered with some trepidation, but Sand's simplicity of manner put him at ease. Among those present were Sand's two children, Maurice and Solange, whom he already knew from her books— probably *Lettres d'un voyageur*—and Frédéric Chopin. Arnold recalled "his wonderful eyes."

The Englishman was pleased to note that there was nothing unconventional in Sand's dress. "She was not in man's clothes, she wore a sort of costume not impossible, I should think (although on these matters I speak with hesitation), to members of the fair sex at this hour amongst ourselves, as an out-door dress for the country or for Scotland." [4]

Arnold records that they talked about the French countryside and the Berry peasants whom Sand had idealized in fiction, and of Switzerland, next on his itinerary. He found her striking, but mainly he was impressed, as were the Brownings, with Sand's "frank, cordial simplicity." [5] From Nohant Arnold went back to England much affected. Clough commented:

> Matt is full of Parisianism; theatres in general, and Rachel in special: he enters the room with a chanson of Beranger's on his lips—his hair is guiltless of English scissors: he breakfasts at twelve, and never dines in Hall, and in the week or 8 days rather (for 2 Sundays must be included) he has been to Chapel *once*. . . . [6]

Although his interest in Sand continued, Arnold was in fact displeased by some of her political activity in 1848, especially two letters she wrote for the newspaper *La Vraie République* expressing disapproval of the new government's policy allowing the provinces to be controlled by the people of Paris. Arnold expressed disapproval of the letters and Sand's elaborate praise for "the people." Five years later he wrote Clough that he was growing tired of his French heroine and in August of 1853, he wrote again to Clough, "I am trying to reread Valentine [sic]—but stick—except in the scenery bits." [7] (These descriptive passages continued to appeal to Arnold twenty years afterwards when he wrote his anniversary article on Sand for the *Fortnightly Review*.)

The clearest evidence of George Sand's influence on Matthew Arnold is to be found, as might be expected, in the many references to Sand and her novels in Arnold's critical writings. Throughout Arnold tends to comment, usually most favorably, on the themes and ideas found in general in Sand's works rather than to offer

critiques of individual works. Also, as in his writings on Byron,
Arnold makes no comment on Sand's sexual vagaries—a point of
some concern to his friend Clough, who tempered his admiration for
Sand with moralistic criticism. (Arnold's biographer Lionel Trilling
suggests wryly that Arnold probably could not "impugn the morals
of a lady he had visited.")

An 1877 essay, when the first anniversary of Sand's death was
drawing near, is Arnold's most important single writing on Sand. In
it Arnold gave reactions to her works and stated the qualities of her
life that pleased him. He stated he would not write a critical survey;
he did not intend to "go regularly through her productions, to
classify and value them one by one." Instead he said that he wrote
the article for those to whom Sand has been a "friend and a power"
and for his own satisfaction. "It is for myself." [8]

As in much of Arnold's criticism, he assumed the role of a
professor determined to correct public taste. Sand, he said, was
much more than a teller of charming stories and a creator of
interesting characters. Beyond that there was more, the "spirit" of
Sand, and to know this spirit, one does not have to read all of her.
Therefore, he picked four books he would have his readers know as
her most representative works. First he included the *Lettres d'un
voyageur,* which had won praise from many people including
Mazzini, George Eliot, Elizabeth Browning, Charlotte Brontë, and
Jane Carlyle. He listed next *Mauprat,* in which Sand idealizes
married love for one person throughout a lifetime. The third of his
choices is the pastoral *François le Champi.* For the fourth he chose
Valvèdre. Interestingly enough Arnold's choice did not include
Lélia, which Mrs. Sells in her work on Arnold and France thinks
influenced Arnold the most, nor did he include *Indiana* or *Valentine,* Sand's earliest and most controversial works. From these
works he argued that one can detect "all the principal elements" of
Sand's literary creations. Arnold identified three elements, "the cry
of agony and revolt, the trust in nature and beauty, and the
aspiration towards a purged and renewed human society," [9] which he
believed evolved into Sand's search for the "sentiment of the ideal
life," a search to which Sand dedicated herself with absolute sincerity.

Arnold strongly commended Sand for saying that if one's search
for a better world were ineffectual, it would be the world's loss and

not the seeker's. To compensate for the ineffectuality of the search, Sand turned from her endeavor to escape the reign of stupidity to her second "element," the love of nature: "George Sand is one of the few French writers who keeps us closely and truly intimate with rural nature. She gives us the wildflowers by their actual names." [10]

Arnold then referred to *Valentine* but did not quote from it, claiming that the language defied translation. He quoted from Sand's introduction to *La Mare au Diable* and he concluded with praise for her closeness of contact with the country; yet he claimed her interest in humanity always emerged to dominate the final picture, and that the central human being in the picture was the French peasant. From him, Sand hoped for the third "element"— the movement toward a renewed human society. Arnold thought Sand forgave the peasant for supporting the apparently conservative Napoleon III because she realized that his rule meant peace and security while other political parties seemed to promise only more strife. In spite of some political backwardness, the peasant under Napoleon had moved forward toward equality, with an increase in self-respect and well-being.

Arnold concluded by stating that the multiplicity of Sand's works might be a hindrance to her fame, but he predicted permanence for this great writer. In extravagant praise he wrote:

> . . . the immense vibration of George Sand's voice upon the ear of Europe will not soon die away. Her passions and her errors have been abundantly talked of. She left them behind her, and men's memory of her will leave them behind also. There will remain of her to mankind the sense of benefit and stimulus from the passage upon earth of that large and frank nature, of that large and pure utterance—the *large utterance of the early gods.*"

Closely allied in theme to the anniversary essay of 1877 is Arnold's contribution to *The Pall Mall Gazette* on August 12, 1885, written when a statue was unveiled in memory of Sand at La Châtre, near Nohant. This article reveals very clearly Arnold's preference for Sand's brand of Romanticism over Realism of any other French writers of the hour, and in it Arnold equated Sand with Wordsworth and Goethe. He also predicted—incorrectly—that the future would bear him out in his preference for Sand over Balzac!

In his criticism and in his poetry, Arnold stated that the best writers bring joy to their readers, and that joy was a quality found in Sand's works but missing in Balzac's. In his essay, "Preface to the First Edition of Poems," in 1853 Arnold had written: "A poetical work, therefore, is not yet justified when it has been shown to be an accurate, and therefore interesting representation; it has to be shown also that it is a representation from which men can derive enjoyment." [12] And in his "Obermann Once More":

> And yet men have such need of joy!
> But joy whose grounds are true;
> And joy that should all hearts employ
> As when the past was new. (ll. 237-240) [13]

Another evidence of Sand's influence on Matthew Arnold is to be found in their common interest in the works of the poet Senancour. The discoverer of Senancour, the author of "Obermann," was Sand's and Arnold's friend, Sainte-Beauve, who declared Senancour the real father of French Romanticism rather than Chateaubriand. It is known that when Arnold died, he had among his books a copy of Senancour's "Obermann" with Sand's preface. And in an explanatory note which Arnold first published in 1868 to "Stanzas in Memory of the Author of 'Obermann'," he sketched in four paragraphs the life of Senancour and commented that his work had passages that "have attracted and charmed some of the most remarkable spirits of this century, such as George Sand and Sainte-Beuve." Arnold's note further related the qualities he listed in his anniversary essay to explain his admiration for Sand: profound inwardness, austere sincerity, delicate feeling for nature, and melancholic eloquence of style. [14] Moreover, Senancour's appeal lay in the stir within him "of all the main forces by which modern life is and has been impelled," and Arnold listed them: the "dissolving agencies" of the eighteenth century, the turmoil of the French Revolution, and a vague promise of a better world to come. Arnold added that his own day was closer to bringing this new world about than was Senancour's own time, an idea Arnold shared with Sand. [15]

Tinker and Lowry in their important commentary on Arnold's poetry see unconscious biography in Arnold's "Obermann" poems stating that he was at work on a compromise that led to a new view of Christianity, which he developed after monumental readings in the works of many authors. His *Literature and Dogma* (1873) strove to relieve British minds disturbed by the higher criticism, pointing out that the Bible was not a scientific work but a literary one, which, if properly understood, deals with man's conduct—and a proper way to achieve that conduct—rather than with creeds.

Both Sand and Senancour were among the contributors to this view. Sand's optimism, however, gave Arnold more inspiration in finding a way to escape the dilemma than did Senancour.[16] They both had lost their faith in the God of the popular creeds, but as Sand herself described the new religion that emerged: "The loss is not loss of religious sense . . . it is quite the contrary, it is a restitution of allegiance to the true Divinity. It is a step made in the direction of the Divinity, it is an abjuration of the dogmas which did him dishonour."[17]

Another theme in Sand to which Arnold responded in his essays says Lionel Trilling, is the exaltation of woman and the claim especially that women are able to experience passion to a degree that men are either unwilling or unable to. To support his thesis, Trilling lists Stendhal, Ibsen, Shaw, and D. H. Lawrence, who have used variations of this theme. Arnold understood, Trilling says, that women look "for more than devotion, that they seek in those they love a strength that need not be always moral."[18] Arnold also chose one of Sand's favorite themes, love, as the basis of social life, fully understanding by "love" that Sand meant "social equality." And to convert the English to this idea, Arnold devoted much energy; his speech on "Equality," for example, was an attempt to popularize this view.

Further evidence of Sand's influence is found in numerous passages copied from Sand's works in Arnold's *Note-Books.*[19] Arnold referred to twelve of Sand's works, and it is known that he owned at least five of them. As was his practice, he returned many times to a favorite passage, even to recopy one he had previously copied. Typical of these passages is one from Sand's *Histoire de ma vie,* in which she discusses the true nature of prayer or a passage dealing primarily with poetry as an emotional release. Many copied quotations express a desire for stability in life. A long passage from *L'Homme de neige,* in 1860, advises against being discouraged and disturbed about the future. In this passage, Sand speaks of forsaking worldly ambitions, scorning mistakes (made when one is young and sometimes frivolous), and advises seeking salvation in work, some twelve hours a day of it, "possible to anyone who is not wretched and unwell." [20]

Passages in 1873 and 1876 relate to one of Arnold's favorite themes: serenity out of morality after the writer has conquered despair. One passage advises that "one must rearrange in order to take the lofty view." [21] In 1877, there occurs the passage from Sand's *Journal d'un voyageur,* "The need to love, the sentiment of the ideal life which in none other than the normal life such as we are called to know it." [22] This line Arnold took, as we have seen, for the motif of his anniversary essay on Sand, published that same year.

In 1882, as Arnold drew to the close of his life, he gained a new interest in Sand through her mystical novel *Spiridion.* Passages that year are many—thirty-four, all from *Spiridion.* Typical is a passage that comments how much more difficult it is to build up (*bâtir*) than it is to tear down (*abattre*) or the passage that sums up theology as "belief, hope, love." [23] One significant passage on old age contrasts optimistically with Arnold's poem "Growing Old." In his own poem, first published in 1867, the last years of life are characterized:

> Deep in our hidden heart
> Festers the dull remembrance of a change.
> But no emotion—none. (ll. 28-30)[24]

Yet the passage from Sand's *Spiridion,* which struck Arnold, states: "Instead of growing morally colder with old age, I feel my heart, vivified and renewed, rejuvenated to the degree that my body leans toward destruction." [25]

Arnold continued copying passages from Sand in the *Note-Books* almost until his death. The last passage from Sand, copied in 1884 and taken from *Jacques,* adds an optimistic note: Florence, one of the characters, asks Jacques if the world is still far from the "shining summit." Jacques replies that the answer is God's secret, but that their world is much closer to perfection than that of "all the people who preceded us." [26]

Thus the *Note-Books* furnish evidence of Sand's importance to Arnold as do his letters, poetry, and his essays. He participated in that intense devotion to Sand which among Victorians became a kind of cult. In Arnold's mind, George Sand was changed into a person much like Arnold himself: the melancholic artist, dissatisfied with the age, yet determined, at the cost of great spiritual exertion, to throw off despair and then to correct the evils of the world. His recognition of her as a symbol of the new woman, as a symbol of political revolt, as a shining example of one in search of *la vie idéale,* reflects the fascination many Victorians felt for George Sand.

NOTES

1. Marcel Moraud, *Le Romantisme français en Angleterre de 1814 à 1848* (Paris, 1933), p. 205.

2. Howard Foster Lowry, ed., *The Letters of Matthew Arnold to Arthur Hugh Clough* (New York, 1832), p. 20.

3. Matthew Arnold, *Mixed Essays* (New York, 1883), pp. 236-237.

4. Ibid., p. 239.

5. Ibid.

6. Frederick L. Mulhauser, *The Correspondence of Arthur Hugh Clough* (Oxford, 1957), I, 178-179. Letter is written to J. C. Shairp and is dated February 22, 1847.

7. Lowry, p. 139. The lack of italics for *Valentine* is Arnold's doing. Victorians were not always careful of punctuation in letters.

8. Arnold, *Mixed Essays* (New York, 1883), p. 240.

9. Ibid., p. 241.

10. Ibid., p. 246.

11. Ibid., pp. 259-260.

12. R. H. Super, ed., *The Complete Prose Works of Matthew Arnold* (Ann Arbor, 1960), I, 2.

13. Arnold, *Works* (London, 1903), I, 312.

14. Kenneth Allott, ed., *The Poems of Matthew Arnold* (London, 1965), p. 129.

15. C. B. Tinker and H. F. Lowry, *Poetry of Matthew Arnold, A Commentary* (London, 1940), pp. 272-274.

16. Ibid., pp. 262-273. See also Lionel Trilling, *Matthew Arnold* (New York, 1939), pp. 272-276.

17. Lionel Trilling, p. 381.

18. Ibid., pp. 381-382.

19. Howard Foster Lowry, Karl Young and Waldo Hilary Dunn, eds., *The Notebooks of Matthew Arnold* (London, 1952).

20. Ibid., pp. 10-11.

21. Ibid., p. 255.

22. Ibid., p. 277.

23. Ibid., p. 383.

24. Arnold, *Works,* I, 58.

25. Lowry, Young, and Dunn, p. 383.

26. Ibid., p. 410.

The Linking of the Georges, Sand and Eliot: Critical Convention and Reality

THELMA JURGRAU
Humanities Division
Empire State College, SUNY
at White Plains

A survey of the views of the late nineteenth century critics shows that both French and English writers have a tendency to link the names of the two novelists George Sand and George Eliot, often on a personal as well as a literary level. The temptation to do so stems apparently from some real and some merely presumed similarities and parallels between these two talented women. Among the first, none is more obvious than that both were women. A typical comment was one which linked the two women not only because of their sex and their names but also because of an assumption that these two authors, simply because they were both women, tended to dwell rather too much on the romantic and even sexual aspects of life:

> There is a kind of love-making which seems to possess a strange fascination for the modern female novelist. Currer Bell and George Eliot, and we may add George Sand, all like to dwell on love as a strange overmastering force which, through the senses, captivates and enthralls the soul. They linger on the description of the physical sensations that accompany the meeting of hearts in love. Curiously, too, they all like to describe these sensations as they conceive them to exist in men. We are bound to say that their conceptions are true and adequate. But we are not sure that it is quite consistent with feminine delicacy to lay so much stress on the bodily feelings of the other sex.[1]

Discussion of their pseudonyms was another way in which critics
saw fit to link the two, and even those who came to praise could
balk at a transparent masculine disguise. George Stovin Venables, a
prolific critic and lawyer, writes about Eliot in *The Edinburgh
Review*: "The great writer, like Madame Dudevant, adopts the
ungraceful disguise of a masculine pseudonym. . . ."[2]

Some took note of the similarly suspect nature of the private lives
of these two women. Jane Carlyle, for instance, is said to have
remarked in answer to her husband's accusation that the Frenchwoman's novels were erotic, that "England had small right to cast the
first stone across the Channel when she had a George of her own
right there in London."[3]

Even the physical appearance of the two women became a basis
for comparison. Charles Eliot Norton, described what he calls "an
odious vulgarizing portrait" of George Eliot which he felt bore a
likeness to its subject and compared it to Couture's well-known
drawing of Sand:

> The head and face are hardly as noble as George Sand's but the lines
> are almost as strong and masculine; the cheeks are almost as heavy
> and the hair is dressed in a similar style, but the eyes are not so deep
> and there is less suggestion of possible beauty and possible sensuality
> in the general contour and in the expression. Indeed one rarely sees a
> plainer woman; dull complexion and dull eyes, heavy features.[4]

The degree to which the names of these two writers are linked in
people's minds becomes most apparent, however, when we see how
often critics comment on the writing of one of the Georges by
comparing her work to that of the other George. Among Eliot's
champions in France, only Emile Jonveaux is mildly disparaging to
his countrywoman when he makes a virtue of Eliot's conscience at
the expense of George Sand;[5] Alexandre Weil intends high praise
for Eliot when he designates her "the George Sand of England;"[6]
Edmond Schérer contrasts the eloquent style of Sand with the more
contained one of Eliot;[7] Brunetière prefers Eliot on the grounds of
what he considers objectivity, and we know that he generally
condemned writers of the Romantic school.[8] The extreme position
of Robert du Pontavice de Heussy, who declares Eliot's novelistic
talents unapproachable by any female writer in France, including
George Sand, is balanced by that of Jules Lemaître, who notes with

distress the air of Protestant conscience in Eliot's novels, quite unlike the typical French atmosphere of Sand and finds the work of the Englishwoman superfluous on the illogical ground that the qualities the public and critics have admired in her exist in the novels of Sand.[9]

The foregoing is not meant to suggest that Eliot enjoyed a large French audience. Indeed, it is the conclusion of John Philip Couch, whose study provided the above information, that the English writer was rather neglected in France. This is less surprising than the fact that Eliot was apparently not preferred to Sand even in England. We have seen the reservations of Venables and of Jane Carlyle. Among those who praise Eliot's literary accomplishments, hardly anyone claims precedence for Eliot over Sand.[10] Sidney Colvin praises both, but is especially tender to Sand.[11] Edward Dowden is the first to complain about Eliot's moralizing endings compared to her French counterpart.[12] Ruskin deplores the author's assumed halo, as well as what he takes to be her Naturalism, countering that "Sand is often immoral; but she is always beautiful."[13] William Henley treats her stern moral attitude with still greater diffidence when he declares that "Herself, too, has been variously described . . . as George Sand *plus* Science and *minus* Sex."[14]

In the year of George Sand's death, Henry James dramatized three recurrent points of view on the two novelists.[15] Not only did he manage more than his contemporaries to focus directly on the works rather than the personalities of Sand and Eliot (probably because as a novelist he would consider that this is where critical attention belonged), but, through the voices of his characters, he approximated for us examples of criticism typically directed toward both writers. Pulcheria speaks as an aesthete who resents both writers because they digress from their subject; Theodora makes clear that, because the writers in question are women, the moral situations presented in their fiction should be subject to special scrutiny; while Constantius expresses the common preference for the French author.

Interest in both of these nineteenth century writers declined markedly in the early twentieth century, although Sand's temporary eclipse seems to have been more complete than Eliot's. By the 1960s, however, partly as a result of the work of Georges Lubin in editing her voluminous correspondence, there was a lively revival of

interest in the life and works of George Sand. It is not surprising
then that, as interest in Sand was reawakened, the linking of the two
Georges in the comments of the critics should once again be
manifest. In the 1960s we again see the names of George Sand and
George Eliot appearing together in the writings of such contemporary critics as K.A. McKenzie, Patricia Thomson, and Paul Blount.
It remained for enthusiasts of women's literature, such as Ellen
Moers, in the present decade, once again to unite the two for their
sex, their male pseudonyms, their unconventional lives, and their
literary achievements, as well as for a similarity in their works.[16]

One may therefore conclude, regarding the critical convention of
linking the Georges, that it has come full circle to compare these two
writers on the personal as well as the literary level, with perhaps this
difference: that, when Eliot was first introduced, it was by way of
the already notorious Sand, whereas, today, the name and novels of
Sand appear to enter in the wake of Eliot.

After noting the ways in which the critics have linked the names
of George Sand and George Eliot, we might ask what the actual
relations between the two may have been and how far may they be
linked legitimately? Many critics, including Paul Blount, Marcel
Moraud, and Gordon Haight, Eliot's official biographer, have
noticed the strong attraction which George Eliot felt for France and
for George Sand. Although we often remember her interest in
German culture, Eliot's interest in the French language, literature,
theater, and history developed early and lasted all her life. The fact
that she changed her name from Mary Ann to Marian is considered
to be a result of her travels to France and Switzerland. She was
fluent in French and even had occasion to use it in a tête-à-tête with
Franz Liszt, which, when she wrote about it afterwards, made her
identify with Sand. Indeed, her good friends the Brays and the
Hennells received many a letter from her requesting Sand's books
or criticism about them, with Eliot always praising or defending
what she called "my divinity."[17]

Gordon Haight cites nine novels of Sand's which Eliot definitely
read, plus *Lettres d'un voyageur.* A review which Eliot wrote in the
fifties about illustrious French women ends with a crescendo of
praise of George Sand:

   ... to this day, Madame de Sévigné remains the single instance of a
   woman who is supreme in a class of literature which has engaged the

ambition of men; Madame Dacier still reigns the queen of blue-stockings, though women have long studied Greek without shame; Madame de Staël's name still rises first to the lips when we are asked to mention a woman of great intellectual power; Madame Roland is still the unrivalled type of the sagacious and sternly heroic, yet lovable woman; George Sand is the unapproached artist who, to Jean-Jacques' eloquence and deep sense of external nature, united the clear delineation of character and the tragic depth of passion.[18]

One reason Eliot gives for the eminence of women in French literary history is sociological and sheds light on her previous denial to her friends that George Sand's morals were attractive to her.

Heaven forbid that we should enter on a defence of French morals, most of all in relation to marriage! But it is undeniable, that unions formed in the maturity of thought and feeling, and grounded only on inherent fitness and mutual attraction, tended to bring women into more intelligent sympathy with men, and to heighten and complicate their share in the political drama.[19]

In commenting on the personal influence of Sand on Eliot, Marcel Moraud goes furthest when he claims that if Eliot's spirit had not been saturated with Sand's romantic notions on love and marriage, she would perhaps have hesitated to form the unconventional union with George Lewes. Paul Blount feels that Moraud's is an extreme position, although he too considers Eliot's praise of Sand's novel *Jacques* as "evidence of Sand's influence on her in the step she finally took with Lewes."[20] Patricia Thomson, particularly susceptible to the George-triangle, calls her 1963 article, "The Three Georges," and points out that it was the intention of Lewes to make the perfect woman novelist out of George Eliot, "a sort of amalgam of the best aspects of Jane Austen and George Sand."[21] The fact that Eliot's fiction does not at all resemble the romantic side of Sand, casts doubt on Thomson's hypothesis. If Lewes was helpful in nurturing the novelist in Marian Evans, it was with sufficient sensitivity to her individual talent to know that Lèlia could not have been one of her potential characters.

Can we find any significance in the fact that both women chose the name George for their masculine pseudonyms? George Sand actually invented her pen name in two stages: "Sand" came from her first collaborator, Jules Sandeau, whose name they shortened when they wrote *Rose et Blanche* (1831). When she went on to write *Indiana* alone, however, she substituted George for Jules. Her own explanation was that the name George seemed to represent her native Berry.[22] The explanation which Georges Lubin gives is related: he explains that the name George, from the Greek word for farmer, suggests a person close to the soil and that the Berrichon population of 1832 was then composed almost entirely of peasants.[23] He notes further that a few of the earliest editions showed the typical French spelling, Georges. But Sand was firm and consistent in using her own version, "George," which leads us to speculate on another reason for the choice. "Georgeon" is a name which inspired the greatest terror among natives of Berry, in central France, where Sand grew up. This rustic demon is the devil himself, who got the name when he was defeated in a battle with Saint George. Sand describes how the peasants' fear extended to a taboo against the writing of the name on any material whatsoever.[24] It is not difficult to imagine Aurore Dupin, in the childish habit of tempting fate, tracing out the letters with her finger and perhaps stopping just short of the last one or two.

Eliot's explanation for her adoption of the name was simpler: "George was Mr. Lewes' Christian name." [25] But considering all that we have noted about Eliot's great admiration for Sand we might easily venture the suggestion that Sand was also in her mind when she chose the name George.

Thibaudet raises an interesting question concerning the two writers. Since Eliot, like Rousseau, was a late starter in novel writing, he believes that had Eliot started earlier, she probably would have written more like Sand.[26] Sand published her first book at the age of twenty-seven (1831), in collaboration with Jules Sandeau. By that time, she had already left her husband, the Baron Dudevant, the year before, after having a second child, two love affairs, and moving to Paris. At the same age, twenty-seven (1846), Eliot's life had been very different. Still very much involved in clarifying her own position regarding the Church, she had completed the enormous labor of translating Strauss' three-volume critical examination of the life of Jesus, which was to have a profound influence on religious thought in nineteenth century England. She was still ten years away from her first published fiction. On the personal side, she had moved to Coventry with her father, had a mildly scandalous incident with Dr. Brabant, and, after a brief spark of attraction, rejected the marriage proposal of a young restorer of paintings. She was still eight years away from her decision to live with the married George Lewes, a liaison which was exclusive for the twenty years that it lasted. Eliot's recuperation from "Strauss-sickness"[27] was aided by reading Sand and Rousseau and defending them against the charges of immorality which her close friends brought. One might say that she was gaining courage for her later tries at liberation, but, in the meantime, was still heavily burdened both by the authority of her father and by her religious problems.

George Sand would go on, in another year, to publish two novels (*Indiana* and *Valentine*) under her own new pseudonym, and to begin *Lélia*. By the age of thirty-two (1838), Sand had managed to effect a legal separation from Dudevant and had published about a dozen novels. At the same age, Eliot, by contrast, had lost her father after arduous nursing care, had returned from a year abroad and had moved to London, where she had a minor involvement with John Chapman and a major one with the *Westminster Review* which he was publishing. In October 1851, she writes to Charles Bray from London: "My only real lasting trouble is my own emptiness."[28]

Thus it is hard to agree with Thibaudet's suggestion. It seems quite clear rather that Eliot would not have written a Romantic novel of the Sand type either at age twenty or twenty-seven, and that by age thirty-two was still further away from it than ever, considering the differences in the lives and careers of the two writers.

Another difference we discern between these two talented women is their views of themselves. George Eliot frequently expresses discontent with her appearance. On the other hand, one rarely finds in the personal writing of Sand any reference at all to her own appearance. Her disapproval of over-concern with one's own person is clear from the preliminary portion of her autobiography: "I have always found it in bad taste to talk excessively about oneself; worse still, to do it with oneself."[29]

To trace these differences in self-esteem back to childhood is beyond the scope of this paper. It should not be out of the way however, to speculate on certain general explanations for such contrasting self-evaluations. For example, it would be accurate to think of Eliot as dominated by patriarchal tendencies and Sand as not. The strong influence of Robert Evans on his daughter and her dependence on him pervade her biography and letters. Here is a typical example: "I and father go on living and loving together as usual, and it is my chief source of happiness to know that I am one item of his." [30] At the age of twenty-four, an age when George Sand was already a wife and the mother of two children, George Eliot was still required to ask her father's permission to remain at the home of friends longer than she had planned. [31] Eliot's biographer devotes a whole chapter to her need for the presence of a male figure and calls it "Someone to Lean Upon."

George Sand's knowledge of her father came to her only through his mother, for he died when she was only four. She heard, for example, how, as a child, he was so spoiled he would ring for a servant to retrieve a dropped pencil. And while she admired what she heard of the man who became a devoted son and husband, her basic father-image was that of the boy her grandmother talked about. Authority figures for Sand were mostly women; her grandmother and her mother, both of whom fought over her and cared for her, seem to have created in her two opposing tendencies: one, mothering, and the other, rebelling.

Sand had the reputation of being as much mother as mistress to her lovers, many of them younger than she. She was also devoted to her own children in a way which meant both mental concern and physical attention. Her son Maurice and his family lived with her at Nohant until she died. She was less successful in holding on to her daughter, Solange, but gave her sincere support until their break, which resulted from Sand's inability to stand by and watch Solange lead a dissolute life. Sand nevertheless continued to give financial support to Solange and her sculptor husband and never let their conflict affect the terms of her will.

The concept of revolution permeated all areas of Sand's beliefs. Tracing back her noble heritage on her father's side, she points out all the enlightened ancestors who even then believed in equality for all, in spite of their rank. About her grandmother, who survived the Revolution and raised her, she proudly tells how she found cartons full of her couplets, madrigals, and biting satires against Marie-Antoinette. Sand's idea of equality is basic; she claims never to have even understood or entertained the idea of inequality. From the lowest of beggars to the highest of kings, she was convinced that God had marked no one either for nobility or slavery. Her theory was that equality went back to primitive times in nature; on this idea she based her religion of humanity. Her interpretation of the French Revolution as the outer manifestation of Christian principles, although a rationalization, is consistent with her generally inspired idealistic personality. There was always at work within her the attempt to make an integrated whole out of nature, religion, society, and then art. She maintained these ideals into old age.

Sand was as proud of the republican branch of her family as of the noble one, but for different reasons which belie any prejudice against marriage. She says: "If it is true that my father was the great-grandson of Augustus II, King of Poland, and if, on this side I find myself in a way illegitimate but nevertheless actual, a close relative of Charles X and of Louis XVIII, it is no less true that I am attached to the people by blood in a way as close and direct; furthermore, there is no taint of bastardy on that side." [32]

In George Eliot we see much more of a tendency toward fragmentation of personality and shifting of opinion over the years. Her early admiration of revolutionary ideas was quickly given a definite boundary outside of the English terrain; she discarded her youthful pietism for a rejection of the Church; she reversed her opinions from adulation to disgust for the poet Edward Young; the same is true for the work of Hannah More; from an innate anti-Semitism she became strongly interested in Zionism. Undoubtedly, the strong split that she felt between her writer self and her personal self is another difference between the two women. Once George Sand adopted her pseudonym, she became George for all, friends and business acquaintances alike, whereas Eliot always remained Marian to her friends, was always surprised to be accepted on masculine terms and wore the male mantle awkwardly. Her father, although holding an extremely respected and responsible position as a steward, was still in the situation of a domestic to the aristocratic families for whom he worked; hence she had difficulty reconciling her social position in any direction, up or down. She was a snob when it came to artistic taste. She said to Sara Hennell, who painted: "How an artist must hate the noodles that stare at his picture with a vague notion it is a clever thing to be able to paint." [33]

George Sand was not only a prolific novelist, she was also a

prodigious writer of personal letters. Sand's correspondence with
Flaubert, for instance, which flourished during the last ten years of
her life (1866-1876), is characteristically full of personal details,
plans for meetings and advice on how to subdue his spleen; it is
equally full of impersonal statements on universal subjects. Often
her arguments with him on the role of the writer take off from
ordinary subjects and rise to a crescendo of sincere rhetoric typical
of her public personality:

> But one writes for all the world, for all who need to be initiated; when
> one is not understood, one rejoices and continues. There lies the
> whole secret of our perservering labors and of our love of art. What is
> art without the hearts and minds on which one pours it? A sun which
> would not project rays and would give life to no one.[34]

Eliot, on the other hand, had few correspondents, and, although
Charles Dickens was a personal admirer and acquaintance, almost
all letters came through Lewes. The fact that Lewes handled all of
her business affairs removed her as possible recipient of much
interesting correspondence. He very generously did this and other
chores to leave her free for writing, but also because she was (unlike
Sand) extremely sensitive to any criticism about her work. Therefore, her letters are characterized by personal details and comments,
and only occasionally does she rise to a statement of general
interest. This is true in her life-long correspondence with Charles
Bray, one of the first intellectual friends she acquired as a young
adult. The following excerpt from a letter to him may be compared
to the Sand quotation for style and content:

> I can't tell you how much melancholy it causes me that people are, for
> the most part, so incapable of comprehending the state of mind which
> cares for that which is essentially human in all forms of belief, and
> desires to exhibit it under all forms with loving truthfulness. Free-
> thinkers are scarcely wider than the orthodox in this matter—they all
> want to see themselves and their own opinions held up as the true and
> the lovely.[35]

The style is typically convoluted, the message veiled and the spirit
depressed and heavy.

To sum up, the differences between Sand and Eliot are more

profound than the similarities which often serve critics as bases of comparison. The events of their lives promoted in Sand a propensity toward romance, in Eliot an accretion of reserve. Temperamentally, Sand was always radiating warmth, while Eliot seems to have been in constant search for a hearth. There may be an explanation for such divergent temperaments in the fact that Eliot suffered from a shortage of mothering and an overdose of fathering, while Sand had, if anything, a surplus of mothering and no fathering at all.

While Sand inclined to egalitarian idealism, Eliot is an elitist and a realist. Though both writers seem to meet on the moralizing function of art, they differ in their perspective—Eliot's from on high, like a preacher's, Sand's on an equal level, like that of a common sufferer, without the condescension of the pulpit. While Sand seems to have followed a single, integrated line in the evolution of her ideas, Eliot seems to have shifted over the years, in a way which indicates less stability. Less self-concerned, Sand found less troublesome the kind of doubts about beauty and ability which Eliot struggled with. The former thus had the freedom to go outside herself in social commitments as well as general objectivity, while the latter became more isolated as time went on, in spite of great professional success.

Eliot never possessed a robust physique (a further contrast to the vigorous health of her French counterpart), and by the time she reached her sixties, there were signs of deep emotional as well as physical strains. The death of Lewes in 1878, which left her so immobilized as to prevent her attending the funeral, was the chief blow to her stability; her publisher, John Blackwood, died within the year, which meant that Eliot had lost another of her pillars. The private personality withdrew further, notwithstanding the many who came to comfort her, including some whose names still impress today—the Burne-Joneses, Benjamin Jowett, Leslie Stephen, Herbert Spencer, the Darwins.[36] Only John Cross, the young banker who had taken charge of her investments seven years earlier, was able to be effectively consoling; their marriage in the spring of 1880 was a great shock to Eliot's few close friends. And it is hard not to view this first marriage of Eliot's at the age of sixty as a delayed concession to the forces of respectability which she had apparently scorned but perhaps covertly craved. Notwithstanding a brief flight into health during their Italian honeymoon, Eliot's physical condition was unable to combat the sore throat which attacked as usual in the winter, and she died on December 22 of the same year, at sixty-one.

While Eliot became even more reserved in later life, Sand appears to have kept expanding and radiating outward. As she approached the age of seventy and began to suffer from an anemia-induced fatigue, she allowed her hectic writing schedule to subside, but her life was nevertheless filled with all forms of activity centered especially around children. She took charge of the education of her granddaughters, danced with them and her grandnephews at the carnival celebrations, put on marionnette shows and musicals in the fall, gave parties for her friends and neighbors every Sunday, and held an annual New Year's masquerade dance and supper. Nor was her love of family travel diminished; her summer trips with Maurice and his family were lengthy and exerting and included mountain climbing. She also was an active and genial hostess for the many visits from admirers foreign and domestic. Like Goethe's home in Weimar, her home in Nohant was a place of pilgrimage for many an adulator.

Even their funeral eulogies confirm the sharp differences between the two novelists. Eliot's are characterized by admiration, respect, and awe, such as Leslie Stephen's opinion that Eliot was "the greatest woman writer who ever won literary fame."[37] On the other hand, Sand's death brought warm responses such as those from Dostoevsky:

> She was one of the most sublime and beautiful representatives of womanhood. . . . It is only in learning of her death that I have understood the large way in which this name figured in my life, the great enthusiasm and adoration which I have devoted to this poet and how much joy and happiness I owe to her.[38]

George Sand, the human being, would be as sorely missed as George Sand, the writer.

ACKNOWLEDGMENT

This paper is an abridgement of Chapter I of a doctoral dissertation, "Pastoral and Rustic in the Country Novels of George Sand and

George Eliot," presented to and accepted by the faculty of the City University Graduate Center in February 1976. It was written under the guidance of Ruth Z. Temple.

NOTES

1. Anonymous review, *Saturday Review,* 9 (April 14, 1860), 470-471, rpt. in *George Eliot: The Critical Heritage,* ed. David Carroll (London: Routledge & Kegan Paul, 1971, pp. 114-119), p. 118. This collection of essays includes that of another critic who bristles visibly at what he deems particularly feminine traits among novelists. In an essentially hostile article reviewing George Eliot's novels in *Home and Foreign Review,* 3 (Oct., 1863, 522-549, rpt. in Carroll, pp. 221-250, p. 241) Richard Simpson, a journalist, Shakespearean scholar and convert to Roman Catholicism writes that:

   a supreme passion is inconsistent with honour and delicacy either in men or women: and both the male and female characters of female novelists are liable to this defect . . . they generally saturate their female characters with passion and sensuality. Mrs. Aphra Behn, Mrs. Centilivre, Madame de Staël, George Sand, the Countess Hahn-Hahn, Mrs. Inchbald, Currer Bell, Mrs. Norton, and George Eliot, simply misuse their sex.

   Such attitudes seem to justify the assumption of masculine pseudonyms on the part of women novelists. The fact that Eliot's first novel received almost unanimous praise perhaps is related to public ignorance of her identity; once exposed as a woman, a new set of values seems to have been attributed to her.

2. [George Stovin Venables] Unsigned review, *Edinburgh Review,* 124 (Oct., 1866), 435-449, rpt. in Carroll (pp. 278-285), p. 278. Lest we delude ourselves that twentieth century critics have given up such sexist observations, the following remark of Harry Levin, "Janes and Emilies, or the Novelist as Heroine," in *Refractions* (New York: Oxford Univ. Press, 1966), p. 257, certainly made with no malicious intention, will serve to disabuse us:

   It may be a coincidence worth noting that in France and England alike the most articul-te lionesses assumed the name of George. There was, indeed, somethi.g mannish about both George Eliot and George Sand; both of them achieved careers by flouting the domestic conditions of the day . . . for both Aurore Dupin and Marian Evans the masculine pseudonym was as much a requisite of a literary profession as a room of one's own and a bank account would be to Virginia Woolf.

3. Quoted by Townsend Scudder in *Jane Carlyle* (New York: Macmillan, 1939), pp. 351-352. Paul Groves Blount's study, "The Reputation of George Sand in Victorian England (1832-1886)," Diss. Cornell 1961, p. 122, shows that "the ethical problem dominated almost all criticism" of the Frenchwoman, with debate centering on Sand's outspoken discussions of marriage and female emancipation. The peak of anti-Sand sentiment was reached in the thirties when such Victorians as John Wilson Crocker (in 1836) held Sand's early novels responsible for actual cases of illicit love, suicide and murder which had come into the French newspapers and courts at that time (pp. 55-59). It is no wonder then that when Eliot became a well-known novelist and was revealed in 1859 as a woman writing under a male pseudonym and living with the married Lewes, similar accusations of immorality were raised against her.

4. Gordon Haight, *George Eliot: A Biography* (New York: Oxford Univ. Press, 1968), p. 410.

5. Emile Jonveaux, "Felix Holt le radical, par George Elliot [sic]," *Le Correspondant,* 69 (25 nov. et 25 déc. 1866), 617-618; cited by John Philip Couch, *George Eliot in France* (Chapel Hill: Univ. of North Carolina Press, 1967), p. 24; in the well-documented study of Couch we learn that Jonveaux's abridgment for serial publication of *Felix Holt* in the untra-conservative Catholic *Le Correspondant* was responsible for the general adoption of Eliot by French readers with family tastes. In a turnabout from his English counterparts, Jonveaux accuses Sand of having—in Couch's interpretation—"deviated from a more pious course in her earlier novels" compared to the exemplary conscience which dominates Eliot's novels.

6. Couch, on p. 38, describes Weil's enthusiastic account of *Daniel Deronda,* addressed in 1876 to an audience of French Jews in the *Archives Israelites.*

7. Edmond Schérer, "Revue de *Daniel Deronda,*" *Le Temps* (6 mars 1877), p. 292, cited by Couch, p. 74. Schérer was chief literary critic for the newspaper *Le Temps* from 1861 to 1885. According to Couch's interpretation, Schérer says: "There are no moments of eloquence, no finished effects, as in George Sand; instead the style is 'plus contenu, son art plus sévère'" (p. 74). His enthusiasm for Eliot waxes a few years later as he discovers in her a combination of the disparate qualities of Balzac and Thackeray in their "social tableaux; Defoe, Dickens and Dumas for adventure stories; and George Sand and Rousseau for 'l'éloquence des passions'" (*Le Temps,* avril 1885, p. 240, cited by

Couch, p. 82). However, when it comes to the subject of love, he simply cannot allow Eliot precedence over Sand; in this case he becomes chauvinistic for his country and his sex when he says, according to Couch: "To write convincingly about love the critic thinks one must either be a man or to have the talent, like George Sand, of being able to 'se désexiser'" (Couch, p. 82).

8. Ferdinand Brunetière, her most important champion, sees fit to praise Eliot at the expense of Hugo and Sand, whom he accuses, according to Couch, of "indiscreetly putting too much of themselves in their works" (p. 122). It was in defense of the English writer against the French Naturalists that Brunetière first brought Eliot's name to the attention of the French reading public. Zola had raised a cry against such respected and powerful publications as the *Revue des Deux Mondes* (Sand's publisher) for sacrificing Naturalism to moralism. They did this, Zola felt, by giving excessive attention to English fiction like that of George Eliot, which was tantamount to pandering to their readers' tastes for the George Sand tradition of "romancier" (Couch, p. 28). By faulting the French Naturalists for a dearth of sympathy, Brunetière was able to raise George Eliot as the prototype of English Naturalism, in which, the critic feels, sympathy is not sacrificed and yet objectivity is maintained. Another aspect of Brunetière's defense of Eliot has to do with what Couch calls "the danger of an excessive and undiscriminating admiration of the Russians" (p. 115) which the critic observed in 1888 and which prompted the following ecumenical question in Brunetière's "Les *Nouvelles* de M. de Maupassant," *Revue des Deux Mondes,* 3° per., 89 (1 Oct. 1888), 693; cited by Couch, p. 115:

> Ne pourrions-nous pas les admirer sans leur sacrifier tout à fait les nôtres? et quand je dis les nôtres, je veux dire aussi bien les Anglais, Dickens, Thackeray, Charlotte Bronte [sic], George Eliot, que Balzac et George Sand?

9. In Couch's words, de Heussy proclaimed that "no one of her sex in France, not even George Sand, can approach her in 'cette profondeur de pensée, cette netteté de vision, cette puissance d'observation, qui sont les traits distinctifs de l'écrivain anglais'" in "George Eliot," *Le Livre,* 10e année (jan. 1889), p. 16, cited by Couch, p. 110. Lemaître, in 1894, expressed the climax of French impatience with foreign influences. Couch quotes Lemaître's virulent essay, "De l'influence récente des littératures du nord," *Revue des Deux Mondes,* 3° per., 126 (15 déc. 1894), 850; cited by Couch, p. 117, in which he finds one George to be enough:

> Il y a sans doute autant de bonhomie robuste et charmante, autant de goût pour la vie simple et les détails familiers, autant de complaisance

et d'art à nous faire sentir, quelle qu'en soit l'enveloppe et la condition
sociale, combien c'est intéressant et digne d'attention une âme humaine;
il y a, je le veux bien, autant de tout cela chez le George d'outre
Manche que chez le George français; je dis qu'il n'en a pas plus, parce
que je crois que c'est impossible. Et ma grande raison, c'est que je le
crois.

10. In his biography of Eliot, Gordon Haight quotes Myers's letter in which
he compares her accomplishment to that of her female predecessors,
including Sand (F.W.H. Myers to George Eliot, Dec. 8, 1872, Yale;
Haight, p. 451):

> You seem now to be the only person who can make life appear
> potentially noble and interesting without starting from any assump-
> tions . . . others who have shown more or less of the same power of
> rising into clear air,—Mme de Staël in *Corinne,* Mrs. Craven in
> *Fleurange,* George Sand in *Consuelo*—have all needed some fixed
> point to lean against before they could spread wings and soar.

11. Sidney Colvin, "Daniel Deronda," *Fortnightly Review,* 20 (July-Dec.,
1876, 601-616), 614-615, claims that

> The art of fiction has reached its highest point in the hands of these
> two women. . . . George Sand excels in the poetical part of her art.
> George Eliot excels in the philosophical . . . George Eliot, while she
> speaks much more to our understanding, never speaks to our imagina-
> tion in so pure, single and harmonious a way as George Sand . . . to
> each her own crown.

12. Edward Dowden, "George Eliot," *Contemporary Review* (Aug., 1872),
pp. 403-422, rpt. in *A Century of George Eliot Criticism,* ed. Gordon
S. Haight (Boston: Houghton Mifflin, 1965, pp. 64-73), p. 72; though
generally sympathetic to Eliot, this critic remarks:

> Maggie returns to St. Oggs: Fedalma and Don Silva part: Romola goes
> back to her husband's house. We can imagine how unintelligible such
> moral situations, and such moral solutions, would appear to a great
> female novelist in France.

13. John Ruskin, "Fiction—Fair and Foul," *Nineteenth Century,* 10 (Oct.,
1881), 516-531, rpt. in *A Century of George Eliot Criticism,* pp. 64-73.
Ruskin insists (on p. 72) that *The Mill on the Floss* be labeled as
"essentially Cockney literature,—developed only in the London sub-
urbs, and feeding the demands of the rows of similar brick houses,
which branch in devouring cancer round every manufacturing town,"
but his true colors emerge when he favors "the really romantic literature
of France. Georges [sic] Sand is often immoral; but she is always beautiful." The fact that Eliot had died the previous year perhaps freed Ruskin
to express himself sincerely with regard to both women writers.

14. William Ernest Henley, *Views and Reviews: Essays in Appreciation* (London: Charles Scribner's, 1890), pp. 130-132, rpt. in *A Century of George Eliot Criticism* (pp. 161-162), p. 162.

15. Henry James, "*Daniel Deronda:* A Conversation," *Atlantic Monthly,* 38 (Dec., 1876), 684-694, rpt. in *George Eliot: The Critical Heritage* (pp. 417-433), p. 422.

16. K.A. McKenzie, "George Eliot and George Sand," *Australasian Universities Language and Literatures Association Proceedings* [2] (1964), pp. 61-62. His is the single study of this century which I have found that deals solely and comparatively with Sand and Eliot. In a brief sketch of what was probably a more extended talk, this critic notices a negative reaction in the work of Eliot to that of Sand but agrees to a strong positive but personal influence. Patricia Thomson, "The Three Georges," *Nineteenth Century Fiction,* 18:2 (Sept., 1963), 137-150. The whole question of morality which is linked with sex in the minds of nineteenth century English critics, has been pretty much ignored in comparisons of the two novelists since the turn of the century. Of our present day critics, only Miss Thomson points out how both women lived outside the legal ties of marriage yet acted as moralists in their fiction. Paul Groves Blount, "The Reputation of George Sand in Victorian England (1832-1886)," Diss. Cornell 1961. Ellen Moers, "Women's Lit: Profession and Tradition," *The Columbia Forum,*" 15 (Fall, 1972; pp. 27-34), p. 27.

17. *The George Eliot Letters,* ed. Gordon S. Haight (New Haven: Yale Univ. Press, 1954), I, 275; subsequently referred to as *Letters.*

18. George Eliot, "Woman in France: Madame de Sablé," *Westminster Review,* 42 (Oct., 1854), 448-473, rpt. in *Essays of George Eliot,* ed. Thomas Pinney (New York: Columbia Univ. Press, 1963), pp. 52-81; subsequently referred to as *Essays.*

19. *Essays,* p. 56.

20. Blount, p. 237.

21. Thomson, p. 143.

22. George Sand, *Oeuvres autobiographiques,* ed. Georges Lubin (Paris: Gallimard, 1970), II, 139.

23. Lubin, "Notes," *OA,* II, 1336, n° 1.

24. George Sand, *Légendes rustiques* (Paris: Calmann-Lévy, 1877), p. 67.

25. J.W. Cross, ed., *George Eliot's Life: as Related in her Letters and Journals* (1885; rpt. New York: AMS Press, 1965), pp. 212-213.

26. Thibaudet, p. 93.

27. *Letters,* I (Cara Bray to Sara Hennell, Feb. 14, 1846), 206.

28. *Letters,* I (Oct. 6, 1851), 365.

29. *OA,* I, 7. (Author's translation)

30. *Letters,* I (Martha Jackson, April 21, 1845), 189.

31. *Letters,* I (Cara Bray, Nov. 20, 1843), 165.

32. *OA,* I, 15-16. (Author's translation)

33. *Letters,* I (April 18, 1849), 281.

34. A. McKenzie (G. Flaubert, Oct. 1, 1866), p. 19.

35. *Letters,* III (July 5, 1859), 111.

36. Haight, p. 532.

37. [Leslie Stephen] Unsigned obituary article, *Cornhill,* 43 (Feb., 1881), 152-168, rpt. in *Carroll* (pp. 464-484), p. 472.

38. Edith Thomas, *George Sand* (Paris: Editions Universitaires, 1959), pp. 126-127; the author quotes Dostoevsky, *Journal d'un écrivain,* 1876 (Author's translation).

George Sand and the Russians

CAROLE KARP
Ann Arbor, Michigan

Nowhere in the world did George Sand's works find a warmer reception than in tsarist Russia, where there formed around her name a veritable cult. Russians of the 1840s who had any pretense to European culture felt compelled to display a "passion" for the works of George Sand.[1] One eye-witness to her enormous popularity in Russia was the international opera star Pauline Viardot, who wrote to her close friend George Sand in 1847 that: ". . . là-bas tous vos ouvrages sont traduits à mesure qu'ils paraîssent, que tout le monde les lit du haut en bas de l'échelle, que les hommes vous adorent, que les femmes vous idolâtrent et qu'enfin vous régnez sur la Russie plus souverainement que le tzar."[2]

Counted among that "tout le monde" to whom Pauline Viardot referred were all the best minds of Russia at the time, all of that newly developing intelligentsia which was as yet so small in numbers, but which soon would begin to reshape the future of that country. The young, yet untried revolutionaries, Alexander Herzen and Michael Bakunin, spoke adoringly of George Sand in their letters and diaries. Vissarion Belinsky, who would soon become the chief literary critic of that important generation known to history as "the generation of the forties," referred to Sand as "the Joan of Arc of our times."[3] Turgenev, who came to know her personally in her later years, wrote a moving eulogy to her in the Russian press in which he called her "one of our saints."[4] And even Dostoevsky, the great spokesman for Slavophile conservatism, worte movingly about the spiritual kinship which he, as a young man, had felt with her works."[5]

Perhaps the most authoritative testimony we have to Sand's

importance in Russian literary history is found in Prince Mirsky's highly regarded *History of Russian Literature.* In it Mirsky credits Sand with being the major source of the Russian realist novel:

"Russian realism," Mirsky wrote, "was born in the second half of the forties. . . . In substance it is a cross between the satirical naturalism of Gogol and an older sentimental realism revived and represented in the thirties and forties chiefly by the then enormously influential George Sand. Gogol and George Sand were the father and mother of Russian realism and its accepted masters during the initial stages."[6]

Dostoevsky has left us added testimony about Sand's triumph in Russia. He wrote in his *Diary of a Writer* in 1876: "I believe I do not err when I say that George Sand—judging at least by my personal recollections—promptly assumed in Russia virtually the first place among a whole Pleiad of new writers who at that period suddenly rose to fame and won renown all over Europe. Even Dickens, who appeared in Russia about the same time as she, was, perhaps, less popular with our public."[7]

There were, however, two distinctly different attitudes toward George Sand in Russia of the 1830s. In the literary circles of Moscow, where the Russian intelligentsia was then developing, George Sand was an object of veneration. Yet, in the dominant St. Petersburg press, which represented the viewpoint of "official" Russia, Sand's novels were severely reproved and frequently censored. Count Uvarov, the Minister of Education, and formulator of the reigning slogan of the day: "Orthodoxy, Autocracy, Nationality," published an official government viewpoint of George Sand's work. In July 1836, his Ministry of Public Instruction announced that the writer who hides herself behind the pseudonym George Sand: "attracts special attention because of her hatred of society and the existing order, her hatred of marriage, her strange disfiguration of women, her effort to shake loose human laws and to attack even those laws which are more sacred. Society and sane critics have answered her with scorn."[8]

Those "sane" critics to whom Count Uvarov was referring were, no doubt, the reactionary journalists, Senkovsky, Bulgarin and Grech, who controlled the Russian press in the 1830's and were known as the "St. Petersburg triumvirate." Their journals, *The Northern Bee, The Library for Reading,* and *The Son of the*

Fatherland, conducted a strenuous campaign to discredit Sand. One Senkovsky article warned the Russian public:

> You need to know that that woman despises all womanliness, even skirts. She dresses herself in male clothing and goes on sprees in that attire, and curses with young men in the streets of Paris. . . . That perfectly well explains to you how she could have written *Lélia.* One Russian traveler who recently returned from Paris . . . told us that he happened to spend an evening with her and a few others in a restaurant, and that on leaving there, she actually asked our compatriot if he had a cigarette.[9]

In yet another article Senkovsky complained:

> Even J.-J. Rousseau never went so far in his *Confessions* as did the writer of *Indiana, Valentine* and *Lélia.* . . . Here there is no beating about the bush, no idle talk, and especially no passing over anything in silence . . . in these books there is something awesome and somber: a woman rebelling against man, her sovereign master. A rebellion filled with bitterness and vengeance, filled with regrets like pride itself is, like the vengeance of Satan in *Paradise Lost.*[10]

Dostoevsky, in his 1876 commemorative article on Sand, reflected on that campaign in the St. Petersburg press aimed at discrediting the French woman writer. "They scared the Russian ladies," he recalled, "particularly by the fact that she wore trousers . . . it was sought to frighten them with the idea of depravity and to ridicule her."[11] In that same article, Dostoevsky also remarked upon the fact that Sand's novels were importers of revolutionary western ideas which the tsarist censors had otherwise banned: ". . . In those days," he recalled, "fiction was the only thing permitted, whereas the rest, virtually every thought, especially coming from France, was strictly forbidden. . . . Nevertheless, novels were permitted. . . . And right here, specifically in the case of George Sand, the guardians committed a grave error. . . . That which in those days burst into Russia in the form of novels . . . proved the most 'dangerous' form . . . there came forth thousands of lovers of George Sand."[12]

However, a recent study revealed that the tsarist censor was not so indifferent to George Sand's work as Dostoevsky, and most everyone, had believed. A soviet scholar named I. Aizenshtok who

made a direct survey of tsarist censorship records, discovered that
George Sand's novels were systematically censored in their original,
and that translations were allowed in abbreviated and "corrected"
form.[13] The leading members of the intelligentsia managed, nevertheless, to read Sand's work in the original. Belinsky, for example,
urged Bakunin not to read her 1842 novel *Horace* in the translation
which was then appearing in a Russian journal, but to read it
instead in the original.[14] That novel drew Belinsky's greatest particular praise. He proclaimed Sand to be "the lode star of salvation and
prophetess of a great future. It's not the first time," he rhapsodized,
"that a woman was the savior of the world."[15]

In stark contrast, then, to the severe reproval of George Sand in
the dominant St. Petersburg press of the 1830s, the newly developing intelligentsia in the Moscow literary circles revered her as their
saint. Timothy Granovsky, a well-known lecturer and writer of the
era, and a member of the celebrated Stankevich circle to which
Belinsky, Bakunin, Turgenev, and many other young upcoming
writers belonged, wrote of George Sand in this way: "I believe her to
be the greatest heart of contemporary literature . . . her sufferings
have often torn from her those cries which the world condemns
because its ears are too feeble."[16]

Sand's novels seem to have had a miraculous effect upon the
young anarchist-to-be, Bakunin, who wrote in French to his family:
"Chaque fois que je lis ses ouvrages, je deviens meilleur—ma foi se
fortifie et s'élargit . . . aucun poète, aucun philosophe ne m'est aussi
sympathique qu'elle, aucun ne m'a aussi bien exprimé mes propres
pensées, mes sentiments et mes besoins."[17]

Odd as it must seem to us today who view Sand's work as so
much idealized, sentimental, wishful thinking, to the young Russian
intellectuals of the 1830s and 40s her novels signified an impatience
with theorizing and a turn toward practical considerations. Bakunin,
for one, noted that Sand's work led him to the realization that: "the
time for theorizing is over." "George Sand n'est pas poète seulement,
mais encore prophète, révélateur," he wrote in a letter to his sisters,
"sa charité est une vraie charité parce qu'elle est pratique. . . . Le
temps de la théorie, Dieu merci, est passé. Tout le monde le sent
plus ou moins; l'aurore d'un monde nouveau nous éclaire déjà."[18]

One by one the young Russian intellectuals abandoned the
German abstract idealism which had dominated their discussions in

the early 1830s and turned toward the French radicalism which George Sand promoted in her novels. The first to make that transition was the man who is known as "the father of the Russian intelligentsia," Alexander Herzen. Sand's mystico-socialist novel *Spiridion* was a major influence in Herzen's life. He read it early in 1839 when it came out in serial form in the *Revue Indépendante* when he was a political exile in a provincial Russian town. His great excitement over *Spiridion* is evidenced by his repeated appeals to a friend in Moscow to forward him the latest issues of the *Revue Indépendante* so that he could read the final chapters of the novel.[19]

After his release from political exile in 1840, Herzen infected Belinsky and others with his enthusiasm for *Spiridion.* Belinsky, who was soon to become a moving spirit of the progressive Westerners, reacted in his characteristically exuberant manner: he suddenly changed courses, renouncing his recent hatred of all things French, and became a fierce champion of George Sand and the humanitarian idealism of Pierre Leroux which she promoted. One chronicler of the period, Ivan Panaev, who claimed to have translated expressly for Belinsky the final chapters of *Spiridion,* witnessed the stunning transformation of Belinsky's attitude toward Sand: "All of his former literary authorities and idols: Goethe, Walter Scott, Schiller, Hoffmann—all paled before her," Panaev recalled. "Now he spoke only about George Sand and Leroux. His enthusiasm was so strong that he decided to study French in order to read them in the original."[20]

Previous to his sudden conversion, Belinsky's opinions of Sand had differed very little from those of the "official" St. Petersburg press. In an 1838 article Belinsky had written:

Indeed, what does present-day French literature have to offer? The reflection of small and worthless systems, ephemeral parties, momentary questions. Dudevant, or that George Sand, so well-known but not at all celebrated, is writing a whole series of novels, one more absurd and more scandalous than the next, in order to promote Saint-Simonian ideas of society. And what are these ideas? O, excellent! Exactly this: that the industrial trend of thought should prevail over the spiritual. . . .[21]

Yet after his conversion to French radical thinking via Herzen and *Spiridion,* Belinsky became the chief spokesman for George

Sand in Russia. From his position as the leading literary critic of the 1840s, Belinsky continuously propagandized for Sand's novels and oversaw their translation and publication in *The Notes of the Fatherland,* the influential journal which he edited. Often his reviews of Sand's novels served as launching pads for protests against the class prejudices of his day. Thus, in his review of *Mauprat* he noted:

> In George Sand there is neither love nor hate for the privileged classes, and there is neither reverence nor disdain for the lower classes of society; for her there aren't any aristocrats or plebeians, for her there are only human beings, and she finds human beings in all levels of society, loves them, has compassion for them, takes pride in them, pities them. . . . Is it not hard to understand after this, how Mrs. Dudevant could have been so defamed by the blind rabble, by the preposterous and ignorant mob, as an immoral writer?[22]

It was also, presumably, difficult for Belinsky to understand how he himself could have been part of that "blind rabble" which had castigated George Sand as a writer of scandalous novels. Now, as a leader of the progressive Westerners, Belinsky repeatedly held Sand's work up as an example of great literature. In an 1846 review, for instance, he predicted that future generations would look back upon the nineteenth century as a barbarous period, but that they would be amazed and delighted to find Byron and George Sand there, just as men of the nineteenth century had been amazed to discover Shakespeare in the midst of the barbarity of the sixteenth century.[23]

In Russian literary history Belinsky is primarily known as the founder of the utilitarian school of literary criticism. His first full-fledged program for that utilitarian or "critical realist" view of literature which would dominate mid-nineteenth century Russian criticism, appeared in an 1842 article in which Belinsky pointed directly to George Sand's work as a guidepost for the art of his time: "Our age," he wrote, "decisively rejects art for art's sake, beauty for the sake of beauty . . .

> George Sand is, without doubt, the foremost poetic glory of the contemporary world. One can choose to disagree with her principles, one can find them false or unacceptable, but it is impossible not to respect her as a human being for whom every conviction is a heart-felt belief. It is for that reason that so many of her works penetrate so

profoundly into our own souls, leaving ineffaceable traces in our memories. It is for that reason that her talent never lessens, but grows continuously stronger and greater.[24]

In 1847, however, Belinsky began to express some reservations about Sand's work. He found that her most recently published novels *Le Meunier d'Angibault* and *Le Péché de M. Antoine* contained fantastic and incredible characters, and that the natural in them was eclipsed by the unnatural. Yet he still continued to have faith in Sand's artistic powers: "This is not a reason for bewailing the decline of her art," he wrote. "The same George Sand gave us *Tévérino* after *Le Meunier d'Angibault,* and *Le Péché de M. Antoine* and *Isidora* were followed by *Lucrezia Floriani*."[25]

The notorious Lucrezia Floriani was the subject of a heated debate between Belinsky and the novelist Ivan Goncharov, who roundly condemned that most liberated Sandian heroine for daring to live alone with her four illegitimate children and for conducting her sexual life in a most unorthodox manner.[26] In the 1850s and 60s that same Lucrezia became the focus of a dispute between conservative Slavophiles and progressive Westerners. To the Slavophiles Lucrezia was a symbol of that ultimate degradation to which they felt sure French socialist theories would lead Russian women. Among the Slavophile journalists who commented indignantly upon *Lucrezia Floriani* was Nikolai Strakhov, the close friend of Tolstoy. He complained that Europe, through writers such as Sand, was inflicting upon Russia all those morbid aspirations with which it was itself struggling. Catholic extremism, Catholic overstated contempt for the flesh, he concluded, was what had necessitated the dissolute reaction of Sand's emancipated heroine, Lucrezia.[27]

The defenders and attackers of Lucrezia Floriani were all voices in the great debate of nineteenth-century Russia on the "Zhenskii vopros" or "the Woman Question." Female emancipation became a sacred radical cause, not only as an issue in itself, but also as a symbol for a general emancipation of the individual from the restraints placed upon him or her by the old tsarist order. In the giant Russian encyclopedia printed in 1894, the *Entsiklopedicheski Slovar,* we find a separate entry entitled *"The Woman Question,"*[28] which informs us that the woman question in Russian "was raised under the direct influence of George Sand."[29]

Almost every issue of *The Contemporary,* the leading radical journal of the 1860s, contained an article on "The Woman Question." The writing staff and editorial board, which included the most important writers of the day, were apparently all devotees of George Sand. This fact is illustrated in an amusing anecdote which Grigorovich, a novelist of the era, related in his memoirs. He told of having warned the young, upcoming Tolstoy not to divulge his negative opinions of George Sand if he wished to make a good impression at a meeting of the editorial board of *The Contemporary*. Tolstoy, however, could not contain himself. After repeatedly hearing Sand's novels being praised, he burst out sharply, declaring that Sand's heroines, if they existed in reality, "ought to be tied to a pillory for the edification of the populace and dragged through the streets of St. Petersburg." [30]

So pervasive was Sand's influence in Russia that a special literary term was created to describe the phenomenon. "Zhorzhzandism" was a commonplace used by critics to categorize the many novels written in the 1840s and 50s which dealt with themes similar to those of Sand's early novels *Indiana, Valentine* and *Jacques*. These popular Russian novels of the "Zhorzhzandism" trend were generally seen as "protests against marriage." They were also literary reverberations of the general interest of the Russian intelligentsia in the "Woman Question."

While the radical Westerners, for the most part, championed George Sand, within the camp of the conservative Slavophiles she also found some support. Khomyakóv, the most influential Slavophile, refused to place the blame for society's corruption upon the influence of George Sand. "The depravity of men," he noted, "presupposes the depravity of women. . . . And thus, the teachings of George Sand are justified." "I don't see why," he concluded, "Lucrezia Floriani would not have been a very nice man, and even a very respectable gentleman." [31]

Although Khomyakóv could not support Sand's feminist and socialist teachings, he acknowledged that her "great artistic talents rise once in a while to irreproachable heights, as for example in *La Mare au Diable*." [32] Other leading Slavophiles also praised *La Mare au Diable,* in which they discerned traces of the Slav world of the "obshchina," that historic peasant commune which they constantly evoked as an ideal to which Russia should revert, rather than follow the path which the Western nations had taken. In an article in *The*

Moskovite, the leading Slavophile journal, a conservative critic, Yuri Samarin, held Sand's novels up as examples of the proper way to depict the lives of peasants. Samarin, like many of his countrymen, praised Sand for rising up against the realistic depictions of peasant life found in French writers such as Balzac.[33]

The Slavophiles appeared to have found in George Sand a confirmation of their theories about the role and mission of the people. Yet their enthusiasm for the Russian peasant had an entirely different basis than Sand's idealization of the French peasant. While theirs was only the ideological form of their effort to hold fast to patriarchal-feudal conditions, Sand's derived mainly from her desire to promote the socialist faith. Her effort to idealize peasant life was all part of her humanitarian dream of convincing the wealthy to renounce part of their goods. Her vision was to bring forth that classless society about which the Slavophiles' opponents, the Westerners, were just beginning to dream. Yet with her sentimental and idealized peasant tales, Sand was an understandable source of inspiration to all her Russian contemporaries, both Westerners and Slavophiles, who sought solace and hope for their nation in the mystical belief in an idealized peasant community.

The thousands of lovers of George Sand in Russia continued to be faithful to her long after her charms had lost their appeal in the rest of Europe. She was equally venerated in Russia by the famous "nihilist" generation of the 1860s as she had been by the important "generation of the forties" which had canonized her as its saint. The Populists, who dominated the Russian intellectual scene in the 1870s and 80s perpetuated the cult of George Sand, not so much because they sympathized with her ideas, as because she had been the educator of the preceding two generations of Russian radicals. In Russia, George Sand's triumph was complete.

NOTES

1. Vladimir Karénine (pseud. of Mme. Varvara Komarova), *George Sand, sa vie et ses oeuvres* (Paris: Plon-Nourrit, 1899-1926), IV, 103-104.

2. E. Séménoff, "1830 et le romantisme russe," *Mercure de France,* CCXXIV (December 15, 1930), pp. 578-79.

3. V.G. Belinsky, *Polnoe sobranie sochinenie* (Moscow, 1953-59), XII, 115. Translations from the Russian are mine.

4. I.S. Turgenev, *Pervoe sobranie pisem I.S. Turgeneva, 1840-1883* (St. Petersburg: 1884), p. 292.

5. F.M. Dostoevsky, *The Diary of a Writer*, trans. Boris Brasol (New York: Octagon Books, 1973), I, 340-47.

6. D.S. Mirsky, *History of Russian Literature* (New York: Vintage Books, 1958), p. 178.

7. Dostoevsky, *Diary of a Writer,* I, 340.

8. Zhurnal Ministerstva Narodnago Proveshcheniia, vol. XI, No. 7, pp. 234-34. Cited in Raoul Labry, *Alexandre Herzen* (Paris: Bossard, 1928), p. 210.

9. *Biblioteka dliia Chteniia,* Vol. XVII, Section 7 (1834), pp. 6-7.

10. Ibid., Vol. III, Section 7, pp. 123-24.

11. Dostoevsky, *Diary of a Writer,* I, 345.

12. Ibid., 344-45.

13. I. Ya. Aizenshtok, "Frantsuzskie pisateli v otsenkakh t͡sarskoi tsenzury," *Literaturnoe nasledstvo* (Moscow: Izdat. Akademii Nauk, 1939), Nos. 33-34, p. 812.

14. V.G. Belinsky, XII, 115.

15. Ibid.

16. N. Stankevich, T. Granovski, *Correspondence* (Moscow: Stankevich, 1897), II, 201.

17. Cited in E. Séménoff, pp. 582-83.

18. Ibid.

19. A. Herzen, *Sobranie sochinenii v 30-ti tomakh* (Moscow: Akademia Nauk, 1954-61), XXII, 10, 13.

20. Ivan I. Panaev, *Literaturnye vospominaniia* (Moscow: Gos. izdat., 1950), pp. 273-74.

21. Belinsky, III, 398.

22. Ibid., V, 175.

23. Ibid., IX, 576.

24. Ibid., VI, 271-79.

25. Belinsky, *Selected Philosophical Works,* trans. Vovchuck (Moscow: Foreign Language Publishing House, 1948), pp. 426-27.

26. I. Goncharov, *Sobranie sochinenii v vos'mi tomakh* (Moscow: Gos. izdat. Khudozh. Lit., 1955), VIII, 57.

27. Nikolai Strakhov, "Mill, zhenskii vopros," in *Borba s zapadom v nashei literature* (St. Petersburg: Dogrodver, 1882), I, 196.

28. The expression "The Woman Question" is a direct translation of the Russian words "Zhenskii Vopros," a term which appeared continuously in mid-nineteenth century Russian journals. The term encompassed all the issues surrounding women's roles and women's rights—issues which dominated the intellectual discussions of the era.

29. "Zhenskii vopros", Entsiklopedicheski Slovar, eds. Brokau and Efrom (St. Petersburg, 1894), XII, 226,

30. A. Grigorovich, "Literaturnye vospominaniia," *Russkaia Mysl,* II (1893), 69.

31. Aleksei S. Khomyakov, *Polnoe sobranie sochinenii* (Moscow: Universitetskaia, 1900), III, 254-55.

32. Khomyakóv, "O vozmozhnosti russkoi khudozhestvennoi shkoly," *Polnoe sobranie sochinenii,* I, 96.

33. Yuri Samarin, "O mneniiakh sovremennika istoricheskikh i literaturnykh," *Moskvitiianin,* II (1847), 205.

George Sand and Ivan Turgenev

LESLEY S. HERRMANN
Department of Modern Foreign Languages
Manhattan College

"Chère Mme Sand, . . . en allant à Nohant, je m'étais promis de vous dire l'influence que vous avez eue sur moi comme écrivain."
Letter from Ivan Turgenev to George Sand, Oct. 30, 1872[1]

The purpose of this article is to establish George Sand as a literary model for Ivan Turgenev, one whom he imitates, adapts, and later outgrows, but never completely discards. I will discuss three aspects of George Sand's rustic trilogy, *La Mare au Diable, François le Champi,* and *La Petite Fadette,* from which Turgenev borrows in his own works: the unifying narrator in *Notes of a Hunter;* the peasant as a moral ideal; and the peasant girl as heroine, a comparison of petite Fadette and Asya.

Turgenev was the only Russian writer who knew George Sand personally, but their friendship did not develop until 1872, when Turgenev was already in his fifties and George Sand nearly seventy. But Sand's influence on Turgenev began in 1834, long before they met, when Turgenev was a sixteen-year-old student at Petersburg University, and George Sand's first novels were attracting notice in the Russian journals of the time.[2] In 1834, Turgenev wrote a poetic drama entitled *Steno,*[3] after the idealistic young poet Stenio, protagonist of George Sand's novel *Lélia,*[4] published in 1833. More than ten years later, when George Sand's popularity in Russia had reached its apogee, Turgenev was writing *Notes of a Hunter* (1847-1852), sketches and observations of peasant life. The first sketch, "Khor and Kalinych," was published in the Russian journal, *The Contemporary* in 1847,[5] the same year that a Russian newspaper

162

noted, "If you do not fall down upon your knees before George Sand, then you are not a contemporary person."[6]

Turgenev's letters to his friends, particularly those to Pauline Viardot, show that he followed the latest literary developments with close attention, and that in this sense, he was indeed contemporary.

Turgenev frequently gave his opinion of George Sand's novels to Pauline Viardot. In January, 1848, Turgenev wrote that he was reading *François le Champi,* the second story in George Sand's trilogy, which was then being serialized in the French *Journal de Débats.*

C'est fait dans la meilleure manière: simple, vrai, poignant. Elle y entremêle peut-être un peu trop d'expressions de paysan; ça donne de temps un air affecté à son récit. . . . Mais on voit clairement qu'elle . . . se plonge avec délices dans la fontaine de Jouvence de l'art naïf et terre à terre.[7]

As his letter shows, Turgenev was very much interested in George Sand's experiments with "l'art naïf," but Turgenev was not the only Russian at this time with a literary interest in peasant life. Under the influence of Auerbach in Germany, Immermann and Gotthelf in Switzerland, and of course, George Sand and Balzac in France, other Russian writers, such as Dmitry Grigorovich and V.I. Dal, wrote about the peasant.[8] But these efforts were either ethnological studies, or else tracts depicting the degradation of the serf and demanding the abolition of serfdom.[9] Turgenev's sketches went beyond ethnology or politics, and he tried to emulate George Sand's literary approach to the life of the peasant.

Sand had entitled her three rustic tales *Veillées du Chanvreur,* (*Evenings with a Hempdresser*) as the stories are united by the presence of a peasant hempdresser, who recounts the original tales to the author in his peasant dialect. Sand felt that if she reproduced the stories as they were "told" to her they would be incomprehensible to the educated reader.

Si je fais parler l'homme des champs comme il parle, il faut une traduction en regard pour le lecteur civilisé, et si je le fais parler comme nous parlons, j'en fais un être impossible, auquel il faut supposer un ordre d'idées qu'il n'a pas.[10]

Her solution to the problem was to retell the stories with just enough of the hempdresser's expressions to add local color, but not so much as to make the stories incomprehensible to her Parisian audience. The result: *François le Champi,* a mixture of dialect and archaic French expressions.[11]

Although Turgenev felt that "elle y entremêle peut-être un peu trop d'expressions de paysan," he faced the same problem as Sand: how to capture the spirit of peasant life without losing either the flavor of peasant speech or the understanding of his reader. Like Sand, Turgenev had to compromise; he, too, invented a narrator, but instead of an uneducated, peasant hempdresser talking to the author, Turgenev chose an educated landowner. The narrator occasionally reproduces peasant dialect,[12] but tells the stories in standard Russian. In this way, Turgenev avoided what he considered the affectation of a peasant narrator.

Turgenev's hunter and George Sand's hempdresser share many qualities, notwithstanding the difference in their social status. Both are wandering outdoorsmen, keenly observant, but with a certain emotional detachment from what they see, since they are not personally involved in the problems of the peasants. Both have a defined status in peasant society and can mix unobtrusively with those they come across. Thus Sand explains the presence of the hempdresser at the wedding of Germain and Marie in *La Mare au Diable,*

> Il est de toutes les solenmités tristes ou gaies, parce qu'il est essentiel-lement érudit et beau diseur, et dans ces occasions, il a toujours le soin de porter, la parole pour accomplir dignement certaines formal-ités, usitées de temps immémorial. *Les professions errantes, qui introduisent l'homme au sein des familles san lui permettre de ce concentrer dans la sienne, sont propres à le rendre bavard, plaisant, conteur et chanteur.*[13]

For the same reasons, Turgenev's hunter is also able to observe the peasants without inhibiting them, since a hunter's presence is an accepted part of the peasant way of life.

"The Singers" illustrates the narrator's function in *Notes of a Hunter* particularly well. In this story, the hunter attends a singing contest between two local peasants in a country tavern. First, the hunter establishes his credibility as narrator.

> "My arrival," he says, "at first rather confused the guests of Nikolai Ivanich" (the tavern-keeper), "but observing that he bowed to me as to an acquaintance, they set their minds at rest and paid me no mind. . . ."[14]

Then, he states his intention: to bring the life of the peasants to the attention of the reader, who knows nothing of peasant customs.

> "Probably not many of my readers have had occasion to look inside a country tavern—but we sportsmen, we go everywhere."[15]

Because they are eye-witnesses to major events in peasant life, both the hunter and the hempdresser convey an authenticity that makes the stories seem realistic and believable, rather than fabrications for the amusement of the reader. George Sand ends *François le Champi* with the playful statement,

> "L'histoire est donc vraie de tous points? . . ."
> "Si elle ne l'est pas, elle le pourrait être," répondit le chanvreur, "et si vous ne me croyez, allez y voir."[16]

George Sand had long considered the peasant as a moral ideal, based on the teachings of her master, Jean-Jacques Rousseau. Her purpose in writing the "romans champêtres" was not, to present an unadorned reality, but rather to search for what she calls "ideal truth," and if in the process, reality is embellished, no harm has been done.[17] Her tales present a poetic dream of the simple life of the tiller of the soil, not the wretched and degraded way of life that Balzac, for example, depicts in his peasant novels. By showing what men ought to be rather than what they are, George Sand preached the same reforms which she had advocated in her didactic socialist novels, and in her early novel *Mauprat,* published in 1837, which envisions a reform of men rather than of institutions.

Turgenev was more realistic than Sand in his approach to the peasant, but on balance, *Notes of a Hunter* favors the peasant rather than the landowner. Like Sand, Turgenev demonstrates the moral authority of certain peasants, notably Lukeria in "The Live Relic;" Kasyan in "Kasyan from Fair Springs;" and Gerasim in "Mumu."[18]

These special peasants are surrounded by an aura of saintliness of which they themselves are unaware; they correspond to George Sand's description of Germain in *La Mare au Diable,*

> "Eh bien! tel qu'il est, incomplet et comdamné à une éternelle enfance, il est encore plus beau que celui chez qui la science, a étouffé le sentiment . . . j'aime encore mieux cette simplicité de son âme que les fausses lumières. . . ." [19]

These peasants with their simple ways demonstrate purity of soul, spontaneous enjoyment of life, sensitivity, and instinctive decency which are intended to inspire the reader with admiration, and in the same manner as George Sand's peasants, to encourage humanity through example.

Lukeria in "The Live Relic" is such a peasant. Afflicted by God for what she considers her "sins," she is completely paralyzed and near death when the hunter pays a visit to her hut in the forest. He is impressed with her simple faith, total selflessness and lack of self-pity.

> "I was amazed," says the hunter, "that she told her story gaily, without groans and sighs, neither complaining nor begging for sympathy." [20]

When he asks what he can do for her to make her life easier, she replies,

> "I need nothing; I am content with everything, thank God . . . but the peasants are poor . . . and if only their rent could be reduced. . . ." [21]

Another gentle peasant is Kasyan, in "Kasyan from Fair Springs." A peasant philosopher with special powers of healing, Kasyan is able to converse with birds and beasts; his fellow peasants consider him a sorcerer, and fear and respect him for his wisdom. Kasyan abhors killing God's creatures,

> "Death runs not," says Kasyan, "nor is there any running from him, but neither should we help him. . . ." [22]

One Russian scholar has drawn a convincing parallel between Kasyan and Patience from *Mauprat*.[23] Both peasants are versions of "holy fools," whose eccentric behavior mysteriously expresses God's wisdom.

Still a third Sandian peasant is Gerasim from Turgenev's 1852 story "Mumu." This tale is not part of *Notes of a Hunter,* but it is both chronologically and thematically related to it. Gerasim is a deaf-mute who keeps apart from the other peasants, but does the work of four men and always pays his taxes on time. He is forced to drown his only friend, a little dog named Mumu, because she snarls at the mistress. Gerasim bears his lot without complaint. Only after Mumu's death, he becomes even more solitary and withdraws from society, his defense against man's inhumanity to man. These three peasant portraits, Lukeria, Kasyan, and Gerasim, are as close as Turgenev ever comes to idealizing the peasants in the manner of George Sand.

Usually Turgenev is much more restrained in his admiration. Even in one of his most lyrical stories, "The Singers," Turgenev admits both the bad and the good in the peasant nature. The tale concerns a singing contest between Yasha, nicknamed the Turk, and a peddler. Yasha's superb singing wins the contest, and everyone in the tavern is overcome with emotion by his song.

> In Yasha's voice . . . the truthful, burning Russian soul rang and breathed . . . and caught at your heart, caught straight at your Russian heartstrings . . . in every sound rang something native and immeasurably broad—like the familiar steppe.[24]

Yet later in the day, the hunter encounters this same Yasha, drunk and sitting bare-chested on a bench, singing a dance-hall tune. To Turgenev the true Russian peasant like Yasha is both the embodiment of the Russian soul and a drunken lout. The sublime Yasha could grace the pages of the "romans champêtres" of George Sand, but the drunken Yasha belongs to a more Balzacian view of life.

Perhaps George Sand's greatest contribution to the peasant novel was her creation of a peasant heroine who would be a worthy successor to Indiana Delmare and Edmée Mauprat. In *Consuelo,* published in 1842, the heroine of obscure background becomes a famous opera singer, but *Jeanne,* published in 1844, was Sand's first attempt to create a simple peasant heroine. Sand was not satisfied with *Jeanne,*[25] and Turgenev, while saying that *Jeanne* was "doux et beau," thought that the heroine was "un peu trop pédante." [26]

After rereading *Consuelo,* he wrote to Viardot,

> Sand often spoils her most fascinating feminine characters by forcing them to be talkative, sober-minded and pedantic . . . even Fadette belongs in this category.[27]

The second part of *La Petite Fadette* indeed shows Fadette transformed from a gamine, mercurial sprite into a didactic young woman. Turgenev may have used Sand's portrait of the early Fadette, the tomboy who becomes a young woman on falling in love, for his own "Asya," published in 1858.

Fadette and Asya resemble one another in appearance, behavior, family background and love. Fadette, when she enters the story, is a fourteen-year-old peasant girl, scorned by the neighborhood for her biting wit and flamboyant disregard for village customs. She is ugly, her clothes are torn, her skin too dark.

> Elle était petite, maigre, ébouriffée et hardie. C'était un enfant très causeur et très moqueur, vif comme un papillon, curieux comme un rouge-gorge et noir comme un grelet. . . .[28]

But her behavior more than her looks arouses the peasants' ire, for she is proud and aloof.

> La petite Fadette prit un air fier et quasi fâché; et se décidant enfin à le regarder, elle le fit d'une manière si méprisante, qu'il en fut tout démonté et n'osa point lui porter la parole. . . .[29]

In truth Fadette is not scornful. She acts this way out of shame for her upbringing; she and her brother, to whom she is extremely devoted, were deserted by their mother, who ran away with a soldier.

When she falls in love with Landry, Fadette blossoms into a radiant young woman:

> Elle devint un peu rouge, pas plus que la petite rose des buissons, mais cela la fit paraître quasi belle, d'autant plus que ses yeux noirs, auxquels jamais personne n'avait pu trouver à redire, laisserent

échapper un feu si clair qu'elle en parut transfigurée . . . la voilà belle par miracle.[30]

Asya, Turgenev's half-peasant heroine, looks remarkably like Fadette: both are small, slim, boyish, dark-skinned, graceful, and with bright, black eyes. The first time he meets Asya, the narrator, identified only as N.N., describes her as "a short, young girl . . . with something peculiar in the form of her dark-skinned, round face with its small slender nose, almost childish little cheeks and bright, bold gaze. . . ."[31]

Turgenev's first draft of "Asya" shows an even closer similarity between Fadette and Asya, although in the final version, Turgenev discarded many details of Asya's appearance and upbringing.[32] In the first draft, the narrator describes Asya as "the girl with the forced laughter and the homely face."[33] In the final version, the narrator simply describes her as "the girl with the forced laughter," and the first time that the narrator meets Asya, he says that she was "adorable."[34]

In the first draft, Asya, like Fadette, does not become beautiful until transformed by love. Also, like Fadette, Asya behaves outrageously out of shame for her family. She is the illegitimate daughter of an aristocrat and a serf; the narrator notes that she does not resemble a young woman of noble birth, but rather is like "a wild tree only recently grafted, or a wine still fermenting."[35]

Once again the rough draft shows a similarity between Fadette and Asya. Turgenev made three notes before writing "Asya;" the smell of hemp reminds him of his homeland; the song of the nightingale; and, most significantly, Asya's sensitivity about her mother.[36] All three of these notes can be connected with George Sand, but particularly the third one with regard to Fadette. Sand makes a special point of stressing Fadette's passionate defense of her mother.[37] Turgenev had originally intended to develop an episode about Asya's upbringing to explain some of her eccentric behavior. In the sketch of her early life, Asya is sent to stay with an aunt, where she lives a lonely, silent life among strangers who do not understand her and consider her haughty and strange.[38] Turgenev completely omitted this scene from the final story, but if we consider Turgenev's original intention, Asya's upbringing is much closer to Fadette's; she was raised by her grandmother and led a solitary existence except for the companionship of her brother because other children considered her too eccentric. Asya is also extremely close to her brother, and spends her time exclusively in his company, avoiding contact with other people.

Both Asya and Fadette are unusually graceful dancers.

> La petite Fadette dansait très bien; il l'avait vue gambiller dans les champs ou sur le bord des chemins, avec les pâtours, et elle s'y déménait comme un petit diable, si vivement qu'on avait peine à la suivre en mesure. . . .[39]

Asya waltzes "beautifully, with enthusiasm" and it is during the waltz that her love blossoms. "Suddenly, something soft and feminine flitted across her virginally severe face."[40]

It is probable that Turgenev had more than one model for Asya. Pushkin's Tatyana, Turgenev's own natural daughter Paulinette, and Pauline Viardot herself are possible sources. If Viardot were a model for Asya, it seems most likely that it is the Viardot on whom the early chapters of George Sand's *Consuelo* are based, when the ugly, dark-skinned young singer falls in love and turns into a beauty.

Nikolai Chernyshevsky, a Russian radical critic of the 1860s, wrote a famous article on "Asya" entitled "The Russian at the Rendezvous," in which he laments that the weak-willed hero of "Asya" unfortunately reflects Russian society. Chernyshevsky says that if the hero had not been afraid to yield to Asya's love, we might have had a poetic tale on the order of George Sand.[41]

Turgenev, by his own admission, used George Sand's work as a starting point for his own search for artistic truth. As he wrote to his friend, the novelist and critic Alexander Druzhinin,

> "for you she [George Sand] represents a delusion to be uprooted. For me she represents incomplete truth when complete truth is unattainable."[42]

NOTES

1. E. Halpérine-Kaminsky, ed., *Ivan Tourguéneff d'après sa correspondance avec ses amis français* (Paris, 1901), p. 153.

2. The notice that they attracted was not always favorable. *The Library for Reading, The Son of the Fatherland,* and *The Northern Bee,* three conservative Petersburg journals, were particularly virulent in condemning George Sand, especially in the 1830s.

3. Turgenev himself many years later describes *Steno* as a "perfectly preposterous work, which, with childish incompetence, I was slavishly imitating Byron's *Manfred.*" Quoted in *Literary Reminiscences and Autobiographical Fragments,* trans. David Magarshack (New York: Farrar, Straus and Cudahy, 1958), p. 105.

4. Vladimir Karenin (pseud. of Varvara Komarova) "Turgenev i Zhorzh Sand," *Turgenevskii Sbornik,* ed. A. F. Koni (Petersburg, 1921), p. 90.

5. N.V. Izmailov, ed., *Turgenev i krug 'Sovremennika'* (Moscow-Leningrad: Akademiya, 1930), p. X.

6. V.F. Botsyanovsky, "Zhorzh Zand v Rossii," *Biblioteka Teatra i Iskusstva,* II (Feb. 1915), 25.

7. Ivan Sergeevich Turgenev, *Pisma,* I (Moscow-Leningrad: Akademiya Nauk, 1965), p. 292. Letter of January 5, 1848.

8. Turgenev discusses these writers in his review of Auerbach's *Schwarzwalder Dorfgeschichten.* See Henri Granjard, *Ivan Tourguénev et les courants politiques et sociaux de son temps* (Paris, 1954), pp. 147-199.

9. Ibid.

10. Preface to *François le Champi* (Paris: Garnier, 1962), p. 215.

11. A.H. Schutz, "The Peasant Vocabulary in the Works of George Sand," *University of Missouri Studies,* II (Jan. 1, 1927), 11.

12. Especially in the stories "The Singers" and "Bezhin Meadow."

13. *La Mare au Diable* (Paris: Garnier, 1962), p. 136.

14. Ivan Sergeevich Turgenev, *Zapiski Okhotnika* in *Sochineniya* (Moscow-Leningrad, 1963), IV, 230.

15. Ibid.

16. *François le Champi,* p. 404.

17. In the preface to *La Mare au Diable,* p. 12, George Sand makes the oft-quoted statement "l'art n'est pas une étude de la réalité positive; c'est une recherche de la vérité idéale."

18. The story "A Live Relic" was not published until 1874 and was later added to *Notes of a Hunter.*

19. *La Mare au Diable,* p. 24.

20. *Zapiski,* p. 355.

21. Ibid., p. 364.

22. Ibid., p. 126.

23. M. Sumtsov, "Vliyanie Zhorzh Zand na Turgeneva," *Knizhki nedeli,* I (1897), 11-12.

24. *Zapiski,* p. 241.

25. Preface to *François le Champi,* p. 216, in which Rollinat finds it incongruous to compare Jeanne to a druidess and to a Joan of Arc.

26. Alexandre Zviguilsky, ed., *Ivan Tourguénev, Nouvelle correspondance inédite* (Paris: Librarie de Cinq Continents, 1971), p. 38. Letter of May 7, 1850. "Les héroines de Mme Sand tombent souvent dans ce défaut—témoin la petite Fadette, Consuelo dans *La Comtesse de Rudolstadt.*"

27. Turgenev, *Pisma,* I, p. 347. This letter is published in Russian because the French original has been lost.

28. *La Petite Fadette* (Paris: Garnier-Flammarion, 1967), p. 83.

29. Ibid., p. 103.

30. Ibid., p. 159.

31. Turgenev, "Asya" in *Sochineniya,* VII, 75.

32. André Mazon, *Les manuscrits parisiens d'Ivan Tourguénev* (Paris: Champion, 1926), pp. 58-59.

33. "Asya," p. 429.

34. Turgenev's narrator calls Asya "very comely," "Asya," p. 75.

35. Ibid., p. 87.

36. Mazon, p. 58.

37. *La Petite Fadette,* p. 138.

38. "Asya," p. 101.

39. *La Petite Fadette,* p. 119.

40. "Asya," p. 101.

41. N.G. Chernyshevsky, *Polnoe sobranie sochinenii,* V (Moscow, 1953), p. 158.

42. Izmailov, p. 197.

The Lélios of Berlioz
and George Sand

ENID M. STANDRING
Department of French
Montclair State College

In an article entitled "French Romanticism and the 'Fraternity of the Arts'" which appeared in the 1969 Fall-Winter issue of *Symposium,* Pierre Moreau, referring to the recently established discipline called "comparative arts and literature," said, "Il y a un danger dans ces relations entre les arts." If there is danger in a composer's trying to use in the art of music the techniques of a painter, a sculptor, a poet, or a novelist, presumably also a literary critic without technical knowledge of the other arts should avoid expressing opinions on works in these media, at least in print. In *Les Grotesques de la musique,* Berlioz qualifies both Balzac and Gustave Planche as madmen, Balzac for his attempt at a technical analysis of Rossini's *Mose* and Planche for his "strange criticism" of Beethoven's *Eroica.*[1] And in his *Memoirs,* he identifies Stendhal as the author of a *Life of Rossini* "full of the most tiresome nonsense about music, for which he fancied he had a feeling."[2] He treated with particular scorn the *dilettanti* of 1832, who applauded Rossini with enthusiasm. It is, therefore, with some trepidation that, as a *dilettante* of 1976, I share with you my impressions of the relations between the literary Lélio of George Sand and the musical hero of Berlioz.

The year of the Lélios was 1832 and the month was December. Aurore Dudevant, already known as Georges [sic] Sand with the publication of *Indiana* and *Valentine,* achieved further success when her story, *La Marquise,* appeared in the *Revue de Paris* of December 2. As in *Valentine,* the theme is the love of a noblewoman for a commoner; the hero of *Valentine* is the nephew of a tenant farmer, sensitive, cultured, and a singer of remarkable talent; the hero of *La Marquise* is an actor.

This typically Sandian theme of a "socially 'impossible'" [3] passion is treated with classical lucidity in the young author's almost forgotten short masterpiece. The eighty-year-old heroine reminisces about her widowhood at sixteen after six months of marriage to a cynical libertine of fifty. Wearied of parrying alone the attacks of the would-be Merteuils and Valmonts on her "virtue," she accepted with distaste an official lover as a protector, for his sword was sharp and his loyalty unfailing.

Her sudden passion for the Italian actor, Lélio, when she first saw him perform in *Le Cid* at the *Comédie Française* and the necessity of hiding this forbidden love by exchanging her loge for an obscure seat and by adopting the disguise of a student gave adventure to the bleak existence of the young widow. For two years she indulged her secret adoration of Lélio, or rather of the heroes whom he portrayed. Indeed, the shock provoked one night by her seeing the actor off-stage, stripped of theatrical illusion, was such that the marquise took to her bed for several days.

Yielding, however, to the insistence of an acquaintance that she go with her to see Lélio in *Cinna,* the marquise, to her amazement, was again captivated by the actor, who finally noticed her emotion. Henceforth, she was aware that he reciprocated her adoration, and the two years of solitary worship were followed by three of a love that was shared.

Hearing that Lélio was to be replaced and was about to leave France, the marquise finally agreed to his plea for a secret rendezvous. He appeared, resplendent in the Don Juan costume which he had worn in Molière's *Le Festin de Pierre*. His ardent declarations that his love for her had transformed and uplifted him, his expressions of respect and veneration, almost induced the marquise to yield to him, as in *Valentine* the heroine finally yielded to Bénédict, but reason prevailed. Admitting the class prejudices inculcated in her since childhood, the marquise declared that they were not the reason for her resistance, but rather the fact that, forced to go along with the eighteenth century, she had been profaned by submitting to the caresses of a man whom she did not love. She would never see Lélio again, but would love him until death.

The *mélologue* in which Berlioz' Lélio appeared, *The Return to Life,* is more typical of the flamboyant romanticism of 1830 than the relatively sober *La Marquise* and, like the latter, a half-forgotten work. It was performed for the first time at the celebrated matinée of December 9, 1832, as a sequel to the revised *Symphonie fantastique,* the two works forming *Episode in the Life of An Artist.* The young composer had borrowed the term *mélologue* from the Irish poet, Thomas Moore, who had written a *Melologue upon National Music,* a work consisting of verse alternating with folk music of various countries. While still "serving time" at the Rome Academy as prize-winner for composition, Berlioz had assembled six earlier works to form the musical part of *The Return to Life:* the ballad on Goethe's poem "The Fisherman" dated from 1827, "Chorus of Shades," "Song of Bliss," and "Aeolian Harp—Recollections" were adapted from the prize cantatas of 1827 and 1829.[4] Jacques Barzun thinks it likely that the "Brigand's Song" was originally the Pirate Song after Victor Hugo.[5] The finale, *Fantasia on Shakespeare's Tempest,* had been heard at the Opera by a meager audience during a real storm and a political upheaval in November, 1830. In order to create a unity from the six disconnected musical pieces and to link the work dramatically to the *Symphonie fantastique,* Berlioz had composed a prose libretto to be spoken, as specified in the instructions preceding his score, by "a first-rate dramatic actor, not a singer."[6]

The instructions begin: "This work should be performed immediately after the Fantastic Symphony, which indeed it supplements and concludes."[7] The characters are divided into "Real Persons" (Lélio, composer; Musicians; Choristers; Friends and Pupils of Lélio) and "Fictitious Persons" (Horatio, Friend to Lélio; A Brigand-chief; Brigands; Ghosts). The theatrical nature of the work is emphasized by Berlioz' requirement that orchestra, chorus, and soloists be placed behind the curtain; that the actor alone should speak and act in front of it and that, upon his exit, at the conclusion of the last monologue, the curtain should rise and reveal all those taking part in the finale.

The opening monologue of Lélio, described in Berlioz' program notes to the *Symphonie fantastique* as a young composer who has attempted suicide by taking an overdose of opium, recalls, as he staggers onto the stage, the lurid dreams provoked by the drug: "The

scaffold, the judges,—hangmen, soldiers,—the screaming mob. . . ."
He refers to the ever-recurring *idée fixe* that represents the Beloved:

> And then, that inexorable melody, which haunted me even through
> the lethargy of my sleep, recalling that image which time had almost
> effaced from my memory, to revive my slumbering sorrow and
> suffering. . . .

Listeners will recall that, in the last movement of the *Symphonie
fantastique,* "A Witches' Sabbath," this theme is deformed, rendered
grotesque and vulgar, for the Beloved appears in the nightmare
recalled now by the artist as a witch:

> To see her,—hear her,—cruel,—cruel! her soft, fair features distorted
> by atrocious irony; the melody of her sweet voice changed to that of a
> howling Bacchanalian. . . . And yet it was she, . . . she herself, yet not
> herself, wearing that impenetrable smile, and leading on the infernal
> dance around my grave.[8]

Discovering the letter of farewell written the previous day to
Horatio, the artist recalls that it was while his friend was singing his
favorite ballad to his own piano accompaniment. Goethe's "The
Fisherman" is now sung behind the curtain by a tenor to a
barcarolle-like six-eight accompaniment, *tempo Andantino.* After
the first stanza, at the appearance of the mermaid, the composer
interrupts with the remark that Horatio had composed the ballad
"imitated from Goethe" five years ago and that he, Lélio, had
created the music: ". . . five years! How I have suffered since then!"
(p. 4) A second interruption occurs after the next stanza, when the
mermaid is luring the fisherman into the ocean depths. Sixteen
measures of the *idée fixe* in cut time *Allegro non troppo* suddenly
intrude into the ballad and Lélio murmurs: "Siren! Siren! Oh God!
my heart will break!" (p. 6) The ballad resumes, Tempo I, *un poco
più mosso ed agitato,* to be interrupted four lines later, when the
fisherman begins to succumb to the mermaid's charm. Lélio remarks: "Yes, yes, alas! I listened but too often." (p. 7) At the end of
the ballad, the fisherman disappears with the mermaid into the
depths.

Lélio then muses on the strangely haunting nature of his memories and on the striking allusion to his own sad past contained in the

ballad. Verses, music, and voice seem to tell him to live on for his art and for friendship's sake. Quotations from Hamlet and recognition of the strong influence of Shakespeare on his art inspire him to compose the "Chorus of Shades," which he imagines being played within him by an "ideal" orchestra (p. 8).

After the Chorus, which laments the horrors and inevitability of Death, played *Largo misterioso,* Lélio pronounces a eulogy of Shakespeare, followed by a virulent diatribe against critics. He wishes to flee "a society worse than hell itself" by joining a band of outlaws in the Kingdom of Naples or in Calabria. He exits, returning with the accoutrements of a brigand. While the brigand chief—"a powerful baritone"—the "ideal" orchestra and chorus perform "The Brigand's Song" behind the curtain. Lélio acts the scene in front of it (pp. 23-50).

The truculence and violence of the brigand theme are followed by silence, tears and sobs, calm, and rêverie. "The Song of Bliss" is performed by a second tenor as the imaginary voice of Lélio, accompanied by his Angel with her harp (pp. 51-58). Sadness again overcomes him. He asks why he cannot find the Juliet, the Ophelia for whom his heart pines, listens with melancholy to the orchestral piece, "Aeolian Harp—Recollections," then calls upon his Mistress, Music, for aid. Thereupon he is inspired to compose a Fantasia on Shakespeare's Tempest, to be executed by his pupils, who must now be assembling. After devoutly invoking Shakespeare, he exits, the curtain rises showing the musicians on their platform and the choristers advancing towards the usual orchestra pit, boarded over for this work. The hero reenters and gives detailed instructions for the execution of the Fantasia (pp. 59-63). According to Dickinson, Berlioz' text calling Miranda to meet her destined husband is in Italian "to keep the audience from looking for clues."[9] The composer compliments the executants on their performance and dismisses them. Part of the orchestra and all the chorus leave the stage, the curtain falls and Lélio remains in the foreground. For the Weimar performance of the work in 1855, Berlioz added a short postlude: fourteen measures of the *idée fixe* played by the remaining members of the orchestra, during which Lélio murmurs: "Once more! Once more—and for ever!" and leaves the stage.[10]

In the *Revue de Paris* of the second half of December, 1832 appeared a biographical article on Berlioz. The writer was his friend, the musicologist Joseph d'Ortigue. Recalling the sudden passion aroused in the young composer for an Irish actress when he first saw her as Ophelia [in 1827], d'Ortigue wrote:

> . . . from that moment, a sudden love, inexplicable in its causes and effects, terrifying in its violence and tenacity, overwhelmed his heart. Such an emotion can only be compared to that extraordinary passion of the marquise of R . . . for the actor Lélio, which a gifted writer has described with such talent in the *Revue de Paris*.[11]

Reporting on the December 9 concert, he remarked that Miss . . . (understand "Smithson") was present and that she was following the script of the melologue with the closest attention. He speculated on how strange she must have felt at hearing the astonishing work that she had inspired and at witnessing the triumph of the artist whom she had formerly disdained and the ingenious means of vengeance that he had employed. While stressing the need for discretion in delicate matters and the reserve with which "this sort of inventory of a living man" should be handled, d'Ortigue continued, "But G. Sand's story is constantly on [the author's] mind, and he cannot help but remember that Lélio finally realized the passion of the marquise and returned her love."[12]

Further evidence of the autobiographical nature of the melologue appears in Berlioz' *Memoirs*. Now defining *Lélio or The Return to Life* as a "monodrama," he writes: "The subject of this musical drama, as is known, was none other than my love for Miss Smithson and the anguish and 'bad dreams' it had brought me."[13] He describes the actress's emotion at the concert, particularly after the intermission:

> But when Bocage, the actor who spoke the part of Lélio (that is, myself), declaimed these lines, "Oh, if I could only find her, the Juliet, the Ophelia whom my heart cries out for! If I could drink deep of the mingled joy and sadness that real love offers us, and one autumn evening on some wild heath with the wind blowing over it, lie in her arms and sleep a last, long, sorrowful sleep!"
> "God!" she thought: "Juliet—Ophelia! Am I dreaming? I can still no longer doubt. It is of me he speaks. He loves me still."[14]

We could argue that the passage of time between 1832 and 1848, when Berlioz began to write his *Memoirs,* must have colored his recollections, but there is testimony much closer to the event. Pourtalès quotes a letter dated January 5, 1833 from Berlioz to Albert Duboys, a friend in Grenoble, in which the composer relates:

> Henriette Smithson was escorted to my concert not knowing that it was given by me; *she* heard the work of which she is subject and the primary cause; *she* wept, she expressed all her enthusiasm to me after the concert. I was introduced to her at *her* hotel; *she* listened to me . . . *she* asked my forgiveness for the suffering that she had unwittingly caused me . . . and finally, on December 18, in the presence of her sister, I heard the words: "Well, Berlioz . . . I love you." [15]

In the same letter, he implores Duboys to guard the secret of his happiness until the time when his parents will have to be informed, adding: "D'Ortigue has been imprudent enough to unveil it partly in my biography in the *Revue de Paris,* have you read it?" In the postscript, he asks his friend for an immediate reply informing him "how they are gossiping about all that in Grenoble. . . . The *Revue de Paris* must have had its effect. . . ." and he concludes: "A love of five years, concentrated, which has resisted everything, even an episodic passion!" [his engagement to Camille Moke] (p. 127). Berlioz' secretive tone and d'Ortigue's veiled references seem strange if we are to believe the second part of Elliot's assertion: "The concert was repeated later in the month [December 30] and in the meantime Berlioz conspired with his friend d'Ortigue to publish in the *Revue de Paris* a full account of the Smithson affair, together with a statement to the effect that Henrietta had been present at the first concert." [16] Wotton even states that "[the] sketch of Berlioz' life, . . . ostensibly written by Joseph d'Ortigue . . . was practically penned by Berlioz himself." Wotton refers to an article by Charles Malherbe in the *Rivista musicale italiana* for 1906 relating "how some manuscript notes of Berlioz were discovered at the Conservatoire— his first attempt at an autobiography—which had been utilized by d'Ortigue." Wotton remarks that much of the two versions is collated and that a paragraph that he quotes from d'Ortigue "like many another, is practically the same in both cases. . . ." [17]

To return to *La Marquise,* some critics have discerned autobiographical elements also in this work. Joseph Barry, for example, who equates the marquise with Sand and Lélio with Marie Dorval, who had become famous on May 3, 1831, in Dumas' *Antony*:

> Nightly [the marquise] steals to the theatre disguised as a man to see [Lélio] perform. Chin resting (*à la* George Sand) on the chair before her, hands clasped on trousered knees, "forehead bathed with perspiration" from the fervor, she followed the actor's every movement, "every palpitation of his breast." [18]

Absent from Paris, George missed the May première of *Antony,* but did attend the first performance of Hugo's *Marion de Lorme* on August 11, when Marie again played opposite Bocage. In her chapter on Mme Dorval in *Histoire de ma vie,* Sand pays tribute to the magnetism of the actress's talent, but mentions that Marie was handicapped by a husky voice.[19] The marquise of her story says the same of Lélio.

Barry's parallel is further reinforced by his translation (pp. 148-9 in his biography of Sand) in which he names "George's own song of songs." It forms part of "Sketches and Hints," is titled "To the Angel without a Name" and sub-titled "Translation."[20] Georges Lubin notes that Sand scratched out the original title "To the Angel Lélio." He mentions the publication of *La Marquise* in the *Revue de Paris* of December 9, [sic] 1832 and the "curious coincidence" of the December 9 performance of Berlioz' monodrama *Lélio or The Return to Life.*[21] Lubin further refers to comments on the "Angel" made by Pierre Reboul in his introduction to *Lélia.* Reboul quotes from Sand's "curious page, claimed, as an afterthought [après coup] to be a translation":

> Why do not men have wings so that they might come at night and fly away in the morning? I prefer thistledown to any man! You blow upon it, and it is lost in the wind. No man ever becomes lighter, evanescing into spirit.[22]

Like Barry, Reboul sees the Lélio of *La Marquise* as Marie Dorval. He stresses the fact that a search for the original of the pretended translation would be vain, and both Barry and Lubin concur that Sand used the term as a screen. George describes Marie's immediate and impetuous response to her letter to the actress requesting to see her. On the very day that Mme Dorval received the letter, she came to Sand's apartment and greeted the author with an effusive embrace (*O.A.,* II, 228). Barry quotes from a letter written by George "to the just-met Marie: Good-bye, great and beautiful one, no matter what, I will see you this evening." Two days later, George canceled an evening with Mérimée, informed Marie soon afterwards that she was "working like a horse" (on *Lélia*) and sent the actress a copy of *La Marquise* (Barry, *op. cit.,* p. 145).

As for Berlioz' work, opinions differ on the origin of the name Lélio. Barzun states:

> The name Lélio, assigned in place of 'the artist' who first figured in his melologue, was explicitly given in the revision of the score in 1855, but it probably dates from 1832 or 1833, for we find the association of ideas mentioned by d'Ortigue in these years . . . and much of what he says can only have come from Berlioz himself.[23]

He notes a possible common source for Sand and Berlioz: Hoffmann's tale *The Empty House* in *Nachtstücke,* II, 1817, "in which the especially intuitive character is so named."[24] Pourtalès states that Berlioz borrowed the name from Sand's *Lélia,* parts of which appeared in the spring of 1833 in the *Revue des Deux Mondes,* and the composer used the masculine form. Barzun objects to this notion on the grounds that *Lélia* came out nearly a year [July 31, 1833] after d'Ortigue's remark establishing the parallel with the earlier tale. Contrary to Pourtalès, Barzun declares that Sand borrowed the name from her own work and turned it into a feminine one. He also points out that there is no parallel between Sand's heroine and Berlioz' artist. George seems to have had a predilection for the name Lélio, since she used it again for the artist-hero of *La Dernière Aldini,* published in 1838.

Fortuitous as they may seem, parallels between the two works other than the same name are striking. The five-year worship of the marquise is for Rodrigue, Xipharès and Hippolyte rather than for the actor who portrays them;[25] the five-year adoration of Lélio the composer for the Beloved of the *idée fixe* corresponds to Berlioz' own five-year love for Ophelia and Juliet rather than for the Shakespearian actress. Thus, each work reflects its creator's passion for the theater and for the theater's greatest writers.

In both works, love is haunting, persistent, obsessive and idealistic. The object of the love has a magnetic charm for the victim. For Sand's marquise, Lélio is a vulture, seizing her as though she were a partridge in the magnetism of his flight, she panting and motionless in the magic circle he traces around her (*La Marquise,* pp. 110-111); for Berlioz' artist, the Beloved is a siren to whom he has listened too often. In each work, the loved person temporarily causes shock and disillusionment in the worshipper. After two years of secret adoration, the marquise cannot believe her eyes and ears when she sees Lélio off-stage, yellow, faded, worn, badly-dressed, and common-looking, shaking hands with the low characters in a café and swallowing brandy, and hears him swearing horribly (*La Marquise,* p. 112). For her, it is a nightmare as hideous as the one recalled by Berlioz' composer-hero when he had seen and heard his Beloved as a witch. However, in each case, the worshipper is again magnetized, "and for ever."

Although love is the primary theme of *La Marquise* and of *Lélio,* both works also contain criticism of certain aspects of society. The marquise recalls that the theater audiences of her youth considered that Lélio overacted and was devoid of taste and feeling; that in her social circles she was judged as disdainful, cold and heartless (*La Marquise,* p. 105). Berlioz' hero attacks "the young theorists of eighty, who wallow in a sea of prejudice" and "those who dare to lay their desecrating hands of corruption upon our master-pieces . . ." (*Lélio,* p. 23). Indeed, the protagonists of both works have an intense feeling of alienation. In retrospect, the aged marquise believes that Lélio and herself were attracted to each other from the extremities of the social scale precisely because of this alienation, for they were not of their time. The only escape for Berlioz' hero as an artist appears to be flight into the primitive life of the bandit.

Coincidence in the resemblances between the situations marquise/Lélio and Lélio/Beloved seems even more evident after investigation of the pre-1832 relations between Sand and Berlioz. Mme Karénine claims that "as early as 1830, George often mentions in her letters the name of Berlioz, who was then so little appreciated in France, but whose *Melodies* and other works were already known and valued in Aurore's little circle of friends." [26] On the other hand, Mme Marix-Spire writes that she has never found anything to confirm Mme Karénine's statement. [27] In Mme Spire's view, George owed her discovery of Berlioz to the distinguished lawyer of

Châteauroux, Rollinat, and to his children, all artistically gifted like their father, to whom George was introduced on November 5, 1831, at the première of *La Reine d'Espagne*. Mme Spire quotes a letter to Rollinat's son, François, in which George requests: "Send me those songs of Berlioz, if they are not being used in your family."[28] And in a letter to Casimir Dudevant dated December 8, 1832, she asks her husband to return to Rollinat "the melodies of Berlioz" that she left on her desk in Nohant.[29]

The resemblances in the relations between the protagonists of the two works might seem less coincidental if it were possible to compare a complete score of *The Return to Life* of 1832 with the Richault and Broude versions, both undated, but both based on the so-called "first" performance of *Lélio; or The Return to Life* in Weimar on February 21, 1855. Barzun mentions that Schlesinger was bringing out three pieces from the Melologue in the spring of 1833 and Pierre Citron declares that *Lélio* and the *Symphonie fantastique* were among the works of Berlioz published by Schlesinger between 1829 and 1846;[30] however, a complete score of the 1832 version seems to be nonexistent today. Hence, it is impossible to determine to what extent, other than the addition of the name Lélio, the scores of 1855 were modified to stress the parallels with *La Marquise* discerned by d'Ortigue.

Moreover, Lubin believes that any letters that Sand may have written to Berlioz must be considered as definitely lost. He did discover three replies of Berlioz to letters of Sand, but observes that the author and the composer do not appear to have maintained a regular correspondence, except for a brief period between 1837 and 1838.[31] There is also no primary evidence of Sand's attendance at Berlioz' matinée of 1832. Mme Spire writes that she probably was "at this celebrated concert of the ninth, which brought together all the Parisian circles of the dandy, the writer and the artist . . ."; Barzun notes her presence "at the concert and also before, at rehearsals," with, among others, Liszt, Chopin, Hugo, Heine, Vigny, Dumas, and Gautier.

In Mme Spire's opinion, owing to the influence of Planche, one of the young composer's adverse critics, George hardly knew Berlioz' music until 1835 (*op. cit.,* p. 274) and did not meet him until that same year. In her *Journal intime,* which Lubin dates from November 15 to 28, 1832, Sand writes: "Save me from fops, I want to see artists. Liszt, [De] Lacroix, Berlioz, Meyerbeer. . . ." (*O.A.,*

II, 960). Mme Spire quotes from letters written by George to Liszt during the autumn and winter of 1834 in which she asks him to bring Berlioz to her home. She seems to have met Liszt, through Musset, during the latter half of October of that year, at the time of her reconciliation with the young poet. To Liszt, she owed her introduction to Chopin, Meyerbeer, and Berlioz (Spire, pp. 393-398).

The earliest evidence of Berlioz' appreciation of Sand's works is quoted by Lubin from a letter written on May 22, 1837, by the composer to Liszt, who was staying at Nohant. Hector asks his friend to compliment Mme Sand on *Mauprat,* which he has just read. However, Lubin points out that there are strings attached, for Berlioz was negotiating with George the possibility of her writing a drama in which Harriet (whom he had married on October 3, 1833) could appear (*Homm. à G.S.,* p. 20). On the other hand, praise for Berlioz as an artist, without strings, appears in Sand's *Letters of a Traveler.* In the sixth of this series dated April, 1835 and addressed to Everard (Michel de Bourges), she declares: "Berlioz is a great composer, a man of genius, a true artist . . . he is very poor, very brave and very proud" (*O.A.,* II, 810). In the *Revue des Deux Mondes* of June 15, 1835, she dubs him a "Promethean genius" (Barzun, I, 270, n. 36). A tribute comparable to the marquise's veneration for the underestimated Lélio appears in the eleventh traveler's letter dated September, 1836, addressed to Meyerbeer:

> Do you remember, maestro, that one evening I had the honor of meeting you at a concert of Berlioz? . . . They played the *March to the Scaffold.* I will never forget your cordial handshake and the emotion with which that hand . . . applauded the great misunderstood artist who is heroically struggling against his unappreciative audiences and his cruel destiny.[32]

It may be concluded that there are many resemblances between the literary and the musical work: autobiographical elements, primacy of love, obsessive passion, abundance of tears and emotional outbursts, exaltation of the artist and the concept of his alienation in a Philistine society. They stem from the fact that Sand's story and Berlioz' melologue are youthful creations in different media of two artists born within a year of each other at the turn of the century. They had similar temperaments, were admirers of Hugo and rebels imbued with the Hernani-type Romanticism of the early 1830's. The circumstances of the creation of the two works rule out any possibility of a direct influence of the novelist on the composer. Sand wrote *La Marquise* during the summer of 1832, while Berlioz was recopying the parts of his melologue at his home town, La Côte Saint-André, biding his time until he felt justified in returning to Paris, which was not until November 7 of the same year. In the absence of evidence of any personal relations between the two and of Sand's attendance at Berlioz' concerts before and during 1832, we may consider the discernment shown by d'Ortigue in his article of December of the same year as forming the link between the Lélios of Berlioz and George Sand.

AFTERWORD

I recently had access to the twenty-page program-libretto published by Schlesinger for the 1832 matinee: *Le Retour à la vie,/ Mélologue,/ Faisant suite à la Symphonie fantastique/ intitulée:/ Episode de la vie d'un artiste,/ Paroles et musique de M. Hector Berlioz./ (Montagnes d'Italie.—Juin 1831.)* (Paris: Bibliothèque Nationale. Musique. Rés. 1924.) A comparison of this booklet with the libretto of the above-mentioned identical Richault and Broude versions based on the Weimar performance of 1855 reveals many revisions. The changes relevant to the present paper are the addition of the name Lélio and the insertion of the *idée fixe* as an interruption in "The Fisherman" and as a coda. Two recent articles by Peter Bloom stress the differences between the melologue of 1832 and the monodrama of 1855: 1. "Une lecture de *Lélio ou Le Retour à la vie.*" *Revue de Musicologie,* Tome LXIII (1977), Nos. 1-2, pp. 89-106. 2. "A Return to Berlioz's *Retour à la vie.*" *The Musical Quarterly,* LXIV, No. 3 (July, 1978), pp. 354-385. In both articles, Professor Bloom expresses the view that, after a lapse of twenty-three years, Berlioz' addition of the name Lélio is unlikely to have been based on the analogy with *La Marquise* suggested in 1832 by d'Ortigue.

NOTES

1. Hector Berlioz, *Les Grotesques de la musique* (Paris: Gründ, 1969), p. 34. English translation mine.

2. Berlioz, *Memoirs,* trans. by David Cairns (New York: Norton, 1975), p. 170, n. 6.

3. Curtis Cate, *George Sand: A Biography* (New York: Avon, 1976), p. 207.

4. Jacques Barzun, *Berlioz and the Romantic Century* (New York: Columbia University Press, 1969), I, 220.

5. Ibid.

6. Berlioz, *Lélio; or, The Return to Life: Lyric Monodrama: Opus 14b* (New York: Broude Bros., n.d.), p. 1. Edition in French, German and English. Eng. trans. by John Bernhoff. Hereafter referred to as *Lélio.*

7. *Lélio,* p. 1.

8. Ibid., p. 2.

9. A.E.F. Dickinson, *The Music of Berlioz* (London: Faber and Faber, 1972), p. 55.

10. *Lélio,* p. 149.

11. Joseph d'Ortigue, "Hector Berlioz," *Revue de Paris,* 45 (Dec. 1832), 286. English translation mine.

12. Ibid., 294-5.

13. Berlioz, *Memoirs,* p. 215.

14. Ibid., p. 216.

15. Guy de Pourtalès, *Berlioz et l'Europe romantique* (Paris: Gallimard, 1939), p. 126. English translation mine.

16. J.H. Elliot, *Berlioz* (London: J.M. Dent; New York: Farrar, Straus & Giroux, 1938, rev. ed. 1967), p. 64.

17. Tom S. Wotton, *Hector Berlioz* (London: Oxford University Press, 1935), p. 25.

18. Joseph Barry, *Infamous Woman: The Life of George Sand* (Garden City, N.Y.: Doubleday, 1977), p. 144.

19. Sand, *Oeuvres autobiographiques* (Paris: Gallimard, 1971), II, 227.

20. Ibid., 617-618.

21. Ibid., 1428. For *La Marquise,* the date December 9 should read December 2.

22. Sand, *Lélia,* ed. Pierre Reboul (Paris: Garnier, 1960), Introduction, p.

xxxix. The English translation of the passage quoted by Reboul is Barry's, op. cit., p. 149.

23. Barzun, op. cit., II, 259, n. 4.

24. Ibid., Cf. E.T.A. Hoffman, *Das öde Haus* in *Fantasio - und Nachtstücke* (Munich: Winkler-Verlag, n.d.), p. 459.

25. Georges [sic] Sand, "La Marquise" *Revue de Paris,* 45 (Dec. 1832), Ill.

26. Mme Wladimir Karénine, *George Sand, sa vie et ses oeuvres* (Paris: Ollendorf et Plon-Nourrit, 1899-1926), I, 312, n.l. English translation mine. The *melodies* are the *Nine Melodies for One and Two Voices* (Paris: Richault, 1830). The words are Thomas Gounet's adaptation of poems by Thomas Moore.

27. Mme Thérèse Marix-Spire, *Les Romantiques et la musique: le cas George Sand* (Paris: Nouvelles Editions Latines, 1954), p. 196.

28. Ibid., p. 250. Quoted from Jules Bertaut, *Une Amitié romantique: Lettres inédites de George Sand et François Rollinat* (Paris: Renaissance du Livre, 1921), pp. 26-27. English translation mine.

29. Quoted in Spire, op. cit., p. 251.

30. Berlioz, *Correspondance générale,* ed. Pierre Citron (Paris: Flammarion, 1972), I, 569.

31. Georges Lubin, "George Sand et Hector Berlioz," *Hommage à George Sand* (Grenoble: Presses Universitaires de Grenoble, 1969), p. 18.

32. *O.A.,* II, 935.

High Analytical Romanticism: The Narrative Voice in George Sand's *Lucrezia Floriani*

ALEX SZOGYI
Hunter College
Department of Romance Languages and Graduate Center
City University of New York

George Sand was possessed of an inordinately deep need to explain herself to the world. She was one of the most articulate women who ever lived. *Lucrezia Floriani,* one of her least known but best novels, is a magnificent fictional account of a great impossible love, its genesis, flowering, and lingering death. Like Benjamin Constant before her and Proust after her (George Sand is so prominently featured in the heritage of the young Marcel—there was a true affinity between their author's works), George Sand equated the duration of a great love with the life and death of a human being. For these writers, the liebestod motif was part and parcel of their fictional weltanschauung. *Lucrezia Floriani,* like the novel *Adolphe,* the opera *La Traviata,* and Proust's *La Fugitive,* is a work of art in which high Romantic passion is wedded to a deep lyrical and psychological analysis. So intent is George Sand in bringing the essence of the story to her reader that she constantly interrupts it, guiding the beleaguered reader to the conclusions, the ironies, and the essence she so passionately needs to tell.

The prurient interest of the work lies in the fact that it may very well have been a fictionalized account of what went wrong with George Sand's and Chopin's celebrated liaison. George Sand once read it to Delacroix with Chopin sitting by admiringly, unable to see himself in the tormented rôle of the jealous lover. Delacroix was

embarrassed to the marrow as he looked from George Sand to
Chopin and back, with neither of them seeming to grasp the
connection between the fiction and the reality. George Sand always
took care to deny that the novel was a barely fictionalized truth.
Georges Lubin, the celebrated editor of her correspondence, when
asked recently whether the novel was actually about the two of
them, flatly denied it. Curtis Cate, in his provocative biography,
patently affirms it and keeps insisting that Sand knew and deliber-
ately set about to portray Chopin in his least flattering aspects. Be
that as it may, the quality of the novel has nothing whatsoever to do
with its roman à cléf aspects: we mention them here to explain why
so much of the novel might depend on the narrator's voice to make
the essential points George Sand insisted on making to her reader.

The nineteenth-century novel is filled with authors penetrating
their narratives. Some did it more subtly than others. In Benjamin
Constant's *Adolphe,* the narrator is a modern La Rochefoucauld,
poeticizing a sad story. Whether the heroine is Mme de Staël, Mme
Lindsay or a generous dollop of both and yet others, the narrator's
voice is a judicious mixture of seventeenth-century psychological
acumen and nineteenth-century sensibility. Stendhal's narrations are
filled with the ironic aperçus of its author, ever on the qui vive, ever
intruding wickedly in on the manuscript, like an oblique mirror
distorting the truth in order to heighten it for us. Balzac is there,
narrating his tale like some master builder, the author of the
Comédie humaine striding godlike in his codifying of human
behavior, a modern Dante, dispensing heaven and hell in an
Olympian and often unsubtle manner. But Balzac's narrative ironies
are always delicious and highly savorable. Flaubert was, of course,
celebrated for not doing any of this, but as we know from canny
studies of *Madame Bovary* that the soi-disant objectivity of Flaubert
was a carefully engineered fictional attitude: one need only read
Madame Bovary's suicide scene to intuit the great care Flaubert
took to make us love her as she destroyed herself. It all culminated
with Proust, whose narrator was a fictional hero of the volume,
indistinguishable from his young hero, Marcel, and somehow linked
to the impassive codifier of human behavior whose analysis of the
meanings of the experiences within the book are infuriatingly
somewhere between modern maxims à la Rochefoucauld and
truisms which any treatise on psychology could reveal. George

Sand's narrator is obviously herself: she has the deep honesty characteristic of her which refuses to mask her identity. She has a direct, palpable relationship with her audience, exhorting them, cajoling them, moving them—forever playing with their sensibilities and refusing to allow them to make up their own minds about what they are reading. Thus, *Lucrezia Floriani* is a truncated novel, a story one recounts to one's intimate friends, which is interrupted by the impression the narrator insists the story should be giving to those assembled. Yet so consistent is the use of this abrupt technique that it finally becomes the raison d'être of the novel. It is as if George Sand realized that all stories are basically alike, all great loves basically as frustrating and containing the same seeds of self-destruction, and so she takes it upon herself to embroider and explain it all. That rich *fioritura* which her voice creates is the deeply felt narrative she is truly telling. In the long run, her novel is *not* the novel itself but the novel of her narrator's own desperation at ever being able to communicate every important moment of the novel.

From the point of view of genre, George Sand struggles with the high passion of the Romantic novel, wishing to temper it and analyze it, thereby taming it and creating a new genre. In the 1857 edition of the work (it had been written in 1846), she discusses her fictional imperatives (all translations are my own):

> In the novel as well as in the theatre, I should like to find the way to ally the dramatic movement with a true analysis of the characters and the human feelings . . . this problem has not yet been resolved for either genre. For twenty-years now, we have been floating between two extremes, and for my part, loving as I do strong emotions in fiction, I have however walked the extreme other way, not out of reasons of taste but because of my conscience, because I saw the other way was being neglected and abandoned by the fashion. I have made every effort, without exaggerating their weakness nor their importance, to retain the literature of my time in a practical road between the peaceful lake and the wild torrent. . . . I come back upon what I have seen and heard, and I ask myself about the whys and the wherefores of the action which moved and carried me away. Then it is that I perceive the suddenincongruities or the false reasons for the facts the torrent of my imagination has pushed forth, scorning the obstacles of reason or of moral truth, and from that point the retrograde movement which pushes me back, as

so many others, towards the smooth and monotonous lake of analysis.[1]
(pp. 1-2)

Emotion recollected in tranquillity? More than that, a definitive attempt on George Sand's part to criticize the Romantic novel.

> *Lucrezia Floriani,* this book composed entirely of analysis and meditation, is therefore nothing but a protest against the excessive use of old-fashioned techniques, those veritable surprise machines, whose qualities and defects seemed, in my view, to disconcert the undiscerning public. (p. 2)

And so, George Sand, wishing to write a better book than some others of her time, opted to criticize the form of the love novel. She was perhaps not aware of her place within a lineage. Certainly, that place has not yet even now been accorded her. But it is fascinating to see how she went about her work. In her own words, the analysis of a feeling is the crux of the matter. "What it is possible to do is to analyze a feeling." And so she tells us how to go about it: the feeling comes first, not the character. She takes on the difficult métier of the anti-Balzac *sans le savoir*: "So that it may have a meaning for the intelligence, by passing through the prism of imagination, we must thus create characters to embody the feeling we wish to describe, and not the feeling for the sake of the character." She admits that it is her way and that she has never found another. At the end of her preface she asks her readers whether her portrait of passion is true and deep and whether it has taught them something. She asks them to reconstruct the characters for themselves as if the author had not been able to do it convincingly enough.

From the very first, in the novel, she speaks directly to the reader, as "benevolent reader." She *tutoie*s the reader in an act of deep literary intimacy. She accuses readers of not being French enough, too much influenced by foreign literatures. She realizes that the French public is being spoiled by its authors and catered to disgustingly. She will do it differently. The reader expects too much of the writer, and gets a surfeit of action. It will soon be too late and authors will have nothing more to do or to say. Boredom will set in with the process. And so, loyal to her forefathers, a little like Alceste in *Le Misanthrope,* when he scores Oronte for his preciosity and prefers an old song of Louis XIII's time, George Sand proposes a narrative sans spice. She refuses the cowardice of surprise.

> Instead of carrying you from astonishment to astonishment, to make you fall at the end of every chapter from a fever of excitement, I'll take you step by step by a little narrow road, making you look straight ahead, behind, to the right, to the left . . . if, by chance, there is a ravine ahead, I'll tell you: "Watch out, there's a ravine." If there is a torrent, I'll help you to pass over it, I won't push you in head first, so that I can have the pleasure of telling others: "Oh, I broke my neck, I didn't suspect; that author played a dirty trick on me." (p. 10)

She refuses to mock her reader, and yet she feels that she will thus be called the most insolent and presumptuous of all novelists and that her readers will leave her flat in the middle, refusing to follow her. She ends her preface by saying she is not afraid to write a bad novel and to take liberties which will result in one. How ironic! The world has never forgotten George Sand (now less than ever), but it has done a good job forgetting her novels, leaving them to dusty oblivion. She was right in some manner: *Lucrezia Floriani* refuses to be a Romantic novel. It doesn't have the genius to become a Proustian mélange of psychology and fiction. Its characters, the passionate actress, la Floriani, who retires from the world to tend her many children and the neurotic prince Karol Roswald, sick in mind and body, who falls in love with her and is nursed back to health by her until the point in which he so destroys her with his fits of jealousy and unreason, reminds us of the narrative rhythm of the ironies implicit in Gide's *L'Immoraliste,* in which the wife saves the husband's life and the husband then sacrifices the wife, though Gide's narrator is a poor mockery of the narrative mode in fiction.

A few examples of her technique will suffice to make her method clear. At one point, la Floriani tells her lover the story of her life. She wishes to elicit his love through explaining herself to him. He, who once loved a pure young girl who died, cannot bring himself to love her as she is. He must fantasize her into an amalgam with the dead woman he still loves. Realizing the essential impossibility of a love between her main characters, the narrator attempts to characterize him and finishes with a Romantic epithet which aptly capsulizes Karol's inability to love:

> Finally, he would have wished to complete the sum of his fantastic
> exigencies, that, without ceasing to be the good, the tender, the devoted,
> the voluptuous and the maternal Lucrezia, that she be the pale, the
> innocent, the severe and the virginal Lucy. That's all he would have
> asked for, this poor lover of the impossible!" (p. 159)

Realizing that her readers must be led to the various climaxes of the
narrative, she takes particular pains in frustrating her reader:

> If I intended that the novel follow modern rules, by cutting this chapter
> at this point, I would leave you till tomorrow, dear reader, in uncer-
> tainty, presuming that you would ask yourself all night long, instead
> of sleeping: "Will Prince Karol leave or will he not leave?" But the high
> notion I have of your intelligence prevents me from using this knowing
> ruse, and I will spare you your torments. You know quite well that my
> novel is not far enough advanced so that my hero could get out of it
> suddenly at this point and despite me. Besides, his flight would be quite
> improbable, and you would not at all give credence to breaking up,
> when it is at its first link in the chains of a violent love.
> Possess your soul in patience, go about your business, and may sleep
> pour over you in white and red poppies. We are not yet at the dénoue-
> ment. (p. 176)

She divides her love affair into the essential stages, somewhat as
Stendhal does in *De L'amour*. The stage that interests her will be the
one Proust studied so well: the *décrystallisation*. And in this next
passage, she hints at the entire novelistic world of a Françoise Sagan
as well as that all-encompassing knowledge of an emotion which is
one of the major qualities of the Proustian narrative.

> Karol loved for love's sake: no suffering could revolt him. He was
> entering into a new phase, the suffering one, after having exhausted
> the intoxication of it all. But the phase of turning cold could never
> happen to him. That would have been physical agony, for his love had
> become his life, and exquisite or bitter, he was not up to extracting
> himself from it for a single instant. (p. 197)

When the narrator speaks directly to the audience, one does not
sense George Sand's gender. However, when she tells the story per
se, her instinctive feminist approach, one of the most valuable

contributions, forms the stuff of her analysis. La Floriani forgives her jealous lover but in her heart she knows it's hopeless.

> La Floriani contented herself with this false reparation; or, tired of the war, she feigned contentment; but, in this, she was quite wrong, and threw herself into an abyss of troubles. Karol got used to, from that very day, believing that jealousy is not an insult and that a woman who is loved can and must always pardon it. (p. 241)

It is in these relatively unguarded moments that the omniscient narrator shares the stage with the implicit narrator, a more vulnerable creature.

Toward the end, however, so passionately is she imbued with the desire to explain why some loves can never last that she arrives at a high plain of narrative lucidity: after a particularly passionate series of stupid outbursts on Karol's part, the narrator takes a paragraph to sum up the essence of what is happening:

> It was true, at the bottom of it all: a nature which is rich with exuberance and a nature which is rich through exclusivity, can never melt into each other. One of them must devour the other and leave only ashes. That is what happened. (p. 251)

Her heroine is finally brought to a form of lucidity, a realization that all her loves have been the same, the first as well as the last, and that she has been duped by them all.

> She went in her memory over the details and the totality of her first passion, and compared them with her last, not to establish a parallel between two men that she had no desire to judge coldly, but to interrogate her own heart about what it could still feel of passion and what suffering it could bear. Insensitively she pictured for herself in order and lucidly the whole history of her life, all her attempts at devotion, her dreams of happiness, all her deception and all her bitterness. She was frightened by the tale that she was telling of her own existence and wondered if it had really been she who had been able to deceive herself so many times, and to know it without crying or going mad. (p. 259)

And thus George Sand, through the immediacy of her almost simplistic analysis rivets her reader's attention to her heroine better than if she had contented herself with allowing the story to tell itself.

She even allows the heroine to go back into her own previous thoughts, so that the intensity of self-discovery is both delivered by the narrator and the inner voice of the character. It comes to a passionate climax in her realization that her love and her life are synonymous. A new cartesian definition is promulgated. Without any hint of parody, George Sand defines the Romantic experience of love in terms of a cartesian imperative:

> "What do you want of me? speak, enlighten; must I abstain from love? Here you send me back to my instinct; am I still capable of loving? Yes, more than ever, since it is the essence of my life, and I feel myself living with intensity through suffering; if I couldn't love any more, I wouldn't suffer any more. I suffer, therefore I love and I exist." (p. 261)

And so Lucrezia Floriani resigns herself to the inevitability of loving a man who can never appreciate the quality of her love. She reasons it out lucidly, painstakingly, logically: "It will be the logical conclusion of my life." (p. 262). The logical conclusion culminates in a violent orgy of self-flagellation, told with a measured calm.

> And so La Floriani was seized by an immense pain by saying an eternal farewell to her dear illusions. She rolled on the ground, drowned in tears. She exhaled sobs which pressed on her chest in suffocating cries. She wished to give herself to a weakness which she felt would be the last, and to tears which would never flow again. (p. 264)

After the calm, the narrator takes over:

> Here I have arrived, dear reader, at the conclusion that I had proposed for myself, and the rest will only be an act of condescension to those who wish for some sort of dénouement. (p. 264)

And then she plays mightily with her reader in an almost miscalculated attempt at contemptuous irony:

> You, sensible reader, I wager you're of my opinion, and that you find conclusions perfectly useless. If I followed my conviction and my imagination in this, no novel would ever finish, so as better to resemble real life. Which are the stories of love which would stop in an absolute manner by a break or by happiness, by an infidelity or a sacrament?

Which are the events which fix our existence in a durable condition? I agree that there is nothing nicer in the world than an old-fashioned conclusion: "They lived many years and were always happy." That was said in antedeluvian literature, in the fabulous ages.
But today we don't believe in anything any more, we laugh when we read this charming refrain.
A novel is never anything more than an episode in life. I have just recounted to you what could be construed as unity of time and place in the loves of the prince of Roswald and the actress Lucrezia. Now, do you want to know the rest? Couldn't you tell it to me yourself? Don't you see better than I where my characters are going? Must you know the facts?
If you absolutely insist, I will not be long, and I will not cause you any surprise, because I am engaged to do so. They loved for a long time and lived very unhappily together. Their love was a battle to the death, to see which would absorb the other. . . Certainly, if you wished to follow it all and analyze it all, there would still be ten volumes to write, one for each year that they were attached to the same ball and chain. . . . (pp. 264–265).

And so she takes her heroine on for another few pages to her ultimate demise. "She was extinguished like a flame deprived of oxygen." (p. 267) The ultimate conclusion is to be expected: "By ceasing to love, she had to cease to live." (p. 270). It is most difficult to know how to end such a novel and she does so, ironically, with the difficulty of recounting how Karol reacted to the death of Lucrezia:

Did he die of it, or did he go mad? It would be too easy to finish with him in this way; I won't say another word. . . . It's enough to kill the main character, without being forced to reward, punish or sacrifice one by one all the others. (p. 271)

The narrative voice of the novel could not have known at the time of the composition of the novel, although she easily suspected it, that in real life it was Chopin who was to die. Perhaps, out of implicit pity, she reversed the order to protect his feelings if he made any connection whatsoever between her narrative and their lives. Their relationship died through many misunderstandings several years before Chopin actually succumbed to his illness, somewhat the way the novel suggests. It is quite possible that George Sand, in her attempt to rebel against the conventional, Romantic novel, and in her passionate zeal for the truth of the human heart and its experience, felt that she had to interrupt the narrative to give the essential abstracted truth. Little did she know or suspect that she was one of the most daring of all those who experimented with the genre and that her novel, which is still virtually unknown, is one of those small chefs d'oeuvre of the nineteenth century which include *Adolphe* and *Dominique,* works which reveal the sensibilities of their authors and thus define an age. Long before Proust, George Sand experienced an obsessive love and attempted to codify the stations of such an experience. Her attempt is all the more moving because it is an off-shoot of one of the most publicized love affairs of the century. And even if ultimately it weren't it testifies to the remarkable sensibility and capacity for experience which is the particular trademark of the life and works of George Sand.

NOTES

1. George Sand, *Lucrezia Floriani* (Paris: Michel Lévy Frères, Libraires-Editeurs, 1857). The author of this study is at present translating this novel which has never been translated before. All selections are the author's own translation.

Name Index

Subject Index